Teacher Evaluation

Studies in the Postmodern Theory of Education

Shirley R. Steinberg
General Editor

Vol. 455

The Counterpoints series is part of the Peter Lang Education list.
Every volume is peer reviewed and meets
the highest quality standards for content and production.

PETER LANG
New York • Bern • Frankfurt • Berlin
Brussels • Vienna • Oxford • Warsaw

Teacher Evaluation

THE CHARGE AND THE CHALLENGES

Edited by **KATE E. O'HARA**

PETER LANG

New York • Bern • Frankfurt • Berlin
Brussels • Vienna • Oxford • Warsaw

Library of Congress Cataloging-in-Publication Data

Teacher evaluation: the charge and the challenges /
edited by Kate E. O'Hara.
pages cm. — (Counterpoints: studies in the postmodern theory of education; v. 455)
Includes bibliographical references and index.
1. Teachers—Rating of. 2. Educational evaluation. I. O'Hara, Kate E.
LB2838.T394   371.1—dc23   2014025275
ISBN 978-1-4331-2355-9 (hardcover)
ISBN 978-1-4331-2354-2 (paperback)
ISBN 978-1-4539-1393-2 (e-book)
ISSN 1058-1634

Bibliographic information published by **Die Deutsche Nationalbibliothek.**
Die Deutsche Nationalbibliothek lists this publication in the "Deutsche
Nationalbibliografie"; detailed bibliographic data are available
on the Internet at http://dnb.d-nb.de/.

Cover drawings by Meghan Rose Majewski

The paper in this book meets the guidelines for permanence and durability
of the Committee on Production Guidelines for Book Longevity
of the Council of Library Resources.

To my husband, Dave Majewski, for his unwavering support—
through deadlines and dog rescue

CONTENTS

ACKNOWLEDGEMENTS

I would like to thank Chris Myers and Shirley Steinberg for the opportunity to make my vision a reality, and to the authors for their insightful contributions. It has been a pleasure to work with all of you on this project.

A heartfelt thank you to my family and friends, especially my dad, Bill O'Hara, for lending his wordsmith skills at a moment's notice; Meg and Will, my children, for their love, laughter, and late night chats; Kathi Cochran and Jim Martinez for their friendship and support; and Georgia, Bennie, and Red for their good company.

INTRODUCTION

Kate E. O'Hara

We are teaching and learning in turbulent times. The idea for this book emerged from the outrage I have felt, and continue to feel, about the onslaught of attacks on public education, the current wave of excessive standardized testing of students, the present-day demonization of teachers, and the push for limited and biased teacher evaluation practices. Twenty years ago, as a classroom teacher in the Bronx, I felt the pressure of teaching curriculum narrowed by standardized exams and teaching under the constraints of "reform" initiatives created by those far removed from daily classroom life. Yet, what I experienced decades ago pales in comparison with the experiences of the in-service teachers I work with today. The toxic education climate is rapidly decaying their morale, their creativity, and their inspiration. In my most recent work with teachers entering the profession, I witness the damaging effects on once energetic and idealistic individuals who are now unsure as to whether they are making the right professional choice, struggling to meet the new scripted requirements of being "allowed" to teach, and fearful of entering their own future classroom stifled with standardization.

However, the neoliberal agenda portrays a very different story, with positive messages relayed about the need for federal funding and monitoring of the education system and the push to move schools from public to private. In a 2012 speech, "Change is Hard," Arne Duncan warned us that "America is slipping," but we'll be okay when we work together, informing us that the "Common Core standards were developed by educators," that as a nation, we all want an evaluation system that is "fair, honest, and realistic" and that teachers "deserve much better pay—especially if it's tied to effectiveness."

The title of the Duncan speech reminds me of the title of Bob Dylan's song, *A Hard Rain's A-Gonna Fall.* In an interview about the song, Dylan explained that it wasn't about atomic rain or fallout rain, but rather, a hard rain, "some sort of end that's just gotta happen" (Cott, 2006, p.7). He goes on to describe his own words:

> In that last verse when I say, 'When the pellets of poison are flooding the waters,' that means all the lies, you know, all the lies that people get told on their radios and in their newspapers. All you have to do is think for a minute. They're trying to take people's brains away. Which maybe has been done already.' (Cott, 2006, p. 8)

Neoliberalism penetrates our common sense understandings (Harvey, 2005), or as Dylan aptly put it, takes our brains away. What Duncan proposes seems to make perfect sense: America is slipping, the Common Core State Standards were developed by educators, we are a unified force in wanting an evaluation system that is fair, honest, and realistic, and teachers deserve better pay, especially if it is tied to their effectiveness. I did not hear Duncan's speech on my radio or read about it in my newspaper; instead, I accessed the script from a federal website. However, regardless of the medium, I am still sickened by the falsehoods presented in his message. But, if the message is laden with lies, where do people find the truth? And, are we looking for one truth? Joe Kincheloe, a brilliant and inspiring teacher, whom I miss greatly, spoke often of multiple truths and urged us to question the notion of "universal truth" (Kincheloe, 2003).

Who, then, questions universal truths and instead speaks multiple truths? The authors in this volume do. As readers, they challenge us to critique, to uncover what is deceptive and misleading, and to envision better ways, multiple ways, of evaluating a teacher.

As I read the chapters and speak with the authors, I am reminded of Foucault's (2001) concept of "parrhesia." One who uses parrhesia is the "parrhesiastes" or the one who speaks the truth. Each contributing author of this volume is a parrhesiastes, for several reasons.

The word parrhesia encompasses more than a singular definition. It has several distinguishable characteristics:

- Parrhesia is aligned to frankness. The parrhesiastes speaks openly and from the heart about his or her opinions through direct words.
- Parrhesia maintains an active relationship with truth. A parrhesiastes says what is true because he or she knows it to be true; the words move beyond sincere opinion to what is known to be true, thus a characteristic of parrhesia is that there is always a correlation between belief and truth.
- Parrhesia is entwined with danger. A parrhesiastes merits consideration only if he or she encounters risk or danger for telling the truth. However, the risk need not be a risk of life but it in some way linked to courage for telling the truth in the face of some varying degree of danger.
- Parrhesia demonstrates the truth to someone else but also has the function and form of criticism. The criticism is toward another or toward oneself, but in either instance, the parrhesiastes is always less powerful than the one with whom he or she is speaking. The parrhesiastes risks his or her privilege to speak freely when disclosing a truth that in some way threatens the majority.
- Parrhesia regards truth telling as a duty. The parrhesiastes is not forced to speak but does so for a moral reason, and oftentimes the act of parrhesia results in yielding a freedom.

Each contributing author is a parrhesiastes, speaking truth through frankness and relating truth that has a certain relationship to their own life in regard to both risk and criticism. In reading the authors' words, you will learn as I did, that their truth telling is a moral duty to improve the well-being of others, paving the way for new freedoms from oppressive practices.

The organization of this book falls under three categories. Section 1, "Critiques and Commentary: Framing the Evaluation Picture," provides readers with a critique of teacher evaluation systems in relation to agendas, expectations, and implementation at the local, state, and national levels. Section 2, "Dis/connecting Practice," illuminates the connections, and more often, the disconnections between preservice and in-service classroom practice and evaluation measures. Section 3, "Envisioning Change," speaks to the possibilities and the channels for reform.

Section 1: Critiques and Commentary: Framing the Evaluation Picture

In the first chapter, **Kevin Froner** and **Nicholas M. Michelli** address the importance of standards and evaluation when applied in the right context and especially when measuring the more significant educational goals in a democracy. They argue that value-added models being adopted and implemented today are problematic and also unreliable when used to make judgments about individual teachers. Froner and Michelli make the unambiguous statement that their opposition to these models not be misconstrued; the authors are not against assessment but rather they hold the strong belief that we are in need of a transparent, authentic assessment for our preservice and in-service teachers. They advise that we be cognizant of the negative effects of value-added measures and recognize "the real danger of all of these approaches to assessment is a severe narrowing of the curriculum and, with the advent of edTPA, the narrowing of pedagogy." Their belief in, and outline of, four purposes of education in a democracy guide us in a framework for promise.

In the second chapter, **David A. Gorlewski** and **Julie A. Gorlewski** contend that edTPA "does not represent *positivism* but a *false positivism* (Saltman, 2012). The language of the rubrics does not, in fact, create objectivity; rather, it presents the *perception* of objectivity." They provide readers a narrative that exemplifies how edTPA's support and assessment system divides the multifaceted and complex acts of teaching and learning into distinct subcategories. Gorlewski and Gorlewski include in their chapter the contention that edTPA's assessment system unquestionably conveys to teacher candidates that the multiple aspects and characteristics of their teaching and learning processes are deemed either important or unimportant, based on the given areas edTPA chooses to rate. This leaves many teacher candidates narrowing their practice by teaching through a standards-based approach.

In Chapter 3, **Mark Garrison** presents the argument that the key problems with test-based teacher evaluation and compensation systems are not simply technical in nature, but instead, they reveal "fundamental problems of both a political and philosophical nature." Garrison takes readers through a review of the meaning, as well as a critique of, the operational theory of measurement. He goes on to make the case that "operationism" is best understood as a political act, documenting the role of operationism in the rise of test-based teacher evaluation systems. Garrison ends his chapter with an invitation to view operationism as "a technique for social control, not for knowledge production that engages the public and serves the common good." He asks readers to learn from past experience and create a new vision and governance structure to guide education.

As the author of Chapter 4, I present readers with accounts of the damaging effects of a neoliberal agenda for education "reform." I critique and analyze universal truths from the federal, state, and local levels and relate stories of the destructive impact at the classroom level, through the eyes of teachers and students. Within a critical framework, I also propose ways to respond to the national rhetoric, uncover multiple truths, and work in solidarity for change.

Section 2: Dis/Connecting Practice

In Chapter 5, **Elizabeth A. Bloom, Barbara Regenspan,** and **Jennifer Mc-Dowall** introduce readers to a conversation among three people: a field supervisor of teacher candidates, a teacher educator/teacher candidate advisor, and a teacher candidate. The three authors are deeply involved with edTPA in different capacities, and they collectively share their negative experiences. Their stories touch on the implementation of edTPA and its negative impact on curriculum development in teacher preparation coursework and in the K-12 classroom, teaching to the test, and the "narrowing and instrumentalizing" of teacher candidate work. A candid depiction of a "failing" teacher candidate is also presented. Bloom, Regenspan, and McDowall ask readers to consider models for resisting edTPA and "other elements of the neoliberal 'accountability' agenda."

In the sixth chapter, **Pamela Althea Joyce, Joy Barnes-Johnson**, and **Joanne M. Carris** incorporate a critical theoretical lens to present their thoughts and observations about the controversial topics of student assessment and teacher evaluation. These three veteran teachers provide insight from pedagogical and ontological perspectives, relating narrative accounts and critiques and challenging readers to ask if the American education system is truly promoting "an umbrella effect of teaching that is all-encompassing and able to produce student achievement results from collaborative efforts based on an awareness of an expansive learning environment." Joyce, Barnes-Johnson, and Carris make the claim that in order to do so, we must facilitate change and innovations with "the force of collective power."

In Chapter 7, **Lynda Kennedy** explores what it means to define quality teaching and learning in regard to social studies and history content. She poses the following questions to readers: What is deemed worthy historical content? What is quality history teaching and learning? Who gets to decide? Kennedy also addresses the training of teachers in social studies and history content areas, teacher effectiveness, and the marginalization of disciplines due to a current emphasis on high-stakes testing in mathematics and English language arts. She ends her chapter with the caveat that "radical change in what we value as essential student learning and what we accept as authentic assessment of effective teaching" is needed.

Section 3: Envisioning Change

In the eighth chapter, **Anne Beitlers** and **Pedro Noguera** bring to the forefront a necessity for additional research on effective teaching as it relates to what teachers understand about meeting the learning needs of their students and how, in turn, this understanding can influence their practice. Beitlers and Noguera argue that to effectively meet the learning needs of students, in particular Black and Latino male students, it is essential that teachers increase relevance in their curriculum. Findings from their research illustrate that although "teachers were knowledgeable about the importance of curricular relevance, they were not effective at infusing relevance into their curriculum." However, the authors also propose that by understanding the contributing aspects of teacher effectiveness, we are then better suited to determine whether current education policies will lead to the improvements in both teachers' effective practice and students' achievement.

In Chapter 9, **Haiwen Chu** and **Gloria Rodríguez Bañuelos** critique teacher evaluation systems, contending that existing definitions of effective teachers and student growth are narrow and misleading. They argue that current systems are characterized by inequitable, hierarchical power relations and lack adequate supports for continued teacher growth. Chu and Rodríguez Bañuelos relate the details of an innovative, alternative model of teacher evaluation that is closely aligned with sustained professional development, classroom observation, and teacher portfolios of student work. They also explore the use of six interconnected domains: vision, motivation, reflection, knowledge, practice, and context.

Jaime E. Martinez completes this volume with a chapter that explores the use of a social therapeutic framework for viewing the philosophical, political, and practical issues related to teacher evaluation. The framework itself allows us to see the teacher as a performer. In schools, teacher performance is typically constructed and constrained by multiple social arrangements. However, from a social therapeutic perspective, a highly scripted performance can move to a performance that engages others to create new ways of being. When looking at producing change in teacher evaluation practices, Martinez advises readers that, "we, revolutionary teachers, will have to take responsibility for creating that change."

Collectively, the contributing authors of this volume skillfully present insightful and intriguing perspectives, inviting us to consider multiple truths. Through their words, they also invite us take their messages and build upon them with our own thoughts, critiques, and voices. In doing so, we each join them in acting as a parrhesiastes.

References

Cott, J. (Ed.) (2006). Radio interview with Studs Terkel, WFMT Chicago, May 1963. *Bob Dylan: The Essential Interviews* (pp. 5–12). New York, NY: Wenner Books.

Duncan, A. (2012). *Change is hard*. Retrieved from http://www.ed.gov/news/speeches/change-hard

Foucault, M. (2001). *Fearless speech*. Los Angeles, CA: Semiotext(e).

Harvey, D. (2005). *A brief history of neoliberalism*. Oxford, UK: Oxford University Press.

Kincheloe, J. L. (2003). *Teachers as researchers: Qualitative inquiry as a path to empowerment*. New York, NY: Peter Lang.

Saltman, K. (2012). *Democratic education against corporate school reform: The new market bureaucracy in U.S. public schooling*. North Dartmouth: Social Policy, Education and Curriculum, Research Unit, North Dartmouth Center for Policy Analyses. University of Massachusetts Dartmouth.

SECTION 1
CRITIQUES AND COMMENTARY: FRAMING THE EVALUATION PICTURE

· 1 ·

TEACHER EVALUATION IN THE CURRENT ERA: IMPLICATIONS FOR TEACHER EDUCATION POLICY AND PEDAGOGY

Kevin Froner and Nicholas M. Michelli

Democracy cannot flourish where the chief influences in selecting subject matter of instruction are utilitarian ends narrowly conceived for the masses, and, for the higher education of the few, the traditions of a specialized cultivated class. The notion that the "essentials" of elementary education are the three R's mechanically treated, is based upon ignorance of the essentials needed for realization of democratic ideals. Unconsciously it assumes that these ideals are unrealizable; it assumes that in the future, as in the past, getting a livelihood, "making a living," must dignify for most men and women doing things which are not significant, freely chosen, and ennobling to those who do them; doing things which serve ends unrecognized by those engaged in them, carried on under the direction of others for the sake of pecuniary reward.

John Dewey, *Democracy and Education*

As public schools prepare for a myriad of new teacher evaluations, including the standardization and in many ways nationalization of our education system, educators (including those in preservice programs) must consider how the emerging culture of accountability, measurement, and general mistrust of teachers will influence their experiences in the classroom. Furthermore, teacher educators must consider how new forms of assessment will likely be used in the evaluation of teacher education programs. As public K-12 schools prepare students for the global economy, it appears that the overutilization of teacher evaluation models tied to state examinations is causing some to reconsider why we educate in a democracy and others to question the very purpose of public education.

As a former dean of education at two universities and a current New York City principal, it is not our intention as authors to claim that the Common Core State Standards, edTPA (derived from California's Performance Assessment of California Teachers and the basis for the evaluation of pre-service teachers in an increasing number of states), or teacher evaluation frameworks are the problem in and of themselves, although we point out issues with some of them. Standards and evaluations can be quite valuable if applied in the right context, especially when measuring the more significant educational goals in a democracy.

We will argue, however, that the value-added models increasingly being adopted, in part as a response to Race to the Top, have proven inherently problematic and unreliable when used to make judgments of individual educators (Amrein-Beardsley, 2008; Darling-Hammond, Amrein-Beardsley, Haertel, & Rothstein, 2012; Ladd & Walsh, 2002). One of our greatest concerns is that as the assessment of public education becomes increasingly centered on high-stakes examinations, components that are not easily measured become undervalued. Furthermore, the effect of the current emphasis on high-stakes assessment jeopardizes the culture and climate of schools by increasing stress for principals, teachers, and students.

Let us begin by examining what we believe to be the earliest contexts for public education, including the democratic and civically inspired pillars of schooling.

Why Educate in a Democracy?

How and why we educate in a democracy is a question that has been explored since the establishment of our common school system at the turn of the 18th century, but the current zeitgeist may find its roots in the early twentieth century with the rarely discussed fracture of the Progressive Era education reform movement. During this period, John Dewey and the pedagogical progressives opened schools built on experiential and authentic learning with an emphasis on the development of student-centered classrooms. Some of these institutions are still open today, ironically operating as elite private schools, serving primarily the most affluent among us. We know that some schools of education still teach Dewey, incorporate the more significant pedagogical ideologies, and prepare candidates who understand constructivism and student-centered learning, but the spirit of the movement has mostly been replaced with the measurable and "scientific."

The current discourse on measuring effectiveness did not begin with No Child Left Behind (NCLB) and Race to the Top (RTTT) but dates back to at least the early 1900s when scientific management swept the private sector and infiltrated our schools (Callahan, 1964). The "cult of efficiency" touched everything and buoyed the reforms of the progressive administrators, who viewed the school as a medium to reform society. A noble idea indeed, but in the end, the progressive politicians built large comprehensive public schools lacking both the rigor from the classic curricula that preceded it and the creativity and inquiry-based approaches fostered by Dewey's pedagogues (Labaree, 2005). The alignment we find today between the private sector and public schools was arguably augmented during this period as curricular reform led to policy aligned with business interests, including the removal of Greek and Latin, which were replaced with vocational programs. The comprehensive factory-like high schools continued well into the 1980s, when our manufacturing sector collapsed and the advent of the knowledge economy required a rethinking of public education and postsecondary training.

The second dominant theme emerging out of the post-Progressive Era and continuing into the second half of the 20th century was the issue of equity. The 1954 *Brown v. Board of Education* decision marked a major turning point in integration and the belief that separate was not equal. This was followed by the Elementary and Secondary Education Act (ESEA) of 1965, the Higher Education Act (HEA) in that same year, and the Individuals with Disabilities Education Act (IDEA) of 1975. It can be argued that all were established to further equal opportunities for educational achievement. The Equality of Educational Opportunity Report published in 1966 (Coleman et al.) emerged from the decade's milieu, finding that economic conditions played the most significant role in student achievement, a reality understood by most. The report also suggested that beyond socioeconomic limitations, teachers provided the greatest opportunity to effect change within schools. This led to decades of research on teacher effectiveness, the growth of value-added models or measures (VAMs), and most recently, econometric education studies that measure students' future economic gains correlated with their teachers' VAM scores (Chetty, Friedman, & Rockoff, 2011; Hanushek, 2008; Hanushek, Kain, & Rivkin, 2005; Haycock & Crawford, 2008; Hopkins & Stern, 1996).

Quantitative research in this field, built on regression analysis that correlates student test scores and future earnings, has been used to bolster the 21st-century economic-education discourse (Chetty et al., 2011; Hanushek, 2010) on the monetary value attributed to quality teaching. The underlying assumptions in such studies have been that effective teachers produce higher student test scores and higher test scores yield more economic opportunities, resulting in higher future earnings for students. The results often produce gross exaggerations and misleading economic implications. With a growing emphasis on public schooling and its role in the economy, we ask the following two questions: What role does civic education and social justice play inside this framework? How is educating for the economy reshaping our goals? Answering these questions is essential to understanding the context for the new evaluation systems and accountability measures.

Teacher Evaluation Systems and Emerging Constructs for Public Schooling

As the new teacher evaluation systems infiltrate nearly every element of public education, including preservice teacher education programs, we find a general lack of resistance to the new measurements beyond very sparse protest and academic critiques that have been overwhelmed by an extraordinary political will to solidify rigid structures for teacher accountability. Systematized and concretized, the art of the possible is being eviscerated in public school classrooms.

VAMs, new teacher performance assessments, and teacher evaluation frameworks have provided means to measure teacher effectiveness and are becoming the dominant instruments for teacher assessment. As the teacher evaluation systems coalesce and align, a construct of teacher accountability has ignited a power transfer from our public schools and schools of education to government bureaucracies and private entities like Pearson. From schools led by educators we are moving to a reliance on complex algorithms that promise to accurately identify teacher effectiveness and student growth. These students are learning and those are not. These teachers are effective and those are not. These programs to prepare teachers are effective and those are not.

Research shows, however, that VAMs have margins of errors so wide that an ineffective teacher might in fact be very effective and an effective teacher might be thoroughly ineffective, depending on the error or variables absent from the algorithm (Briggs & Domingue, 2011; Darling-Hammond et al., 2012). Politicians and pundits now call for the release of teacher ratings, and scores have been published for school districts and individual schools. What we find is an environment of mistrust, competition, and at times disdain for educators, a culture often absent in many other developed nations. Finland, often cited as an exemplar in public education, has only one major standardized test, and the responsibility of student assessment is afforded to educators, who enjoy a highly regarded status shared with the Nordic nation's doctors and lawyers. The teachers, not the state, oversee student progress, the design of rigorous assessments, and the creation of learning experiences that encourage the growth and development of all students (Sahlberg, 2007).

The solidification of the current public education construct in the United States is doing just the opposite, with standardized testing at almost every grade level, evaluation frameworks tied to unreliable VAMs, and new performance assessments that appear to transfer the responsibility of evaluating preservice teachers, at least in part, from faculty in schools of education and K-12 schools to Pearson, a multibillion dollar international education company. Furthermore, as the Council for the Accreditation of Education Programs (CAEP) finalizes its new standards, it is clear that VAMs and new teacher evaluations will weigh heavily on schools of education as evidence of success.

Albert Einstein, in several contexts, said, "Not everything that matters can be counted, and not everything we count matters." What a perfect statement describing the dilemma we face, as some of the most significant goals of public education have become minimized by the overemphasis of testing. In the current public education environment, we find that everything not reduced to quantifiable form is deemed less important or simply ignored.

There is serious evidence, beginning with NCLB, that when the focus of tests is on one or two content areas—in this case language arts and mathematics—those subjects become the focus almost exclusively, with a great deal of time devoted to test preparation. The net effect is a narrowing of the functions and objectives of education to what is included on those tests.

Pillars of Public Schooling

We believe that there are four purposes of education in a democracy. The first purpose is to prepare students with a deep knowledge of subjects to the level that they can think critically about that knowledge. The second purpose is that learning to live and communicate in a socially just democracy is the very foundation of a civically educated society. This means that we must teach students to listen carefully to others and their positions, to argue for their own position effectively and with evidence, and to compromise within the limits of integrity. The third purpose is to prepare students to take advantage of life's chances to reach the highest possible levels in society. This involves helping them know what is needed for success and to imagine themselves in colleges and positions that they may not have considered.

Maxine Greene's (2001) admonition that "we cannot become what we cannot imagine" (p. 47) says a great deal. Do we foster imagination, helping students envision what they can become while raising their hopes and expectations? Do we provide opportunities for them to interact with professionals to understand what they do? Not if we are simply preparing them to take high-stakes tests. The fourth purpose of education is to prepare students to lead rich and rewarding personal lives by helping them develop a love for both fiction and nonfiction, to engage with art, to critique what they read, to become physically fit, and to have a global perspective. Anyone looking at K-12 public schools in our society, and, increasingly, at colleges of education, might conclude that indeed, education exists to prepare students for high-stakes tests.

The Case of Louisiana and the Expansion of Value-Added Models

Louisiana was one of the first states to have extensively implemented VAMs. In 1999, the state's "Blue Ribbon Commission for Teacher Quality" mandated a redesign of all programs and the addition of more rigorous requirements. Beginning in 2010, Louisiana moved to a system of evaluating all public classroom teachers and principals based on student growth on standardized tests as reflected in their RTTT application. Fifty percent of the evaluation of teachers was to be based on student test score data and evidence of growth (Deshotels, 2010).

Another outcome of the work of this commission required the redesign of all programs to prepare teachers as well as to secure national accreditation, an accountability system dependent on performance scores to be published for each university, and development of a value-added system to assess teacher preparation programs and teachers (Fleener & Exner, 2011, p. 27). To accomplish this, an extensive student data system was developed with the qualities required for VAMs, such as linking students to individual teachers across years. This was the first instance where a state adopted the practice of using the effectiveness of graduates of college teacher education programs in raising the standardized test scores as the measure of the success of a program. There is much to be learned from this experience, which is likely to spread to other states in light of current policy and practices.

Among the most potent criticisms of value-added systems is the focus on the assessment of individual teachers and high-stakes decisions for these teachers. Louisiana avoided this criticism, at least with respect to teacher education, by aggregating graduates of given programs rather than reporting individual teacher scores. Fleener and Exner (2011) identified four ways in which the Louisiana system differs from other VAMs:

1. The system has the capability of providing effect scores for individual teachers, but to date the system's scores are aggregated by teacher education programs and not intended for use in assessing individual teachers.
2. The system compares first and second year teachers against experienced teacher's scores.
3. Scores are aggregated further by subject areas taught, providing a report for programs with data (those using standardized tests). In the case of Louisiana, these were mathematics, social studies, English language arts, science, and reading. So there is data for teachers of mathematics by the program they graduated from, for teachers of social studies, etc.
4. Based on the outcomes, programs are ranked in one of four "bands" ranging from programs for which graduates perform at a higher level than experienced teachers, programs where the effect is somewhat better than experienced teachers, those where the effect for new teachers is typical of new teachers, programs where the effect of new teachers shows them to be generally less effective than teachers, and programs where beginning teachers score below the mean of other new teachers at a statistically significant level. (pp. 33–34)

There is one other important variable. Not all graduates of a program are included in the assessment; in fact, the results include only about 16% of teachers graduated in a given cohort, excluding 84% of the graduates. Why are they excluded? Teachers are excluded if they teach an area not tested in Louisiana, such as foreign language or physical education. Teachers are excluded if they teach in private schools. Teachers teaching in a grade where tests are not used are excluded. The result of such a significant narrowing of the sample is that cohort data may not be representative of the teacher effectiveness of a university's graduates (Fleener & Exner, 2011, p. 36).

So, in Louisiana, the use of aggregated scores rather than scores for individual teachers does respond to one criticism of VAMs—that it is not reliable enough to make high-stakes decisions for individual teachers. Furthermore, it does not eliminate criticism questioning the validity and reliability of using K-12 standardized test scores to accurately assess postsecondary preservice education programs.

College leaders using this system conclude that it does not provide useful information for program improvement (Fleener & Exner, 2011). For example, the reported differences among the various bands provided no guidance on how to use the data for real program change. The positive effect of not including data on individual teachers also has the effect of not being able to determine whether the cohort reported is in fact representative.

Louisiana provides a good example of extending VAMs beyond individual teachers to their education programs and the limitations implicit in the model. How do we account for teachers in areas that are not assessed? How do we interpret the meaning of the scores? Do they take into account the contexts in which teachers teach?

The Case of Florida: A Political Victory

In Florida, as in many states in the past decade, policymakers focused on teacher education as the culprit of unsatisfactory results in the public education system. The dissatisfaction of policymakers and the rapid increase of new teachers because of a class size reduction initiative led to the emergence, in a short period of time, of a number of alternative routes to teaching. These included the American Board for the Certification of Teacher Excellence, Educator Preparation Institutes, and professional training options. Some of the options involved community colleges and four-year colleges. None of the alternatives, however, were explicitly tied to teacher candidate evaluations; nevertheless, concern mounted from college faculty and deans of education.

The perceived crisis in K-12 public education and the conclusion that teachers were to blame culminated in the introduction of Senate Bill 6 (2010), which proposed the enactment of the following changes:

- Decrease the ability of local school boards and school districts to make a wide array of decisions having an impact on local schools and replacing them with a one-size-fits-all approach mandated from Tallahassee.
- Require that all teachers be retained, certified and compensated based on student test scores on standardized tests, not years of experience or degrees held.
- Penalize school districts that even consider length of service or degrees held when determining compensation or reductions in force.
- Order that teachers be issued probationary contracts for up to five years; then an annual contract every year after that…eliminating tenure.
- Mandate more standardized testing for students (end of course exams for all subjects) and for teachers (additional certification requirements).
- Exclude the salary schedule as a subject of collective bargaining. The state will decide what categories of differentiated pay will be provided.
- Grant to the state a much greater hand in all assessments.
- Abolish an effective and popular program that rewards those who become National Board Certified Teachers, a rigorous national program that awards certification after a yearlong, independent review of a teacher's work in the classroom and knowledge of their field. ("Florida Teachers," n.d.)

Many, including then Governor Crist, who had succeeded Jeb Bush, objected to the bill, saying the following:

> Florida is truly blessed to have such high quality teachers who have made our education system one of the best in the nation. SB 6 punishes the teachers who delivered these stunning educational gains. It lashes out at the teachers who have made Florida schools a model for the nation, the same teachers, Governor Crist says we're "blessed" to have in our classrooms. Nevertheless, if bills like SB 6 pass, they won't be in our classrooms much longer. ("Florida Teachers," n.d.)

Simultaneously, a companion bill was introduced in the Florida House and members felt that they had their "marching orders," with no change possible to the nearly identical bills. Not only would the legislation effectively have ended tenure for K-12 educators for whom tenure was possible, but it would have eliminated the role of higher degrees in salary, requiring that compensation be based on student standardized test scores. Thus the bill had required further development of a value-added system.

The response around the country was strong and critical. *The Washington Post*, for example, published a piece entitled, "Disaster for Florida Teachers: Senate Bill 6" (Strauss, 2010):

> Support by President Obama and Education Secretary Arne Duncan for using student standardized test scores as one measure to evaluate teacher performance gives license for legislators to take that thinking to extremes. That's what is happening in Florida, where the state Senate is considering legislation, Senate Bill 6, that would, if passed, go a long way toward destroying the teaching profession in the state. (para. 1–2)

Senate Bill 6 and its companion bill never became law. The lobbying was extraordinary, with the governor receiving more than 100,000 calls and emails from educators across the nation. At the time, Governor Crist was in a race for the Republican nomination for the U.S. Senate against current Senator Marco Rubio. The governor took the initiative to veto the bill, some say, because he was behind in the Senate race and had nothing to lose (Emihovich, Dana, & Vernetson, 2011). No one believes that the pressure to change teacher education and evaluate candidates is over, but for now, it has been limited (Strauss, 2010).

edTPA and Teacher Education

In 1998, the California State Board of Education, in part as a means to maintain common standards for the emerging pathways into teaching, mandated that all California candidates seeking a preliminary teaching credential pass a state-approved teaching performance assessment with demonstrated validity and reliability to supplement training, course assignments, and supervisor evaluations. Work began in earnest to develop an assessment system with a consortium of educators from public and private universities across California (Darling-Hammond & Hyler, 2013), leading to the Performance Evaluation of California Teachers (PACT). The PACT was to assess the degree of competence of candidates to

- Plan lessons based on California standards and take account of English learners and students with other learning challenges.
- Teach the standards based lessons in California classrooms.
- Plan and administer student assessments based on the lessons.
- Reflect on their own instruction.
- Examine student work and assessment results as evidence of the effectiveness of instruction and then to use the knowledge gained in planning the next lesson. ("Teacher Performance Assessment," n.d., p. 1)

Evaluators of the PACT are university faculty or K-12 educators who are trained to assess the evidence provided by teachers as part of their performance tasks. The document further reports that PACT is intended to be used

- As part of the recommendation of a candidate for a credential.
- As an indicator of the effectiveness of the teacher education program.
- By the candidate to evaluate his or her progress and needs.
- As evidence of a candidate's development for use in a beginning teacher induction program. ("Teacher Performance Assessment," n.d., p. 2)

The California Commission on Teaching also published a handbook for developing a "teaching event" (incorporating instruction, assessment, and reflection) for 18 subject areas, including elementary literacy and mathematics, art, health, science, and agriculture. In addition, the PACT has accompanying rubric handbooks ("Performance Assessment for California Teachers," n.d.) that provide four categories for each standard to be used in making judgments, and candidates are rated 1 to 4 based on the evidence provided.

The Teacher Performance Assessment (TPA), now referred to as edTPA, is based on the work developed by PACT. Like PACT, it is intended for use with teacher candidates and is a means of assessing classroom performance by observing teaching. edTPA is emerging as a major element in certification, adopted by a number of states, including New York, and endorsed and supported by the American Association of Colleges for Teacher Education. Like the PACT, edTPA requires students to develop evidence of teaching ability from a single subject-specific learning segment and represented by lessons from that segment. Evidence from that segment includes lesson plans, student work, analysis of student work, and reflective commentaries, along with video clips of instruction.

Imagine the mass of data that will be created when every candidate produces a portfolio with the required elements. Recognizing the task and the cost, the developers decided to invite Pearson, a British corporation and perhaps the largest publishing house in the world, to assist. Preservice teachers are to pay for the evaluation, with the cost estimated at $300 per candidate. Candidate data is then sent to Pearson, where it is designated to trained evaluators. Evaluation is not conducted by the college or university faculty who have taught, nurtured, and supervised the candidate; it is conducted by Pearson assessors. To some, this seems reasonable. In fact, the process, including Pearson's involvement and the use of external assessors, is parallel to the approach taken by the National Board for Professional Teaching Standards. Darling-Hammond recognized that some characterize edTPA as the corporatization of teacher education, but said the following:

> Nothing could be further from the truth. Like the National Board portfolio, edTPA was not developed, nor is it owned by Pearson. Like assessments in other professions, it was developed—and is guided—by a consortium of professional educators. These individuals make decisions about design, the scoring process, and the qualifications of those asked to score (accomplished teachers and teacher educators). Instructors and supervisors continue to teach, observe, support and evaluate candidates as they always have. (Darling-Hammond & Hyler, 2013, para. 20)

For others, the authors included, there are some unanswered questions and concerns about the impact of edTPA. For one, we know that in the university system where we work, methods classes now include preparation for edTPA, focused on the classroom behaviors evaluated. Here, the same criticism that we leveled at NCLB applies: the preparation has narrowed the curriculum largely to what is measured by edTPA. While edTPA does not itself connect to value-added assessments, some states adopting edTPA are using value-added assessments and tying success in this demonstration of student learning measured by standardized tests to continued tenure and salary increases. We do not know the results of any studies of the correlation for edTPA and future success, but there are preliminary studies involving the PACT, a very similar instrument.

A study by Darling-Hammond, Newton, and Wei (2012b) found that there were small but statistically significant correlations between success on the PACT and the later achievement of a candidates' students measured by VAMs. Furthermore, it showed that the strongest effects were for mathematics in middle school, where content-specific pedagogy and knowledge are often highly variable (Darling-Hammond, Newton, & Wei, 2012). Part of the validation of edTPA may be correlating candidates' scores on the instrument with the value-added gains of their students.

Finally, while California colleges and universities could identify their own faculty and K-12 partners to serve as evaluators after extensive training, in the case of edTPA and the Pearson model, the evaluation is farmed out to educators trained by Pearson. The concern is simple. College faculty and K-12 mentors have had a significant role in the preparation and recommendation of students for licensing. That responsibility is now shifted to the core of assessors identified for edTPA and employed by Pearson. Surely, as noted, college faculty and K-12 mentors will continue to teach, observe, and assess students, but success on edTPA has become the essential requirement for certification in states where it is adopted. Candidates may have the recommendation of their college and university faculty for certification but will not be certified without a score based on the assessment of the outside evaluator.

On balance, we certainly accept the arguments put forth that to become a profession, teaching must move to assess candidates on measures designed by and endorsed by members of the profession, as, it is argued, is the case with PACT. We hope that as this measure is used, and if a correlation with value-added tests is implemented, the broader purposes of educating in a democracy are not lost.

Conclusions

In examining the research on teacher evaluations and the implications for teacher education, we have come to several conclusions about the new assessments.

First, the momentum of the evolution of edTPA and the value-added assessment of teachers can be traced to the requirements of RTTT, specifically, its requirements for assessment and the development of large data sets to enable VAMs. Second, given that pressure, it seems inevitable that the use of quantitative outcomes, including VAMs to evaluate candidates for teaching, teacher education institutions, and practicing teachers and principals, will continue to grow. We must be cognizant of the effects of such measures on school climate and personal well-being of educators and do what we can to mitigate the effects. Third, in voicing opposition to these measures, we must be very careful to avoid the appearance that we are against assessment. We are not. We need clear, open, authentic assessment that takes place in a learning community. Fourth, there is a very important lesson from the Florida case.

Opposition from educators to a Draconian measure can pay off. The governor vetoed the legislation that was described as about to "destroy the teaching profession in Florida." We know that there were extenuating circumstances, namely the governor's standing in the race to be the Republican nominee for the Senate. He had nothing to lose. Nevertheless, he did the right thing and, anticipating the consequences, he left the Republican Party to become an independent. Political action is important, and when it involves a local issue, it can be successful.

Finally, the real danger of these approaches to assessment is a severe narrowing of the curriculum and, with the advent of edTPA, a narrowing of pedagogy. The evidence that preparing for edTPA displaces other pedagogical curricula in methods courses is an example we have experienced in our own work. As Albert Shankar said, "What matters is what we measure." Are we certain that we are measuring all that we hope for as outcomes of education in our evolving democracy?

References

Amrein-Beardsley, A. (2008). Methodological concerns about the Education Value-Added Assessment System. *Educational Researcher, 37*(2), 65–75.

Briggs, D., & Domingue, B. (2011). *Due diligence and the evaluation of teachers: A review of the value-added analysis underlying the effectiveness rankings of Los Angeles Unified School District teachers by the Los Angeles Times*. Boulder, CO: National Education Policy Center. Retrieved from http://nepc.colorado.edu/publication/due-diligence

Callahan, R. E. (1964). *Education and the cult of efficiency*. Chicago, IL: University of Chicago Press.

Chetty, R., Friedman, J. N., & Rockoff, J. E. (2011). The long-term impacts of teachers: Teacher value-added and student outcomes in adulthood. NBER Work. Pap.17699.

Coleman, J. S., Campbell, E. Q., Hobson, C. J., McPartland, J., Mood, A. M., Weinfeld, F. D., & York, R. L. (1966). *Equality of educational opportunity*. Washington, DC: U.S. Government Printing Office.

Darling-Hammond, L., Amrein-Beardsley, A., Haertel, E., & Rothstein, J. (2012). Evaluating teacher evaluation. *Phi Delta Kappan, 93*(6), 8–15.

Darling-Hammond, L., & Hyler, M. (2013). The role of performance assessment in developing teaching as a profession. *Rethinking Schools*. Retrieved from http://www.rethinkingschools.org/archive/27_04/27_04_darling-hammond_hyler.shtml

Darling-Hammond, L., Newton, S. P., & Wei, R. (2012). *Developing and assessing beginning teacher effectiveness: The potential of performance assessments*. Stanford, CA: Stanford Center for Opportunity Policy in Education. Retrieved from http://edpolicy.stanford.edu/publications/pubs/657

Deshotels, M. (2010, January 21). *Teacher evaluation models*. Retrieved from http://louisianaed ucator.blogspot.com/2010/01/teacher-evaluation-models.html

Dewey, J. (1916). *Democracy and education*. Retrieved from http://www.gutenberg.org/files/852/852-h/852-h.htm

Emihovich, C., Dana, T., & Vernetson, T. (2011). Changing needs: The gauntlet of teacher education reform. In P. M. Earley, D. Imig, & N. M. Michelli (Eds.), *Teacher education policy in the United States: Issues and tensions in an era of evolving expectations* (pp. 47–69). New York, NY: Taylor & Francis.

Fleener, M. J., & Exner, M. J. (2011). Dimensions of teacher education accountability: A Louisiana perspective on value-added. In P. M. Earley, D. Imig, & N. M. Michelli (Eds.), *Teacher education policy in the United States: Issues and tensions in an era of evolving expectations* (pp. 26–46). New York, NY: Taylor & Francis.

Florida teachers express opposition to Senate bill 6. (n.d.). Retrieved from http://feaweb.org/florida-teachers-express-opposition-to-senate-bill-6

Greene, M. (2001). *Variations on a blue guitar: The Lincoln Center Institute Lectures on aesthetic education*. New York, NY: Teachers College Press.

Hanushek, E. A. (2010). *The economic value of higher teacher quality*. Cambridge, MA: National Bureau of Economic Research.

Hanushek, E. A. (2008). Teacher deselection. *Stanford University*. Retrieved from http://media.trb.com/media/acrobat/2009-10/49898689.pdf

Hanushek, E. A., Kain, J. F., & Rivkin, S. G. (2005). *The market for teacher quality*. Cambridge, MA: National Bureau of Economic Research.

Haycock, K., & Crawford, C. (2008). Closing the teacher quality gap. *Educational Leadership, 65*, 14–19.

Hopkins, D., & Stern, D. (1996). Quality teachers, quality schools: International perspectives and policy implications. *Teaching and Teacher Education, 12*(5), 501–517.

Labaree, D. F. (2005). Progressivism, schools and schools of education: An American romance. *Paedagogica Historica, 41*(1–2), 275–288.

Ladd, H. F., & Walsh, R. P. (2002). Implementing value-added measures of school effectiveness: Getting the incentives right. *Economics of Education Review, 21*, 1–17.

Performance assessment for California teachers. (n.d.). Retrieved from http://www.pacttpa.org/_main/hub.php?pageName=Supporting_Documents_for_Candidates#Handbooks

Sahlberg, P. (2007). Education policies for raising student learning: The Finnish approach. *Journal of Education Policy, 22*(2), 147–171.

Senate Bill 6. (2010). Retrieved from http://archive.flsenate.gov/data/session/2010/Senate/bills/analysis/pdf/2010s0006.ed.pdf

Strauss, V. (2010, March 24). Disaster for Florida teachers: Senate bill 6. *The Washington Post*. Retrieved from http://voices.washingtonpost.com/answer-sheet/education-secretary-duncan/a-disaster-for-teachers-in-flo.html

Teacher performance assessment. (n.d.) Retrieved from http://www.pacttpa.org/_files/Main/CalTPAPromo-Policy.pdf

· 2 ·

PRODUCING PROFESSIONALS: ANALYZING WHAT COUNTS FOR EDTPA

David A. Gorlewski and Julie A. Gorlewski

We are not new to the lesson planning process. As former high school language arts teachers, K-12 language arts coordinators, and district level leaders, we have been immersed in issues related to curriculum development, standardized testing, and faculty development for a long, long time. Our move to higher education placed us in teacher education programs where we taught curriculum planning to childhood, secondary, and special education candidates for nearly a decade. We think we have a pretty good understanding of what a good lesson plan looks like and how the learning objectives should include content, a behavior, and a listing of the conditions and criteria to measure the meeting of the objective and verify individual understanding, and we both stress to our students—all teacher candidates—the critical importance of connecting the stated objective to the steps of the lesson and, ultimately, to the evaluation.

Often, these are difficult concepts for teacher candidates to master, and one wonders if any teacher ever really "masters" anything in the profession, given differences in learners, the environment, the culture of an organization, and the changing concepts of what it means to be an educated person. Some teacher candidates pick up the lesson planning process quickly, but others struggle to see the difference between *telling* (essentially lecturing or demonstrating) and *teaching* (a much more complicated process that includes pre-assessing, scaffolding, planning multimodal instruction, providing guided practice, and developing an evaluation tool that adequately assesses knowledge and understanding). But, with additional explanations, the use of exemplars, and student-to-student collaborations, teacher candidates eventually gain an understanding of how to write a lesson plan and deliver instruction.

Today, we are in a new era of accountability where outside agents (currently, the state in cooperation with private entities) develop, administer, and evaluate tests of teacher candidates as the last *gateway* to certification to (allegedly) provide assurance of competence and professionalism. These tests are, of course, layered onto an array of measures of competence found in any teacher education program: teacher candidate entrance examinations, coursework, classroom observations, and student teaching (with its recordkeeping, logs, reflection papers, and competency checklists, among other assignments). Yet, the perception is that teacher candidates must pass through still another gateway to prove that they are competent and that teaching is a *profession*. This goal has manifested itself in the form of edTPA – the Teacher Performance Assessment in Education. In short, any teacher candidate applying for initial certification in New York State on or after May 1, 2014, must take and pass this evaluation.

Structure of the Chapter

This chapter provides a literature review addressing the nature of the Global Education Reform Movement (GERM), standardization and the use of rubrics (the critical component in evaluating the submissions of edTPA documents), and teacher identity. It then focuses on how edTPA's evaluation process, driven by the content of the rubrics used to evaluate the documents submitted by teacher candidates, determines what skills and dispositions are privileged, what skills and dispositions are marginalized, what appears to count as "effective" teaching and learning and, ultimately, how it affects the development of teacher identity. As certified (and former) language arts teachers, we analyze edTPA rubrics for English language arts, an area in which we have some expertise.

Thesis

In this chapter, we argue that edTPA, a support and assessment system that scores on numeric scale lesson plans, lesson delivery, and lesson evaluation, as well as various "commentaries" on those processes, does not represent *positivism* but a *false positivism* (Saltman, 2012). The language of the rubrics does not, in fact, create objectivity; rather, it presents the *perception* of objectivity.

We also argue that edTPA's support and assessment system divides the complex acts of teaching and learning into discrete subcategories and that this separation has the potential to turn teaching into a mechanistic activity wherein the delivery of knowledge and skills can become a set of steps to be "checked off" so that a scorer can mark (that is, note) the completion of a particular task.

And finally, we show how edTPA's support and assessment system is actually quite *deficient* in its rating of teacher candidates by elaborating on what the process *does not measure*, that is, teacher qualities and skills that, through their absence, are implicitly seen as *unimportant*.

Literature Review

GERM: All education, including teacher education, occurs in particular social contexts. In fact, a more accurate representation would include concentric circles of contexts, from the most personal and local to the universally expansive global milieu. Therefore, any analysis of the interrelations among teacher development and assessment must be linked to, and considered in light of, the social contexts in which they occur. For purposes of this chapter and in concert with the notion of concentric circles of contexts, the discussion involves the GERM, standardization and rubrics, and the development of teacher identity.

In introducing his discussion of the GERM, Sahlberg (2006) traced three phases of reform that have shaped the educational landscape over the past half century:

> The first was the age of optimism and innovation (up to the late 1970s)....Education reforms were based on large-scale curriculum reforms, increased professional autonomy of teachers and school-driven improvement through innovations. The fact that student populations were relatively homogenous and students with special needs were taught in specific institutions increased the high expectations for implementing innovations. The second phase was the age of complexity and contradiction (late 1970s to mid-1990s). Education reforms focused on increasing external control of schools, teachers and students through inspections, evaluations and assessments that led to an increase of regulations in schools and decreased autonomy of teachers. At the same time, however, the neo-liberal movement increased the freedom of choice

in education. Student populations became more diverse[,] creating a need for inclusive approaches and shifting the emphasis to learning for all. The third phase is the age of standardization and marketization (mid-1990s to date). Education reforms have been designed based on centrally prescribed curricular, learning and assessment standards monitored through intensive assessment and testing and on increased competition between schools. Therefore, teachers are losing their professional autonomy and learning is being focused on successful performance in standardized tests. (pp. 260–261)

Salhberg asserted that reforms have shifted the discourse around public education from (a) optimism and innovation, to (b) complexity and contradiction, to (c) standardization and marginalization. The shifts, as he noted, have been influenced by the intensifying effects of neoliberalism, so to understand the trajectory of the context of reform, it is important to understand neoliberalism. David Harvey (2005) described it as follows:

> Neoliberalism is in the first instance a theory of political economic practices that proposes that human well-being can best be advanced by liberating individual entrepreneurial freedoms and skills within an institutional framework characterized by strong private property rights, free markets and free trade. The role of the state is to…guarantee…the proper functioning of markets….[and] if markets do not exist (in areas such as….education, health care, social security and environmental pollution) then they must be created, by the state if necessary. (p. 159)

On its surface, the logic of this language seems innocuous, especially since so much of Western society is saturated by its effects. Giroux (2003), however, explained the dangers of neoliberalism with respect to public institutions and democracy:

> Neoliberalism defines society exclusively through the privileging of market relations, deregulation, privatization, and consumerism. Under the reign of neoliberalism, the social collapses into the private, part-time labor replaces full-time work, trade unions are weakened, everybody becomes a customer, and the exchange of money takes precedence over social justice, socially responsible citizens, and the building of democratic communities. (p. 3)

> Struggling for democracy is both a political and educational task. Fundamental to the health of a vibrant democratic culture is the recognition that education must be treated as a public good—a crucial site where students gain a public voice and come to grips with their own power as individual and social agents. (p. 162)

Since public education relies on a belief in, and support for, the public good, neoliberalism represents a perilous approach to social policy. A neoliberal approach to education subordinates humans and human interaction to the power and economic needs of "the market," a model that is premised on a false objectivity that privileges the desires of the wealthy and powerful while marginalizing the public good and reducing the vitality of the kind of diverse citizenry that sustains a democracy. The GERM is built on, and provides, the infrastructure for the continued escalation of neoliberalism in education, a movement that has, in the United States as well as in many parts of the world, contributed to the increased use of standardized assessments to measure student learning, teacher effectiveness, and school success.

Despite a plethora of research documenting the negative effects of high-stakes standardized assessments, particularly with respect to students in schools serving poor and working-class communities, results of these assessments are increasingly being used to rank schools and evaluate teachers. Today, assessments linked to the recently adopted national curriculum based on the Common Core State Standards are being implemented in a majority of states in the United States—a mandated aspect of states that sought funds related to Race to the Top legislation. In teacher education, this movement toward standardization has manifested itself in the New York State Education Department's adoption of edTPA as a requirement for initial certification. Focused on large-scale, competitive, individualistic and privatized notions of education based on market-based values such as choice and standardization, all of these initiatives are derived from, and contribute to, the intensification of neoliberalism in education.

Because neoliberalism and GERM are intertwined, the features and principles of each are interrelated. Furthermore, since private enterprise (as opposed to the public good) benefits from neoliberalism, its reforms are "often promoted through the interests of international development agencies and private enterprises through their interventions in national education reforms and policy formulation" (Sahlberg 2012, para. 3). Sahlberg (2012) described the materialization of GERM reforms as having emerged since the 1980s and involving five common characteristics worldwide:

> First is **standardization** of education….Since the late 1980s centrally prescribed curricula, with detailed and often ambitious performance targets, frequent testing of students and teachers, and test-based accountability have characterized a homogenization of education policies worldwide, promising standardized solutions at increasingly lower cost for those desiring to improve school quality and effectiveness.

A second common feature of GERM is *focus on core subjects* in school, in other words, on literacy and numeracy, and in some cases science…

The third characteristic that is easily identifiable in global education reforms is *the search for low-risk ways to reach learning goals*…. The higher the test-result stakes, the lower the degree of freedom in experimentation and risk-taking in classroom learning.

The fourth globally observable trend in educational reform is *use of corporate management models* as a main driver of improvement. This process where educational policies and ideas are lent and borrowed from [the] business world is often motivated by national hegemony and economic profit, rather than by moral goals of human development….

The fifth global trend is adoption of *test-based accountability policies* for schools. In doing so[,] school performance—especially raising student achievement—is closely tied to processes of accrediting, promoting, inspecting, and, ultimately, rewarding or punishing schools and teachers. Success or failure of schools and teachers is often determined by standardized tests and external teacher evaluations that devote attention to limited aspects of schooling, such as student achievement in mathematical and reading literacy, exit examination results, or intended teacher classroom behavior. (para. 5–10)

The multifaceted effects of GERM policies on public education are well documented; the effects on teacher education are beginning to emerge. Education, including teacher education, is an intensely human endeavor, one that cannot be reduced to a discrete set of technical specifications or easily standardized and evaluated skills delivered in a systematic, structured manner. Learning is not guaranteed by neatly designed modules, and it cannot be thoroughly assessed through rankings based on scoring binaries, no matter how technologically innovative their packaging. Regardless of the intent of its developers, edTPA is an apparatus that is likely to sustain and promote the tenets of GERM.

Standardization, Rubrics, and Teacher Development: Contemporary discourse around educational reform frequently conflates standards and standardization. The distinction is critical:

Standards involve the development of clear, meaningful expectations. The concept of standards is desirable; no one would opt for low standards or no standards…. Parents and citizens expect teachers to set and maintain high standards for students; without high expectations, opportunities are lost. Potential is wasted. Standardization, on the other hand, implies distance, objectivity, and fairness. Standardization connotes a one-size-fits-all approach, upholding the notion that "fair" and "equal" are synonymous…such an approach is, at best, unjust. At worst, it is ruinous. (Gorlewski, 2012, p. 84)

The standards and accountability movement has been accompanied by the rise of rubrics. Purported to inject objectivity, reliability, and validity into otherwise subjective assessments, rubrics have become a key aspect of evaluating the performances of students and teachers. Designed to provide specific guidelines to enable students to demonstrate knowledge, skills, and dispositions that meet particular standards, rubrics reap critiques from those who reject their claims of legitimacy from both ends of the spectrum—educators who find them too restrictive and those who find them too undefined. Both sets of critics agree that rubrics are imprecise. Their condemnation differs about whether the ambiguity ought to be addressed by seeking greater specificity in descriptors and improved calibration among scorers or whether the ambiguity ought to be embraced so that assessment can become more holistic. Kohn (2006) explained:

> Now some observers criticize rubrics because they can never deliver the promised precision; judgments ultimately turn on adjectives that are murky and end up being left to the teacher's discretion. But I worry more about the success of rubrics than their failure. Just as it's possible to raise standardized test scores as long as you're willing to gut the curriculum and turn the school into a test-preparation factory, so it's possible to get a bunch of people to agree on what rating to give an assignment as long as they're willing to accept and apply someone else's narrow criteria for what merits that rating. Once we check our judgment at the door, we can all learn to give a 4 to exactly the same things. (p. 13)

Kohn's description of an essential flaw of using rubrics for high-stakes purposes illuminates the danger of perpetuating the notion that numbers attach credence and remove bias—thus establishing significance. This perspective is, of course, wrong. Like examination questions, rubrics determine what counts in instruction; while they may conceal bias, they do not remove it. Given the escalating pressure toward positivism, toward assigning numerical values to entities to rank them, our chapter focuses on how the use of rubrics on high-stakes standardized assessments can distort the process of development it is meant to support. Invoking Mabry, Kohn continued, describing concerns about using rubrics to assess student writing:

> This attempt to deny the subjectivity of human judgment is objectionable in its own right. But it's also harmful in a very practical sense. In an important article published

in 1999, Linda Mabry, now at Washington State University, pointed out that rubrics "are designed to function as scoring guidelines, but they also serve as arbiters of quality and agents of control" over what is taught and valued. Because "agreement among scorers is more easily achieved with regard to such matters as spelling and organization," these are the characteristics that will likely find favor in a rubricized classroom. Mabry cites research showing that "compliance with the rubric tended to yield higher scores but produced 'vacuous' writing." (p. 13)

It is evident that, like standards, rubrics are neither inherently good nor evil; their impact is derived from their use. It is important, then, to consider how edTPA rubrics will be used in the teacher certification process. Will they be used as part of a formative process of ongoing assessment to develop the knowledge, skills, and dispositions necessary for teacher candidates to facilitate student learning? And, in an effort to model critical analysis of curriculum and assessment for teacher candidates, will the rubrics themselves be subject to questions and critique? Or will they be used on an episodic basis, to assign a score and rank candidates and the programs that prepare them? Will the high-stakes nature of the criteria established on the rubrics solidify into an official, measurable definition of what it means to teach? And how will the use of rubrics on this evaluation instrument affect the identity construction of future teachers?

An essential aspiration of teacher education programs is to produce educators with a deep understanding of the social foundations of practice, passion about content knowledge, and dispositions such as tenacity, compassion, curiosity, and commitment to equity and justice. Unfortunately, high-stakes assessments such as edTPA tend to reduce the likelihood that candidates will reach this aspiration. Kohn (2006) noted the following:

> Studies have shown that too much attention to the quality of one's performance is associated with more superficial thinking, less interest in whatever one is doing, less perseverance in the face of failure, and a tendency to attribute the outcome to innate ability and other factors thought to be beyond one's control.

> What all this means is that improving the design of rubrics, or inventing our own, won't solve the problem because the problem is inherent to the very idea of rubrics and the goals they serve. This is a theme sounded by Maja Wilson in her extraordinary new book, *Rethinking Rubrics in Writing Assessment*. In boiling "a messy process down to 4–6 rows of nice, neat, organized little boxes," she argues, assessment is "stripped of the complexity that breathes life into good writing." High scores on a list of criteria for excellence in essay writing do not mean that the essay is any good because quality is more than the sum of its rubricized parts. (p. 14)

Although Kohn (2006) and Wilson (2006) are referring to writing, teaching is analogous: it is a messy, human process that cannot be assessed in technical ways that ignore the complexity of the process and context. Because assessment drives curriculum and instruction, edTPA and its associated rubrics will certainly influence teacher education programs. Curriculum will be narrowed to emphasize assessed criteria and address related descriptors; therefore, teacher educators will be faced with the same dilemma currently faced by K-12 public school teachers: "Either our instruction and our assessment remain 'out of synch' or the instruction gets worse in order that (candidates)…can be easily judged with the help of rubrics" (Kohn, 2006, p. 14).

As Kohn noted, the use of rubrics is not a matter of improvement. If the focus remains on implementation, that is, the *how* of assessment, then the *why* will be discounted. These conditions undermine the development of dispositions related to inquiry, since candidates are, in effect, being discouraged from considering the purpose of the assessment.

Day, Kington, Stobart, and Sammons (2006) explained the importance of the context in which teacher identities are constructed, during induction and beyond:

> Teachers in all countries need support for their commitment, energy and skill over their careers if they are to grapple with the immense emotional, intellectual and social demands and as they work towards building the internal and external relationships demanded by ongoing government reforms and social movements….
>
> Sustaining a positive sense of effectiveness to subject, pupils, relationships and roles is important to maintaining motivation, self-esteem or self-efficacy, job satisfaction, and commitment to teaching; and although this research shows consistently that identity is affected, positively and negatively, by classroom experiences, organisational culture and situation-specific events which may threaten existing norms and practices (Nias, 1989; Kelchtermans, 1993; Flores, 2002), successive reform implementation strategies have failed to address the key role played by these, and thus, paradoxically, fail to meet the standards' raising recruitment and retention agendas which they espouse. (p. 614)

Extending and connecting these concepts, Hodkinson (2005) identified "troubling dualisms" that are reinforced by dividing teaching and learning into categories convenient for standardized assessment. These disquieting dualisms include false distinctions between mind and body, individual and social, process and product, and formal and informal learning. Furthermore, Hodkinson expanded the notion of false distinctions to include disciplinary boundaries:

> To start at the most general level of abstraction, learning in all situations can usefully be understood as complex and relational, with no simple lines of cause and effect, and no factors or influences that are self-evidently more significant or foundational than others. More specifically, it is helpful to integrate these four dualisms in all learning situations. That is, except for very specific purposes, we should always see learning as embodied, as individual and social, as the integration of product and process, and as the integration of formal and informal. (p. 116)

The Format of edTPA

When completing edTPA's assessment system, teacher candidates must submit documents supporting three separate tasks: (a) planning for instruction and assessment, (b) instructing and engaging students in learning, and (c) assessing student learning (SCALE, 2013, p. 1). These tasks are supposed to cover three to five lessons or at least three to five hours of instruction (SCALE, 2013, p. 9). The second task, instructing and engaging students in learning, includes a component called the "Learning Segment" (SCALE, 2013, p. 6). To address this portion of the evaluation, teacher candidates are required to "videotape your teaching and select 2 video clips (no more than 10 minutes each in total running time)" (SCALE, 2013, p. 8), in addition to providing detailed responses to prompts that appear in the form of various questions and directives. For example, in the planning task, each teacher candidate must provide a "commentary" related to the use of academic language, knowledge of their students, and knowledge of related research and theory (SCALE, 2103, pp. 10–12). In the instruction task, candidates are asked to develop a positive learning environment, engage students in meaningful tasks, and write a "commentary" on these events (SCALE, 2013, pp. 20–21). In the assessment task, candidates must select an assessment tool, administer it, analyze the results, provide appropriate feedback, and discuss the next steps to be taken—all as part of an evaluation "commentary" (SCALE, 2013, pp. 28–30).

Each task (planning, instructing, and evaluating) is rated using *five* scoring rubrics—so a total of 15 rubrics are employed by the evaluators. These rubrics are designed using a five-point system with 1 being the lowest level and 5 the highest. Like all rubrics, edTPA versions represent gradations of achievement, with a score of 1 generally indicating the *absence* of a particular quality (for example, the *absence* of content accuracy, evidence, alignment, or justification) and a score of 5 indicating the *presence* of a high quality of, for example, accuracy, alignment, justification, and so forth.

In between, the scores of 2, 3, and 4 are differentiated by *degrees* of a particular quality. For example, in ELA Rubric 1, a candidate's connection to a concept could be described as "vague" and earn a 2, "clear" and earn a 3, or "clear and consistent" and earn a 4 (SCALE, 2013, p. 14).

After an analysis of the 15 rubrics used to evaluate edTPA submissions for English language arts, we will answer each of the following questions: (a) What does the language used in the rubrics imply about *evaluating* the act of teaching? (b) What does the language used in the rubrics imply about the *teaching/learning process*? (c) By its absence, what is implicitly seen as *unimportant* in the teaching/learning process? (d) What do these answers say about the formation of teacher identity? Note: In response to a draft of this chapter, an edTPA representative wrote the following: "It has never been our assertion that a single assessment can possibly measure ALL aspects of teaching. As explained in our design, edTPA is intended as part of a multiple measures system and leaves the assessment of many valued aspects of teaching to the PROGRAMS to determine. Our design is deliberate" (N. Merino, personal communication, January 29, 2014). This contention is addressed at the end of the chapter.

Evaluating the Act of Teaching

First and foremost in the world of edTPA, one will find a culture of positivism, the belief that the activities in a classroom can be quantified. In fact, by the very nature of a five-point rubric, implicit in the edTPA assessment process is the belief that a *quality* (such as "providing evidence") can be *quantified* (with a number from 1 to 5). This was seen throughout the rubric analysis. Yet, the candidate behaviors or the lesson characteristics that are being quantified often defy quantification. By way of an example, we focus on edTPA English Language Arts Rubric 2 and Rubric 5—the only two rubrics specifically related to students with special needs, as evidenced by references to "IEPs and 504 plans" (SCALE, 2013, pp. 15, 18). Both of these rubrics appear in the planning task section. Following are both rubrics and our analysis of each.

Rubric 2—Planning to Support Varied Student Learning Needs

How does the candidate use knowledge of his/her students to target support for students to comprehend, construct meaning from, interpret, and respond to complex text?

Level 1—There is little or no evidence of planned support OR Candidate does NOT attend to requirements in IEPs and 504 plans.

Level 2—Planned supports are loosely tied to learning objectives or the central focus of the learning segment AND Candidate attends to requirements in IEPs and 504 plans.

Level 3—Planned supports are tied to learning objectives and the central focus with attention to characteristics of the class as a whole AND Candidate attends to requirements in IEPs and 504 plans.

Level 4—Planned supports are tied to learning objectives and the central focus. Supports address the needs of specific individuals or groups with similar needs AND Candidate attends to requirements in IEPs and 504 plans.

Level 5—Planned supports are tied to learning objectives and the central focus. Supports address the needs of specific individuals or groups with similar needs. Supports include specific strategies to identify and respond to common errors and misunderstandings AND Candidate attends to requirements in IEPs and 504 plans.

As we analyze this rubric, there are several points worth noting. The differences between Levels 2 and 3 are minimal. Level 2 refers to "planned supports" being "loosely tied" to learning objectives, while Level 3 sees the "planned supports" as simply "tied" to the objectives. Here, candidates and evaluators alike are being asked to respond to a quality (connectedness) as a matter of degree ("tied" versus "loosely tied").

Additionally, the conjunction "or" in Level 2 is changed to "and" in Level 3. This rating seeks to differentiate "learning objectives" from the lesson's "central focus" which, we argue, is a distinction without a difference. The essence of any lesson plan is the *objective* which, by definition, is the *central focus* of the lesson. The objective stipulates the content, student behavior, conditions under which the student will demonstrate knowledge, understanding or a skill, and criteria—the standard of performance that must be met. In short, the objective *is* the central focus of a lesson. One cannot separate the objective from the central focus, yet the application of edTPA Rubric 2 forces the candidate (and the evaluator) to make such a distinction. The term "central focus" appears in the glossary of the edTPA Secondary English Language Arts Assessment Handbook. It is defined as, "A description of the important understandings and core concepts that you want students to develop within the learning segment. The central focus should go beyond a list of facts and skills, [it should] align with the standards and learning objectives, and address subject-specific components in the learning segment" (SCALE, 2013, pp. 44–45). The glossary, however, does not include a definition of the term "learning objective." We believe that there is no definition listed because there is no difference between the two terms, making the "or" and the "and" distinction confusing for both the rater and the student.

Rubric 5—Planning Assessment to Monitor and Support Student Learning

How are the informal and formal assessments selected or designed to monitor students' progress toward the standards/objectives?

Level 1—The assessments only provide evidence of students' literal comprehension of text. Assessment adaptations required by IEP or 504 plans are NOT made OR Assessments are not aligned with the central focus and standards/objectives for the learning segment.

Level 2—The assessments provide limited evidence to monitor students' abilities to construct meaning from, interpret, and/or respond to complex text during the learning segment. Assessment adaptations required by IEP or 504 plans are made.

Level 3—The assessments provide specific evidence to monitor students' abilities to construct meaning from, interpret, and/or respond to complex text during the learning segment. Assessment adaptations required by IEP or 504 plans are made.

Level 4—The assessments provide multiple forms of evidence to monitor students' abilities to construct meaning from, interpret, and/or respond to complex text during the learning segment. Assessment adaptations required by IEP or 504 plans are made.

Level 5—The assessments provide multiple forms of evidence to monitor students' abilities to construct meaning from, interpret, and/or respond to complex text during the learning segment. The assessments are strategically designed to allow individuals or groups with special needs to demonstrate their learning. Assessment adaptations required by IEP or 504 plans are made.

In analyzing this rubric, we must note that the nature of Individual Education Plans (IEPs) and 504 plans is that, by law, these documents *prescribe* and *specify* the type of adaptation and level of curricular modification a teacher is required to provide. These are nonnegotiable practices with legal underpinnings. This edTPA rubric, by its design, attempts, yet again, to differentiate the concept of *evidence* among Levels 2, 3, and 4 with phrases like "limited evidence," "specific evidence," and "multiple forms of evidence" (SCALE, 2013, p. 18). These category descriptions are not mutually exclusive. "Limited evidence" is not the same as "specific evidence." One could provide "limited evidence" that happens to be very "specific." Additionally, one could provide "multiple forms of evidence," all of which lack specificity.

Once again, the use of the rubric forces candidates and evaluators to make distinctions between and among these categories.

An additional aspect of Rubric 5 is worth noting. Level 5 (the highest rating an evaluator can give) includes all of the characteristics of Level 4, with an interesting addition: "The assessments are *strategically designed* [emphasis added] to allow individuals or groups with special needs to demonstrate their learning." How can an evaluator know that the assessment was *strategically designed?* And, given the prescriptions of IEPs and 504 plans, aren't all modifications and adaptations *strategically designed* by Committees on Special Education?

Quantifying a Complex Process

As noted earlier, edTPA's assessment system for gauging competence in teaching English language arts requires the use of 15 different scoring rubrics. Consequently, the act of planning a lesson, executing it, and evaluating student learning is divided into 15 different subcategories.

In the five rubrics under the planning task, teacher candidates are required to show how "plans build" students' abilities to work with complex text; how they use "knowledge of his/her students" to meet learning goals; how that knowledge is used "to justify instructional plans"; how they will "identify and support language demands" associated with the learning; and how the "informal and formal assessments" were selected. These highly interrelated qualities are scored as discrete skills.

Similarly, the five rubrics used to assess instructional skills are designed to evaluate the candidate's ability to "demonstrate a positive learning environment," "actively engage students," "elicit responses to promote thinking," "use textual references," and "use evidence to evaluate and change teaching practices." Since a portion of this section is based on the video submitted by the candidate, distinctions are being made between and among very similar categories. For example, what does a "positive learning environment" (measured by Rubric 6) look like to an observer? Does it include the active engagement of students (measured by Rubric 7)? And wouldn't this active engagement "elicit responses to promote thinking" (as measured by Rubric 8)? Again, edTPA's assessment process asks students and evaluators to separate these pedagogical skills as if each is significantly different.

The third portion of edTPA's evaluation process is the assessment section. Here, teacher candidates are asked to integrate evaluation into their lessons and to use evaluation in a formative way to, in a sense, *assess their own teaching* by *assessing student learning.* The difference between summative and formative assessment is significant, and edTPA's use of this concept is commendable (although it uses the terms "formal" and "informal" rather than "summative" and "formative"). Rubrics 11 through 15 (SCALE, 2013, pp. 31–35) divide what should be a recursive process into a separate set of actions to be taken by the teacher candidate who is asked to do the following: collect and analyze evidence of student learning. This involves the presentation of student work in some type of visual form: a chart, a graph, a spreadsheet, a pie chart, and so forth. A narrative may be developed in place of a visual presentation (Rubric 11). Candidates must also differentiate types of feedback (Rubric 12), provide opportunities to use the feedback (Rubric 13), use the assessments to prove student mastery of content-related language (Rubric 14), and apply this information to plan subsequent lessons (Rubric 15). The related "commentary" on this section appears designed to synthesize these concepts. Nonetheless, the material is *rated* as a set of separate skills.

What Is Missing?

The analysis of the 15 rubrics used in edTPA's assessment system for English language arts teacher candidates provides a glimpse into what teacher skills, dispositions, characteristics, and selected strategies are privileged and, by their absence, marginalized.

The elements privileged were elaborated on in the previous sections. They include quantitative analysis (graphing, charting student outcomes), direct instruction (that is, teacher-centered instruction and teacher-led discussions), and standards-based instruction. In fact, the Secondary English Language Arts Assessment Handbook for edTPA states that lesson plans should include "state-adopted student content standards and/or Common Core State Standards that are the target of student learning. NOTE: Please list the **number and text** of each standard that is being addressed" (SCALE, 2013, p. 10). In addition, edTPA's assessment system shows a preference for core area subjects (English language arts, science, mathematics, and social studies) and explicit teaching (that is, teaching to the test/assessment that is developed as part of the planning process).

However, a great deal of what is considered effective teaching is not measured by the process. These include qualitative analyses that often focus on sociological and cultural phenomena like attitudes and dispositions. Personal attitudes, perspectives, and experiences appear to have no place when looking at education through the lens of edTPA. Therefore, relationship building, a key component of effective teaching, is not rated through this assessment system. Rubric 6 (learning environment) lists candidate behaviors, such as "demonstrates respect" for students and "creates a positive, low-risk social environment," but these characteristics cannot be measured in two 10-minute video snapshots. Relationship building often takes place outside the classroom through teacher-student interactions between class periods, in corridors, before and after school, and through connections made in clubs and on sports teams. Because edTPA is a quantitative enterprise, qualities such as attitudes, dispositions, and values (the love of learning, the desire to read, respect for classmates, etc.) are not measured because they defy measurement.

Other important teacher qualities not rated by edTPA include knowledge of learner development (made impossible to measure due to the aforementioned snapshot evaluation) and, under the heading of "Professional Responsibility" as listed in the InTASC Standards (the Interstate Teacher Assessment and Support Consortium), edTPA is silent relative to skills and qualities such as "professional learning and ethical practice" and "leadership and collaboration." Note: edTPA's Secondary English Language Arts Assessment Handbook acknowledges several national organizations, including "…the Interstate Teacher Assessment and Support Consortium…for their pioneering work using discipline-specific portfolio assessments to evaluate teacher quality" (SCALE, 2013, copyright page). Nonetheless, edTPA's support and assessment system falls far short of assessing and evaluating InTASC's own listing of teacher dispositions.

Group work and, by definition, cooperative/collaborative learning are not measured in any of the 15 rubrics. In fact, the guidelines in edTPA's Secondary English Language Arts Assessment Handbook specifically direct candidates not to include work produced collaboratively as part of the assessment portion. Individual work is the only acceptable indicator of achievement (SCALE, 2013, p. 27).

Since the lesson plans must be standards based, all other philosophical approaches to teaching and learning are not acceptable. Consequently, other approaches to teaching, such as multicultural education, interdisciplinary teaching, and constructivist education, to name a few, would represent square pegs in the round hole of edTPA.

Summary and Conclusion

The edTPA assessment system, which now represents the final gateway for teacher candidates to gain initial certification, has the capacity to shape teacher identities by explicitly and implicitly sending powerful messages about what constitutes good teaching. These include the belief that pedagogical practices and related outcomes can and should be quantified, that the best way to quantify these practices and outcomes is through a rubric, and that rubrics offer "objectivity" and clear evidence of gradations of performance; in short, that performances can be rated with a number and that there are recognizable differences between, for example, a 2 and 3 or a 3 and a 4.

In addition, edTPA's assessment system views teaching as discrete sets of categories (e.g., "planning") and that the planning process can be further divided into subcategories (planning for understanding, planning to support varied student learning needs, etc.). This categorization implies that teaching is a mechanistic process and that the delivery of knowledge and skills can be listed and, eventually, "checked off" a list.

As a direct result of the aforementioned suppositions regarding teaching, edTPA's assessment system implicitly tells teacher candidates that many aspects of the teaching/learning process are not important simply because they are *not rated* or that they are *difficult to rate*. These elements include particular strategies such as group work and cooperative/collaborative learning. The process eschews any form of introducing content and concepts outside of a standards-based approach. Teacher candidates who believe in, or have a talent for, teaching through interdisciplinary, multicultural, or constructivist lenses are forced to teach according to a standards-based approach, as directed by edTPA guidelines. What's more, edTPA's assessment system does not, and cannot, measure critically important characteristics of teachers and learners. Earlier in this chapter (under the heading "The Format of edTPA"), we quoted directly from an edTPA representative who asserted that edTPA is intended as part of a multiple measures system and that the assessment of many valued aspects of teaching (here, our implication is the evaluation of teacher dispositions) is still determined by the respective teacher education program. We wish to make two points relative to this assertion:

First, we believe that teacher dispositions can only be evaluated over a long period of time. The nature of edTPA's assessment system makes the evaluation of dispositions impossible for two reasons: (a) The assessment itself is a snapshot of teacher candidate competency, and (b) the anonymous evaluators never meet or interact with the teacher candidates. Ironically, edTPA's assessment system for "planning for instruction and assessments" directs candidates to "provide relevant context information" when developing a lesson (SCALE, 2013, p. 6). Clearly, knowledge of the students, the school, and the community are seen by edTPA as important. Yet that same system is *not designed* to identify and take into account the "relevant context information" about the candidate being evaluated because characteristics such as self-discipline, positive dispositions toward school and learning, determination, building and sustaining relationships, and the exhibition of values (such as cooperation and fairness) defy quantification.

Second, to contend that these "many valued aspects" are left up to the respective teacher education program is to create a false equivalent. We (teacher education programs and edTPA) are not partners in this enterprise. The fact is that performance on edTPA's assessment system *trumps* a candidate's performance in the teacher education program. In short, if a candidate shows competence in all areas of the teacher education program—entrance and exit examinations, class work and all the outcomes associated with it, as well as student teaching and the exhibition of numerous competencies—failure to meet the established "cut point" on edTPA's assessment system will prevent the candidate from gaining initial certification. Therefore, teacher education programs and edTPA are not partners in the final evaluation.

Finally, one would expect an effective teacher to be a life-long learner— someone who continues to participate in professional learning experiences; one who behaves in an ethical manner; and one who understands and practices leadership and collaboration with colleagues and with the community that he or she serves. These are all critically important dispositions for teacher candidates to exhibit. However, such qualities cannot be measured through a standardized test. As noted earlier, dispositions are not episodic; they reflect attitudes, behaviors, and preferences exhibited over a long period of time. The fact that edTPA's assessment system is silent on these dispositions implies that they have little value in the world of education.

As teacher educators committed to the development of future teachers who embrace, embody, and enact dispositions that foster equity and social justice through critical evaluation and thoughtful action, we seek to reveal the deficiencies of edTPA's assessment system while emphasizing the importance of human interaction, social engagement, and the common good.

References

Day, C., Kington, A., Stobart, G., & Sammons, P. (2006). The personal and professional selves of teachers: Stable and unstable identities. *British Educational Research Journal, 32*(4), 601–616.

Giroux, H. (2003). *The abandoned generation: Democracy beyond the culture of fear.* New York, NY: Palgrave Macmillan.

Gorlewski, J. A. (2012, May). Standards, standardization, and student learning. *English Journal, 103*(5), 88–89.

Harvey, D. (2005). *A brief history of neoliberalism.* Oxford, UK: Oxford University Press.

Hodkinson, P. (2005). Learning as cultural and relational: Moving past some troubling dualism. *Cambridge Journal of Education, 35*(1), 107–119.

Kohn, A. (2006). The trouble with rubrics. *English Journal, 95*(4), 12–14.

Sahlberg, P. (2012, April 2). *Global educational reform movement is here!* Retrieved from http://pasisahlberg.com/global-educational-reform-movement-is-here/

Sahlberg, P. (2006). Education reform for raising economic competitiveness. *Journal of Educational Change, 7*(4), 259–287.

Saltman, K. (2012). *Democratic education against corporate school reform: The new market bureaucracy in U.S. public schooling.* North Dartmouth: Social Policy, Education and Curriculum, Research Unit, North Dartmouth Center for Policy Analyses, University of Massachusetts Dartmouth.

Stanford Center for Assessment, Learning, and Equity (SCALE). (2013, September). *edTPA Secondary English Language Arts Assessment Handbook.* Stanford, CA: Author.

Wilson, M. (2006). *Rethinking rubrics in writing assessment.* Portsmouth, NH: Heinemann.

· 3 ·

MEASUREMENT AS POLITICS BY OTHER MEANS: THE CASE OF TEST-BASED TEACHER EVALUATION

Mark Garrison

Since the Obama administration initiated its Race to the Top competitive grant programs, many states across the country have instituted new legal and policy frameworks for the evaluation of public school teachers and principals to receive Race to the Top funds (Baker, Oluwole, & Green, 2013). While these value-added and similar methods of evaluation and compensation have been tried long before the Race to the Top era (Garrison, 2011; Gratz, 2009; Kupermintz, 2003; Podgursky & Springer, 2007), the Race to the Top competitions have proved decisive in spurring their adoption by states (Learing Point Associates, 2010).

There is now a growing body of literature effectively critiquing the validity and reliability of using student standardized test scores for the evaluation of teachers and principals (Baker et al., 2010; Baker et al., 2013), and while this literature often points to the negative consequences of these policies, there is a need for a broader examination of the political, social, and philosophical implications of this policy move led by state and federal officials and the army of so-called school reformers that has grown from the ranks of large for-profit corporations, private think tanks, and venture philanthropies (Saltman, 2010).

This chapter presents the argument that current test-based teacher evaluations and compensation schemes (TBTECs) rest on the fundamentally flawed and arbitrary practice of the operational theory of measurement (or operationism) and that this critique enables a deeper political, social, and philosophical analysis of TBTEC regimes, using New York State as a case in point. The chapter challenges critics and the public to consider the veiled expression of arbitrary power at work in the imposition of methods for ranking the effectiveness of educators.

Measurement's Political Imposter

While critiques of high-stakes testing run almost as rampant as the testing mania itself, less attention has been paid to the scientific roots of high-stakes testing, including its use for the evaluation of education professionals.[1] While commentators and scholars alike readily oppose the obsession with measurement (Ball, 2012; Ravitch, 2013), little attention has been paid to the fact that the science of measurement behind the pseudo-accountability movement is of a *very particular kind*. In fact, the current practices labeled *measurements* do not meet the criteria for measurements. Few education professionals have engaged in serious discussions about the philosophy of science that guides current education efforts, let alone the social, political, and ideological workings that specifically accompany this particular brand of measurement. Particularly lacking is a critical examination of the operational theory of measurement (or operationism) in pushing the agenda of which these tests are central.

A Critique of Operationism

Mainstream social science, in particular psychology and especially psychometry, practice a particular theory of measurement known as the operational theory of measurement or the theory of scales of measurement (the scales are nominal, ordinal, interval, and ratio). The practice of operationally defining concepts is a linchpin to the daily practice of research workers, especially in psychology and education. It is this operationism in particular that is the object of this discussion, although it is important to keep in mind that the entire measurement edifice is ultimately at issue. In case the point gets lost, the argument is not against *measurement*, but rather, against its political impostor.

What is operationism? Operationism (sometimes called operationalism) assumes that a theoretical concept can only be deemed scientific if it is *defined empirically*. When it comes to matters of education and psychology, this almost always translates to the idea that concepts are to be defined by how they are measured.[2] Operationism "is based on the intuition that we do not know the meaning of a concept unless we have a method of measurement for it"; operationism can thus be understood as "a theory of meaning" (Chang, 2009, p. 1). The current notion of measurement that informs education policy discourses is fundamentally linked to the practice of operational definitions.

Originating among physicists in the 1920s, the operational doctrine was quickly and widely adopted by psychologists and other social scientists looking to claim the status accorded the physical sciences. While physicists and leading philosophers of science came to reject operationism as the 20th century progressed, psychologists ignored these developments and carried on with operationism in a manner critics have likened to religious dogma, with Leahey (1980) arguing that, "'operational definition' has become an empty liturgical phrase" (p. 127). And despite developments in the philosophy of science contrary to the practice, psychologists wanted "to stay as close to pure operationism as possible.... And they persisted (and persist still) in attempting to 'define' each theoretical term empirically even after the positivists have given [operationism] up..." (Leahey, 1980, p. 133; see also, Green, 1992).

A widely known example of operationism comes from proponents of intelligence testing, with their famous dictum that intelligence can be defined as the ability to do well on their intelligence tests (Block & Dworkin, 1976; Green, 1992). The problem of defining intelligence was "solved" by this slight of hand, one that eschewed silly validity discussions and got on with the real work of measuring. While even casual observers recognize the tautological nature of the aforementioned formulation, fewer discern the antitheoretical and arbitrary stance embedded in the idea that it is possible to measure something without knowing something about its nature, that is, without a clear object of measurement (for more on this, see Berka, 1983; Block & Dworkin, 1976). Debates about whether intelligence tests measure nature or nurture, for example, leave intact the suspect method of operationally defining intelligence, where test results are simultaneously assumed to be the effect of a trait (intelligence) and the means for defining that trait. This is akin to offering as scientific the definition of heat as the movement of mercury in a glass tube. It is—at best—a gross form of reductionism.

Importantly for the topic of interest here, this method allows one to promote an understanding of how the world works without having to go through the trouble of theoretical proofs. Intelligence test score variation is often presented as caused by variations in the amount of intelligence in the tested population.[3] This logic is evident in all manner of discourse about everything from international test score comparisons to narratives about failing urban schools. Based on the operationist framework, tests of academic achievement define effective education. Thus, differences in test scores between schools or school systems are, *ipso facto*, taken to represent differences in school quality, because school quality has been operationally defined as student performance on tests of academic achievement. This stands despite the fact that school quality was never theoretically treated and that quality is a culturally bound value statement. Never mind that achievement itself is operationally defined as the percentage of correct answers on an achievement test. Concepts such as school quality are simply forcibly hitched to tests of student achievement without any argument regarding attribution, that is, demonstrating that the results of the latter were caused by the former. But this is not simply a matter of incompetence. As argued later in the chapter, the fundamental assumptions that guide these otherwise curious practices make sense when examined as a political project.

Far from clarifying the meaning of school quality, or increasing our collective understanding of educational attainment, the operationist framework creates greater confusion (see Leahey, 1980, pp. 134–135). Worse still is the now common practice of rebranding long-standing measures of student achievement as measures of school quality. Here is a good example: Officials from the New York State Education Department (NYSED) have recently rebranded the National Assessment of Educational Progress (NAEP) a measure of "career and college readiness." On the basis of this evidence-free assumption, officials argue that NAEP-aligned tests are a sound basis for determining the effectiveness of educators and education systems. NYSED Deputy Commissioner Slentz (2013) wrote the following:

> [T]he Common Core State Standards and accompanying assessments that measure student progress on these standards are closely aligned with the knowledge and skills measured by the NAEP. New York State educators and parents will now have an accurate indicator of how our students are performing and their progress toward college and career-readiness. (p. 3)

But such practices do not constitute a measurement. Instead, they impose value-laden meanings regarding the worth of human beings and forms of education practice (Garrison, 2009). To elaborate this point, two key assumptions of the operational doctrine should be examined: (a) All concepts worthy of the moniker science must come in degrees or be measurable (for an extended critique of this, see Garrison, 2009), and (b) the meaning of scientific concepts can only be generated by behavioral responses to researcher-induced stimuli (e.g., questionnaires, tests, etc.).

E. L. Thorndike, the famous early 20th-century psychometrician, forcefully promoted the first assumption noted in the preceding paragraph. He argued that, "whatever exists at all exists in some amount." But he never discussed purely qualitative entities, such as the common *pilsner*, the *feline*, the *wooden* chair, and the *human* being, none of which by their nature come in degrees— although, in the last example given, the framers of the U.S. Constitution appear to have disagreed, rendering African Americans and Native Americans a fraction of the value of British colonists (Garrison, 2009, pp. 34–35).

Thus, operationism, intimately connected to psychometric practice, insists that scientific concepts (knowledge) require quantification. It is important to emphasize that operationism is premised on and closely related to the idea that a purely qualitative phenomenon must be rendered in quantitative fashion for analysis. The leading proponent of the operationist notion of scales of measurement (nominal, ordinal, interval, ratio), S. S. Stevens (1946), defined measurement thusly in his seminal paper, "On the Theory of Scales of Measurement": "We may say that measurement, in the broadest sense, is defined as the assignment of numerals to objects or events according to rules" (p. 677). This notion formally instituted the idea that measurement is both a mere convention (and thus, ultimately arbitrary) and that all phenomena must be defined and analyzed quantitatively. To resolve debates among scientists about the nature and meaning of measurement, Stevens proposed a series of levels or scales that would allow various forms of quantitative treatment. And while acknowledging the trouble with forcing a purely qualitative phenomenon into quantitative reasoning with his nominal level, he moved ahead anyway. Stevens wrote the following:

> The nominal scale is a primitive form, and quite naturally there are many who will urge that it is absurd to attribute to this process of assigning numerals the dignity implied by the term measurement. Certainly there can be no quarrel with this objection, for the naming of things is an arbitrary business. However we christen it, the use of numerals as names for classes is an example of the "assignment of numerals

according to rule." The rule is: do not assign the same numeral to different classes or different numerals to the same class. Beyond that, anything goes with the nominal scale. (p. 679)

As long as the rules for numeral assignment are clearly specified, measurement is said to be taking place. It is simply a matter of convention, one that promotes the quantitative treatment of a purely qualitative phenomenon. And so, the operational method simply does not give rise to measurement in the manner that a thermometer measures heat phenomena.

With respect to the second point, the idea that scientific meaning and thus knowledge are generated in the act of measurement of behavioral responses to stimuli (the only thing advocates claim is capable of objective study) has had profound consequences for psychology and education. What is not widely known is that the operational doctrine is in essence a behaviorist doctrine, especially of the Skinnerian kind:

> [O]perationism is not the theoretically neutral procedure its advocates pretended it to be. It makes assumptions about the nature of reality; it especially assumes the truth of physicalism. Given this assumption, psychological Behaviorism follows, for mind as a non-physical entity, cannot exist. Rather than merely choosing between alternative viewpoints as its adherents maintain, Operationism supports only one viewpoint, Behaviorism. (Leahey, 1980, p. 134)

Thus, operationism is premised on a deep skepticism regarding the existence of a mental phenomenon; in fact, human will itself is disregarded. Human agency derived from conscience is banned from scientific discourse. All research activity is reduced to the generation of stimuli and recording of responses of subjects. There are grave implications if such a view guides educators.[4]

Operationism as Governance

Standard critiques from philosophers of science overlook the social, political, and ideological content of operationism. Arguably, it is not simply a flawed theory of meaning and invalid guide for the development of theoretical concepts. Operationism serves to construct and impose meaning through ranking the results of stimulus-response regimes, which limit human agency to responding to performance mandates. This imposed meaning is a component of a particular mode of governance. To introduce these ideas, two brief examples are offered.

Take the performance levels created by NYSED as an example. The quality of being proficient is operationally defined by NYSED as a student achieving a "3" or better on state exams; in turn, the cut score that establishes the boundary between the levels (say between levels 2 and 3) is also defined on the basis of the will and belief of (mostly secret) cut score committees and the authorities they report to (for a useful discussion of NAEP cut scores, see Koretz, 2008; and for a general critique of standards as cut scores, see Glass, 1978). Under this regime, teachers and students alike are to be singularly driven to move to the next rank to be considered effective. This is to be the purpose of their work, its meaning. Intentional or not, this doctrine yields to a view that knowledge claims and meaning are limited to those who control the ranking apparatus. The testing expert is the only source of knowledge and conveyer of meaning and truth. The experiences students or teachers have with a test are irrelevant, unless, of course, those experiences are themselves operationalized. Instead of being called on to help researchers understand patterns of educational performance, teachers and students are viewed as invalid and irrelevant sources of knowledge about the reality of which they are a part and help construct.

Another example of operationism as governance can be found, again, with intelligence testing. By defining intelligence as the ability to do well on intelligence tests, tests of intelligence become the official and culturally dominant understanding. What follows is that millions of human beings come to conclude that they are "not intelligent"—despite not knowing what intelligence is or if it can be measured—simply on the basis of answering incorrectly arguably meaningless analogy questions and other invented games of overpaid technocrats.

This practice does not enable the study of teaching and learning. Rather, it serves to enforce a particular vision for, and understanding of, education and society, a vision that is quite suitable to defending extreme levels of social inequality. Thus, these examples show that standards in the form of tests and performance levels can be examined as governing tools, mechanisms for controlling vision and influencing social philosophy. This perspective highlights that setting, maintaining, and policing standards is a claim to, and right of, authority, whether the standards are for commerce or education:

> The right to determine measures is an attribute of authority in all advanced societies. It is the prerogative of the ruler to make measures mandatory and to retain the custody of the standards.... The controlling authority, moreover, seeks to unify all

> measures within its territory and claim the right to punish metrological transgressions. (Kula, as quoted in Garrison, 2009, p. 8)

The perspective emphasizes that standards reflect the outlook, values, and beliefs of those who establish them. Standards and measuring practices have a symbolic character. Examples of this are numerous and wide-ranging, from the theological significance of "just measures" in Muslim and Judeo-Christian texts, to the folk wisdom of peasants regarding measures of vodka at the local tavern (Garrison, 2009, p. 11). In each case, the standard becomes a means for regulating, interpreting, and judging human behavior.

A particular form of governance by way of standards is found in the now popular idea of personalized learning, which is premised on B. F. Skinner's "learning machine" (McRae, 2013). This view of learning denies the social, cultural, political, and even emotional context in which knowledge is created and learning takes place. McRae (2013) wrote the following:

> Adaptive learning systems (the new teaching machines) do not build more resilient, creative, entrepreneurial or empathetic citizens through their individualized, linear and mechanical software algorithms. Nor do they balance the desire for greater choice, in all its manifest forms, with the equity needed for a society to flourish. Computer adaptive learning systems are reductionist and primarily attend to those things that can be easily digitized and tested (math, science and reading). They fail to recognize that high quality learning environments are deeply relational, humanistic, creative, socially constructed, active and inquiry-oriented. (Introduction section, para. 5)

But it is important here to ask the following: Is the move away from the social, cultural, political, and even emotional a result of the relative difficulty of measuring a social, emotional, or moral phenomenon (a failure of science), or are the social, emotional, and moral phenomena irrelevant or counter to the project of which operationism is a part? If the aim is the manipulation of subject behavior and belief through stimulus-response regimes, signaling to the subject what adjustments reformers deem successful, the social, political, emotional, and moral become irrelevant. While many decry the measurement obsession for resulting in a valuation only of what can be measured, the more accurate picture is that the operational doctrine and the data it yields result in measuring as a means for the imposition of a value system, an unexamined and hidden structure that establishes frameworks for making judgments about individual and collective life. In this sense, operationism is a method of cultural politics: operationists measure to make meaning, not to discover it.

The current mechanistic practice of testing—where students are stimulated and then compelled to respond, and now, with TBTEC, teachers are positioned as the causal factor in this stimulus-response chain—is not a reflection of the limit of science but rather a model of how to live. Teacher and student identity, their social being, their purpose, is narrowly rendered from within this framework of performativity (Ball, 2012). This is not a flaw. It is *the way*.

Ball's (2012) notion of performativity assumes the operational stance, and although operationism precedes the neoliberal age, there is little doubt that it—and its offspring test-based accountability—has never been more prominent than in the present context. His elaboration of the notion and central role of performativity in governance is useful in thinking about the political essence of the operational doctrine. "[M]easurement, or to be more precise *performativity…*is a vital component of both management and enterprise," where, in effect "organizations are 'enabled' to think about themselves differently, in terms of, or in relation to their performance" (p. 30). For Ball, "performativity is the quintessential form of neoliberal governmentality, which encompasses subjectivity, institutional practices, economy and government. Performativity invites and incites us to make ourselves more effective, to work on ourselves, to improve ourselves and to feel guilty or inadequate if we do not" (p. 31). Importantly for this discussion, he noted that performativity "operates within a framework of judgment within which what 'improvement' and 'effectiveness' are, is determined for us, and 'indicated' of us by measures of quality and productivity" (p. 31). Put differently, human action is directed by the practice of operationally defining effectiveness by those who get do the defining: Submission to arbitrary power—undisclosed and increasingly unelected and taking the executive form in this neoliberal age—has been successfully rebranded, "meeting the standard."

Ball (2012) argued that the "first order effect of performativity in education is to reorient pedagogical and scholarly activities towards those which are likely to have a positive impact on measurable performance outcomes…and as such it is a deflection of attention away from aspects of social, emotional or moral development that have no immediate measurable performance value" (p. 34). That is to say, through performativity, the purposes for which people are to work and live are controlled.

Again, the problem is not that these practices evidence error or invalidity. For those who organize this reorientation, it is precisely for the deflecting function that such methods are adopted. It is no accident, to take one simple but important example, that the current pseudo-accountability regime structures discourse about public school performance such that the well-documented role of poverty in explaining differential educational outcomes is effectively ignored, even though it can be measured (Berliner, 2012). Put differently, while Berliner (2012) argued that the majority of test score variance can be attributed to out-of-school factors related to unequal distribution of wealth, current policy targets teachers and principals who, while certainly able to make a difference, are not the primary reason for unequal educational outcomes and not a logical place to begin to solve that problem. By adopting a method that ostensibly controls for out-of-school factors, the operational definition of effective teacher functions to deny that we must confront poverty to improve the quality of education for students living in poverty. Since poverty has been controlled for by the formula, we don't need to talk about it.

The Arbitrary Content of the Operational Method

Recall that scaling is the process of assigning numbers or labels to whatever one is measuring and that such scaling activities serve to provide empirical bases for defining theoretical concepts. Now consider that there are two notions of arbitrary. The first is best understood if we take the measurement of temperature as our example. Here, there are two scales, but their ability to measure temperature (at least for daily use in terms of reporting weather) is equally useful. The choice of numbers for the scale—for example, the Celsius scale marks zero degrees as the freezing point of water at some defined height above sea level, and so forth, while freezing is indicated by 32 degrees in the Fahrenheit scale—is in itself arbitrary, although the number systems are not arbitrary, in that each corresponds to actual heat phenomena.

But there is another aspect of arbitrary, one that exists with cut scores or performance levels. The rendering of the categories of basic or proficient in education, again, is arbitrary in the sense of the labels and numbers used (e.g., 1–4 could be 100–400). But these levels are also arbitrary in the political sense: of power or a ruling body, unrestrained and autocratic in the use of authority. So-called performance levels in fact embody both forms of arbitrary. Taking the NAEP example again, Koretz (2008, pp. 185–189) showed that cut score committee members, who literally sit in a room and imagine how, for example, a "proficient" student should respond, and on the basis of this collective imagining, determine proficiency levels, are inherently arbitrary.

While the process is not without method, it is, nonetheless, political. And as it remains largely secret, and those involved largely unaccountable to any public, it is properly considered arbitrary in the political sense. The entire educational measurement apparatus now operates in this manner.

Test-Based Teacher Evaluation and Compensation: An Overview

An essential feature of the changes to the evaluation of educators is the use of student performance on legally mandated (high-stakes) standardized tests to determine teacher and principal effectiveness. States have taken various approaches to revising their laws, and while in general many states are similar in requiring objective student performance data to be used in evaluating teachers, they differ in both the degree and specificity of such requirements. Taken together, however, there is a relatively consistent legal framework among the states, clearly linked to Race to the Top funding requirements (Baker et al., 2013). A key feature of these frameworks is the adoption of the method of ranking the effectiveness (ultimately used to make employment decisions) of educators based on changes in student performance on standardized tests over time. Positive change in student test scores is defined as growth or the value added to students by their classroom teacher. Teachers whose students show more test score growth, on average, are thus defined as more effective, relative to other teachers. On the basis of these calculations of growth and other means for evaluating teachers (such as classroom observations), educators are placed in one of typically four or maybe five categories of effectiveness, with the lowest category being ineffective. It is in this general manner that teacher effectiveness is measured.

There are two general models that have been adopted by states for measuring teacher effectiveness with student achievement data: so-called *value-added models* (VAMs) and *student growth percentiles* (SGPs). While much work has been done to document the problems with VAMs, until recently researchers have not chosen to evaluate SPGs for their validity for estimating teacher effectiveness, "because they are not designed to infer teacher effectiveness" (Baker et al., 2013, p. 7). A main difference between the two models is that while VAMs pretend to be able to isolate the specific affect of one teacher on the performance of his or her students, SPGs make "no attempt (by design) to consider other factors that contribute to student achievement" (Baker et al.,

2013, p. 9). According to Baker and his colleagues (2013), New York State has adopted a hybrid model, where SPGs are conditioned on the progress of students with similar score histories (then rendered as *mean growth percentiles*, or MGPs, for each teacher's classroom); ostensibly, this controls for the influence of students' social background. However, Baker et al. reported the following:

> [New York] State's own technical report found[,] "Despite the model conditioning on prior year test scores, schools and teachers with students who had higher prior year test scores, on average, had higher MGPs. Teachers of classes with higher percentages of economically disadvantaged students had lower MGPs (American Institutes for Research, 2012, p. 1)." (p. 8)

The Operational Basis of Test-Based Teacher Evaluation and Compensation

VAMs fail to theoretically examine the concept of effective teacher (for a presentation of the variety of models now being used, and their atheoretical nature, see Baker et al., 2013). It might, in fact, be more accurate to say that this method for identifying effective teachers ignores much of what is known about teaching and learning, let alone measurement. Needless to say, evidence of the operational doctrine is immediately visible. Kupermintz (2003) studied the validity of one of the most well-known, influential, and long-standing models, the Tennessee Value Added Assessment System (TVAAS). Although Kupermintz did not locate the problems he documents as originating with the operational doctrine, his critique clearly evidences the problems that have been identified here. He wrote the following:

> A typical interpretation for the between-teacher variability in TVAAS teacher effects is that "the single largest factor affecting academic growth of populations of students is differences in effectiveness of individual classroom teachers" (Sanders, 1998). The conclusion is based on the empirical finding that "differential teacher effectiveness is a strong determinant of differences in student learning" (Darling-Hammond, 2000). The statement appears to imply that there are two distinct variables—teacher effectiveness and differences in student learning—and that the former causes the latter. Unfortunately, such causal interpretation is faulty, because teacher effectiveness is defined and measured by the magnitude of student gains. In other words, differences in student learning determine—by definition—teacher effectiveness: A teacher whose students achieve larger gains is the effective teacher. TVAAS divides teachers into five effectiveness groups according to their ranking

among their peers in terms of average student gains. To turn full circle and claim that teacher effectiveness is the cause of student score gains is at best a necessary, trivial truth similar to the observation that "all bachelors are unmarried" (2003, p. 289)

TVAAS, a major inspiration for the models now being imposed across the United States, is premised on faulty logic. Teacher effectiveness is operationally defined as student gains on state-mandated tests. No further argument is necessary.

In discussing the validity of models of teacher effectiveness, Baker and his colleagues (2013) elaborated these problems further: "As framed in teacher evaluation legislation…that measure is typically characterized as 'student achievement growth,' and it is assumed that one can measure the influence of the teacher on 'student achievement growth' in a particular content domain" (p. 14). They continued:

> At issue are policies involving teacher "evaluation" and more specifically evaluation of teacher effectiveness, where in cases of dismissal, the evaluation objective is to identify particularly ineffective teachers. In order to "evaluate" (assess, appraise, estimate) a teacher's effectiveness with respect to student growth, one must be able to "infer" (deduce, conjecture, surmise) that the teacher affected or could have affected that student growth…. To make an *inference* about teacher effectiveness based on student achievement growth, one must *attribute* responsibility for that growth to the teacher. In some cases, proponents of student growth percentiles alter their wording for general public appeal to argue that SGPs are a measure of student achievement growth, and that obviously student achievement growth is a primary objective of schooling. To that end, they argue that therefore, teachers and schools should obviously be held *accountable* for student achievement growth. Where *accountable* is a synonym for *responsible*, to the extent that SGPs were designed to separate the measurement of student growth from attribution of *responsibility for it*, then SGPs are also invalid on their face for holding teachers *accountable*. For a teacher to be *accountable* for that growth it must be *attributable* to them and one must be using a method that permits such *inference*. (p. 14)

And, to base a ranking system on top of such invalidity is yet another mark of an arbitrary authority. Yet, if we carefully consider the theoretical concept that reformers refuse to render in theoretical terms, we will see, as is the operational habit, that it connotes an implicit understanding of how the world works. First, note that effective means *outcome*. The phrase teacher effectiveness suggests, by the force of the formulation, *outcomes or products of teaching*. Logic would follow that teachers produce learning. And, the most obvious place to go looking for some learning is, of course, with those students who engaged in work under the direction of their teacher. Further reinforcing the mechanistic view of education is the very notion of value added itself, which, by simple force of language, reframes students as things that are acted on by workers preparing commodities for market. These notions serve to construct and then impose through the force of policy an understanding of teaching and learning as discrete activities and products amenable to mechanistic thinking, where A effects B yielding to C, a naïve Newtonian-like rendering of the physics of education.

Teaching and learning cannot, with such definitions, be understood as a social practice, a process that cannot be singularly reduced to either the teacher or the student or even to the parent or the community, as education is bound to a historical and cultural movement. Simply put, teacher effectiveness presents learning as a teachers' product when in fact learning is caused by the activity of the learner in his or her real living, social context, of which, indeed, educators are a part (Schlechty, 2011).

Of course, the problem is that while researchers and statisticians may think they are estimating the effect of a teacher on a student's score growth, the altered wording, noted by Baker and colleagues (2013) for public consumption, is no aberration or strained effort to communicate complex information. The aim is rather to operationally define effective teacher. The aim is not to identify effective teachers but to change and narrow what it means to be a teacher on the basis of a behaviorist outlook. The operational definition relocates the social responsibility for the results of educational efforts to individual teachers and other education workers as if they work outside of a social and historical context. In this case, the operational method becomes the practical means for decontextualization and shifts discourse away from the otherwise obvious social factors that systematically determine differential educational outcomes on the basis of structural inequalities in which individuals find themselves. This is politics by other means.

The Political Functions of Measuring Effectiveness in New York State

New York State has enacted what is known as the Annual Professional Performance Review (APPR), which establishes the framework for evaluating public school teachers and principals (charter schools are, interestingly, exempt from some APPR requirements; see Chuang, 2012). While state law has been amended to demand that student achievement data be used to evaluate teachers and principals, the New York State Board of Regents and the agencies they oversee are responsible for translating the legal statutes into state policy. A labor attorney (Viswanathan, 2010) summarized section 3012c of New York State Education Law as follows:

> Section 3012c of the Education Law ("3012-c")…contains the new comprehensive Annual Professional Performance Review ("APPR") system for teachers and principals. For the 2011–2012 school year, the new APPR system applies only to evaluations of teachers in the common branch subjects or English Language Arts, and Math in grades four through eight, as well as building principals. The new APPR system will apply to all teachers and principals effective in the 2012–2013 school year. The APPR system requires teacher and principal evaluations to result in a single composite score made up of the following components.
>
> Forty percent of the composite score must be based on student achievement measures; with 20 percent based on student improvement on state exams (or other comparable local exams), and the other 20 percent based on local measures of student achievement which must be established through the collective bargaining process.
>
> The remaining 60 percent of the APPR score must be based on evidence of overall teacher effectiveness, as determined through locally developed measures (established through the collective bargaining process), and in accordance with standards determined by the Commissioner of Education….
>
> The composite score must be a significant factor in employment decisions, including, but not limited to, promotion, retention, tenure, termination, and supplemental compensation. The APPR composite score will result in teachers and principals receiving a rating of either: (1) Highly Effective; (2) Effective; (3) Developing; or (4) Ineffective. In connection with this rating system, Districts are required to create Teacher Improvement Plans ("TIP") and Principal Improvement Plans ("PIP") for those teachers and principals who receive ratings of either Developing or Ineffective. Two consecutive annual ratings of "Ineffective," will be deemed to establish a "pattern of ineffective teaching or performance" which may be a basis for just cause removal of a teacher or principal. (para. 3–6)

There are significant political as well as ideological implications of APPR. First among those is the further erosion of what is left of "local control" in New York State. While the aforementioned formula appears to leave the majority of teacher evaluation (60 points) to local school districts, Baker et al.

(2013) and Burris (2011) argued that it is the standardized testing portion of the evaluation system that is decisive in placing teachers in one of the four effectiveness categories. Burris showed that "low student achievement measures…will doom a teacher with even perfect teacher achievement in [the locally developed measures category]" to at best a rating of "Developing" (p. 1). For example, a teacher who receives all 60 points from her districts (a perfect score), but only yields 2 points in each of the test-based portions (which comprise 40% of the formula), will have a final score of 64, which falls in the ineffective category. Teachers with large numbers of students with special needs may be especially likely to experience this scenario, as those students are less likely to show test score growth. What is significant, but rarely mentioned, is how this formula effectively removes personnel decisions from the district, as effectiveness ratings are now *de facto* based on state tests and their arbitrarily determined cut scores, not decisions by staff or school boards.

One of Baker et al.'s (2013) major arguments is with respect to *due process*. If teachers are terminated on the basis of MGPs that in fact cannot be attributed to them, and these MGPs are shown to be unstable or unreliable, serious due process claims may arise. But the question is not simply whether APPR will serve to violate teachers' rights, but rather, if in the current climate, courts will uphold teachers' rights. Bold declarations by former New York City Mayor Michael Bloomberg and other reformers of a desire to impose massive teacher firings and increase class size betray a link between the operationism at work and a political aim that is served by defining teacher effectiveness as growth in student test scores (Burris, 2011). Add to this the known correlation between student social background and MGPs and one does not need a crystal ball to see where state education officials and their army of "reformers" wish to go. APPR sets up a regime where educators are in fact punished for working with students living in poverty, those who are not native English speakers, and so on. An important detail here is again made by Burris (2011): A normal curve is assumed in the scaling of the performance rankings, such that, for example, 50% of all teachers in New York State should be rated either "Ineffective" or "Developing." Thus, the outcome of the operational definition of effective teacher as growth in student achievement is the creation of the conditions for large-scale teacher terminations, part of the larger effort to dismantle public education (see Glass, 2008).

An Invitation

While we readily talk of and critique "the test," we are far less inclined to examine the power regime of which the test is an instantiation, a symbol of the regime's valid meaning that organizes our experiences. Operationism is, in the end, a technique for social control, not for knowledge production that engages the public and serves the common good. And as a form of control, it was not and never can be neutral in the political sense, as it assumes a definite view regarding the manner in which society should be organized and governed, a view that the public has rejected. For this reason, critiques should not be limited to the technical failings of tests. So where does this analysis take us?

Many of the key questions about educational assessment have been strangely separated from work to build democratic living and theories of the relationship among education, school, and society, as if the idea of self-government somehow does not apply to attempts to evaluate our collective efforts and institutions. These seemingly technical tasks, including key problems of measurement proper, appear to have been shunned by many who see more important work elsewhere. Yet, the evaluation of education professionals is no more or no less a proper field of action for the basic tenets of democratic living. For starters, one should have a say over the methods that are used to make judgments about oneself, one's place of work, and one's community. Assessment, then, is no less a proper object of political action than are concerns over taxes or war or the Common Core standards.

To assess is to raise those fundamental questions of purpose, for without purpose in mind, how can one assess or evaluate an individual activity, an organization, or an institution? Educators, researchers, social scientists, and the public at large need to start from the beginning. What goals do we as a society want our educational institutions to serve, and who should be involved in setting those goals? How should we determine if we are meeting those goals, and who should be involved in setting standards used to make such determinations? To confront the problem of arbitrary authority that has been identified requires far more than exposure of the arbitrary authority. It requires a new vision to guide education and a new governance structure that is consistent with that vision.

But to do this, we also need to systematically sum up what has been learned over 150 years of past experience with public education and the manner in which we have assessed. Naturally, many feel compelled to defend public education, as we knew it. But history does not rewind. In this sense, scholars in particular can be valuable by leading a range of efforts aimed at summing up the experience of public education in the United States with the goal of identifying and elaborating for public discussion what we might wish to keep, and what we have learned from, but never wish to repeat. We should work to construct a collective memory that serves us in this present period, where the very dignity and idea of the public, of public education, and of the possibility of democratic living, are under attack.

Notes

1. By this I do not reference the numerous reports challenging the validity and reliability of high-stakes testing; these are useful but challenge the regime only from within the dominant scientific framework, which many, including myself, believe is the larger issue. It was for this reason Ken Saltman organized a panel presentation on "Resurgent Positivism, Corporatism, and the Politics of Knowledge in Educational Reform and Research" at the American Educational Studies Association in November of 2010. This chapter is inspired by the presentation I delivered at that time (Garrison, 2010).
2. A historical overview of the philosophy of science, and in particular, the role of positivism and neo-positivism in the development of operationism by physicists (who later rejected the practice) and its adoption by psychologists in particular, is beyond the scope of this presentation. Useful presentations can be found in these works: Chang, 2009; Green, 1992; Leahey, 1980.
3. Note that the theoretical framework assumed here works whether one assumes a "hereditarian" or "environmentalist" stance (see Garrison, 2009). For a general discussion of the atheoretical nature of "IQ," see Block and Dworkin (1976).
4. It should be noted that the problem is not with statistics or necessarily even with quantitative methodologies, per se. The problem rests with confounding meaning with a truth claim and attempting to resolve that problem by asserting that "true meaning" necessarily results from operational forms of measurement and denial of nonquantitative properties of phenomena.

References

Baker, B. D., Oluwole, J. O., & Green, P. C. (2013). The legal consequences of mandating high stakes decisions based on low quality information: Teacher evaluation in the Race-to-the-Top era. *Educational Policy Analysis Archives, 21*(5), 1–71.

Baker, E. L., Barton, P. E., Darling-Hammon, L., Haertel, E., Ladd, H. F., Linn, R. L., …Shepard, L. A. (2010). *Problems with the use of student test scores to evaluate teachers.* Washington, DC: Economic Policy Institute.

Ball, S. J. (2012). *Global education inc.: New policy networks and the neo-liberal imaginary.* New York, NY: Routledge.

Berka, K. (1983). *Measurement: Its concepts, theories, and problems* (A. Riska, Trans.). Boston, MA: Kluwer.

Berliner, D. (2012). Effects of inequality and poverty vs. teachers and schooling on America's youth. *Teachers College Record, 116*(1). Retrieved from http://www.tcrecord.org/content.asp?contentid=16889

Block, N. J., & Dworkin, G. (1976). IQ, heritability, and inequality. In N. J. Block & G. Dworkin (Eds.), *The IQ controversy* (pp. 410–540). New York, NY: Pantheon.

Burris, C. (2011). Why APPR will be so damanging to educators. Retrieved from http://roundtheinkwell.files.wordpress.com/2011/12/why-appr-will-be-so-damaging-to-educators1.pdf

Chang, H. (2009). Operationalism. In E. N. Zalta (Ed.), *Stanford encyclopedia of philosophy* (pp. 1–43). Retrieved from http://plato.stanford.edu/archives/fall2009/entries/operationalism/

Chuang, C. (2012). Additional guidance regarding educator evaluation for charter schools participating in Race to the Top. Retrieved from http://www.p12.nysed.gov/psc/documents/CSeducatorevalguidance_090712.pdf

Garrison, M. J. (2009). *A measure of failure: The political origins of standardized testing*. Albany: State University of New York Press.

Garrison, M. J. (2010). *Testing for corporatist order and private control in the no longer liberal state.* Paper presented at the annual conference of the American Educational Studies Association, Denver, CO.

Garrison, M. J. (2011). On the origin and political significance of test-based teacher evaluation and compensation. *Journal of Inquiry and Action in Education, 4*(1), 49–67. Retrieved from http://digitalcommons.buffalostate.edu/jiae/vol4/iss1/3/

Glass, G. V. (1978). Standards and criteria. *Journal of Educational Measurement, 15,* 237–261.

Glass, G. V. (2008). *Fertilizers, pills, and magnetic strips: The fate of public education in America.* Charlotte, NC: Information Age.

Gratz, D. B. (2009). *The peril and promise of performance pay: Making education compensation work.* Lanham, MD: Rowman & Littlefield Education.

Green, C. D. (1992). Of immortal mythological beasts: Operationism in psychology. *Theory & Psychology, 2,* 291–320.

Koretz, D. M. (2008). *Measuring up: What educational testing really tells us.* Cambridge, MA: Harvard University Press.

Kupermintz, H. (2003). Teacher effects and teacher effectiveness: A validity investigation of the Tennessee Value Added Assessment System. *Educational Evaluation and Policy Analysis, 25*(3), 287–298.

Leahey, T. H. (1980). The myth of operationism. *The Journal of Mind and Behavior, 1*(2), 127–143.

Learing Point Associates. (2010, May). Evaluating teacher effectiveness: Emerging trends reflected in the state phase 1 Race to the Top applications. Naperville, IL: Author. Retrieved from http://www.learningpt.org/pdfs/RttT_Teacher_Evaluation.pdf

McRae, P. (2013). Rebirth of the teaching machine through the seduction of data analytics. *ATA Magazine, 93*(4). Retrieved from http://www.teachers.ab.ca/Publications/ATA%20Magazine/Volume-93/Number-4/Pages/Rebirth-of-the-teaching-machine.aspx

Podgursky, M. J., & Springer, M. G. (2007). Teacher performance pay: A review. *Journal of Policy Analysis and Management, 26*(4), 909–949.

Ravitch, D. (2013). We cannot "measure what we treasure." Retrieved from http://dianerav itch.net/2013/05/02/we-cannot-measure-what-we-treasure/

Saltman, K. J. (2010). *The gift of education: Public education and venture philanthropy.* New York, NY: Palgrave Macmillan.

Schlechty, P. C. (2011). *Engaging students: the next level of working on the work.* San Francisco: Jossey-Bass.

Slentz, K. (2013). *Implementation of the common core learning standards.* Albany: The State Education Department, University of the State of New York. Retrieved from http://www.engageny.org/sites/default/files/resource/attachments/field-memo-transition-to-common-core-assessments.pdf

Stevens, S. S. (1946). On the theory of scales of measurement. *Science, 103,* 677–680.

Viswanathan, S. (2010). New York's overhaul of teacher and principal evaluation procedures. Retrieved from http://www.nylaborandemploymentlawreport.com/2010/10/articles/public-employment/new-yorks-overhaul-of-teacher-and-principal-evaluation-procedures/

· 4 ·

EVALUATING TEACHERS: MAKING MEANING OUT OF THE MADNESS

Kate E. O'Hara

We are in a tumultuous time in public education and teachers are at the heart of the conflict. From politicians to practitioners, the evaluation of teachers is at the forefront of national discussion. Although it is a universal goal to support effective teaching and improve student learning, a divide on the topic has emerged and is growing deeper.

In August 2012, at a meeting in Maryland with 850 Baltimore County teachers, U.S. Secretary of Education Arne Duncan stated, "Change is always hard, and top-down accountability too often feels punitive. At the end of the day, accountability comes from within—from teachers holding themselves to high standards because they take their profession seriously and want to see children succeed."

Who would argue against that goal of accountability? It's the account-ability system that is called into question. As a former secondary classroom teacher and K-12 teacher educator, and now a professor in the field of teacher education, I have yet to meet a teacher who has not taken his or her "profes-sion seriously." On the contrary, the teachers I know and work with struggle daily to be treated as a professionals. They diligently toil to provide their stu-dents with meaningful learning experiences, and they donate their time well beyond the traditional school day, exemplifying "accountability from within."

And yet these teachers are expected to produce modules of test prep, as they have been reduced to "unskilled laborers who deliver the correct goods to the students—nothing more, nothing less" (Kincheloe, 2005, p. 90).

Even more absurd, Mr. Duncan, is the notion that someone would not "want to see children succeed." As Ken Robinson (2010) once quipped, "And people say we have to raise standards as if this is a breakthrough. You know. Really? Yes. We should. Why would you lower them?" (1:31–1:39). Notions of high standards and accountability are common sense; however, "change is hard" when practices that stand in contrast to the democratic purposes of education are in place.

For the dedicated teachers who strive to create learning opportunities that move beyond a reductionist viewpoint, to those who foster criticality and differentiation within a complex, democratic curriculum, a neoliberal agenda has permeated public education, complete with a new vision of what it means to teach, to learn, and to participate in society. This neoliberal framework has become so embedded in our common sense understandings that it reshapes those understandings, masks other realities, and influences the way we operate in the world (Harvey, 2005).

Ira Shor (2009) further explains:

> Neo-liberalism, the dominant ethos of both major parties, has a number of familiar markers: consolidation of enterprises into massive multi-nationals ("corporate con-glomeration," "globalization"); outsourcing of work to cheap labor sites anywhere in the world ("race to the bottom"); conversion of work from full-time to contingent and part-time staffing (adjunct abuse in English especially); defunding "public goods" like parks, public schools and public higher education, public housing, and public hospitals, in favor of "private goods" like fees for park use, health clubs and luxury spas, managed health care, vouchers and charters in K-12, condos and gated communities, and subsidized development ("privatization"); increasing inequality as wealth transfers from the public sector to the corporate one and from the bottom 60% of families to the top echelons ("end of the American Dream," "death of the middle class"). (p. 14)

In the neoliberal framework, school principals serve as managers and teachers as workers, with their teaching void of intellectual activity, driven by stan-dardized tests, performance outcomes, and narrow accountability measures; thus the spotlight is on teachers bearing sole responsibility for failure. "It is now common sense to give credence to models of teaching and learning that assume individuals succeed because of their agency and persistent efforts. It then follows that lack of success can be linked to lack of effort, in which case accountability measures can be invoked (Tobin, 2011, p. 13).

From news reports across the nation, we read of teachers defending themselves against new accountability measures and evaluation systems that have been imposed upon them, accountability measures and evaluation systems that are too often biased and unreliable. And, although teachers have an obvious influence on student achievement, at the same time, they do not control it. For those working in the K-12 classroom, student achievement is not part of a cause and effect relation. In fact, research reveals that gains in student achievement are influenced by much more than any individual teacher. Other factors include the following:

- School factors such as class sizes, curriculum materials, instructional time, availability of specialists and tutors, and resources for learning (books, computers, science labs, and more);
- Home and community supports or challenges;
- Individual student needs and abilities, health, and attendance;
- Peer culture and achievement;
- Prior teachers and schooling, as well as other current teachers;
- Differential summer learning loss, which especially affects low-income children; and
- The specific tests used, which emphasize some kinds of learning and not others and which rarely measure achievement that is well above or below grade level. (Darling-Hammond, Amerein-Beardsley, Haertel, & Rothstein, 2012, p. 8).

Teachers also report that in classroom practice, the implementation of existing evaluation systems creates a curriculum shift to "teaching to the test" and teaching only the subjects of standardized exams. As a result, essential instructional time is lost and replaced with test prep.

This is disheartening, to say the least.

At the Start

David Byrne once warned, "And you may ask yourself: Well…. How did I get here?" Well, let us go back 30 years. In 1983, the National Commission on Excellence in Education issued a report that examined the quality of education in the United States, complete with statistics and fear-instilled messages that our education system was in crisis and our school-aged children had fallen out of first place in a race where few understood the rules and parameters. "A Nation At

Risk" criticized and chastised America's schools and called for a host of reforms, which moved public education into the limelight and to the top of the national agenda. But with that limelight emerged the dark shadow of school bashing and misguided "reforms" that in many ways only compounded the problems identified in the original report (Bracey, 2008; Graham, 2013).

The data and statistics that were supposedly solid ground for building "A Nation At Risk" were later found to be made of quicksand. Dean Paton (2014) clarifies:

> For a document that's had such lasting impact, "A Nation At Risk" is remarkably free of facts and solid data. Not so the Sandia Report, a little-known follow-up study commissioned by Admiral James Watkins, Reagan's secretary of energy; it discovered that the falling test scores which caused such an uproar were really a matter of an expansion in the number of students taking the tests. In truth, standardized-test scores were going up for every economic and ethnic segment of students—it's just that, as more and more students began taking these tests over the 20-year period of the study, this more representative sample of America's youth better reflected the true national average. It wasn't a teacher problem. It was a statistical misread.

> The government never officially released the Sandia Report. It languished in peer-review purgatory until the Journal of Educational Research published it in 1993. Despite its hyperbole (or perhaps because of it), "A Nation At Risk" became a timely cudgel for the larger privatization movement. With Reagan and Friedman, the Nobel-Prize-winning economist, preaching that salvation would come once most government services were turned over to private entrepreneurs, the privatizers began proselytizing to get government out of everything from the post office to the public schools.

> Corporations recognized privatization as a euphemism for profits. "Our schools are failing" became the slogan for those who wanted public-treasury vouchers to move money into private schools. These cries continue today. (para. 9–11)

Privatization does become a euphemism for profits, with private, for-profit vendors selling lesson plans, educational software, textbooks, and student assessments. James C. Scott (1990) explained that "whenever one encounters euphemism in language it is an nearly infallible sign that one has stumbled upon a delicate subject…the imposition of euphemisms on the public transcript plays a similar role in masking the many nasty facts of domination " (p. 53).

Teachers are now dominated by an outside force, dictating what they should and should not do in their classrooms, all under the guise of "reform." A middle school English language arts teacher lamented:

> I don't really teach any more…. I mean I do, kind of. I used to teach a great unit on
> poetry and I would incorporate music, even dance. Now, I am always doing test prep.
> (sighs) My school just bought more practice tests and state approved materials.

Since "A Nation At Risk" was published, the "reforms" continue, with the Elementary and Secondary Education Act (ESEA) of 1965 reauthorized in 2002 as the No Child Left Behind (NCLB) Act, followed by the Obama administration's release in 2010 of "A Blueprint for Reform," addressing the issues created by NCLB and calling Congress for reauthorization. However, Congress was unable to agree on a set of reforms.

> Because Congress would not act to reauthorize ESEA, the Administration moved
> forward to offer states flexibility within the law—as authorized by provisions in the
> law itself—to pursue comprehensive plans to improve educational outcomes for all
> students, close achievement gaps, and improve the quality of teaching. (Whitehouse.
> gov, n.d., para. 5)

Forty-five states, the District of Columbia, Puerto Rico, and the Bureau of Indian Education have submitted requests for ESEA flexibility; as of February 2014, 42 states, the District of Columbia, and Puerto Rico have been approved for ESEA flexibility (U.S. Department of Education, 2014). However, this is not without a catch. In exchange for this new "flexibility," states must adopt "college and career ready standards; new teacher and principal evaluation systems—based in part on student growth; new assessments that measure student growth; and differentiated accountability systems" (Council for Exceptional Children Policy Insider, 2013, para. 2).

And so, the layers of a top-down system of accountability begin to unfold.

Impact on Local Layers

All state educational agencies (SEAs) seeking ESEA flexibility are required to submit a request to the U.S. Department of Education describing how they will meet a particular set of principles, one of which, *Principle 3: Supporting Effective Instruction and Leadership*, requires an SEA to develop and adopt guidelines for local teacher and principal evaluation and support systems (U.S. Department of Education, 2012).

In New York State, home to the largest system of public schools in the United States, a new teacher evaluation law requires 20% of a teacher's evaluation to be based on student growth on standardized tests, 20% on locally selected measures of student performance, and 60% on locally negotiated measures of teacher effectiveness. Under the plan, which is now implemented in New York City as well, teachers are rated Highly Effective, Effective, Developing, or Ineffective, on a corresponding scale from 0 to 100 (McAdoo, 2013; NYSUT, 2012).

Under this new legislation, for the 20% designated for locally negotiated measures, districts are to develop their own assessments or choose from a list of state-approved vendors. John B. King, commissioner of education of the State of New York, stated that local districts can develop their own assessments and do not have to purchase them from vendors. However, it is required that the locally developed assessments be

> "rigorous and comparable" and conform with psychometric standards to ensure validity (they test what they are supposed to test) and reliability (the measurement is consistent). Unless school districts have the resource capacity to employ testing experts to ensure that the locally designed assessments are valid and reliable, many school districts will choose from the state-approved list in order to minimize litigation when student test scores affect a teacher or principal's evaluation score. Vendor costs for the local exams vary widely. (Mitchell, 2012, p. 8)

The terms *choice, state approved,* and *flexibility* return us to a point made earlier: dialogue at the national level, the public transcript of the power holders, is marked with euphemisms imposed by the dominant, obscuring negatively valued actions, avoiding offense, and providing a benign look. However, the self-interested adaptation of descriptions and appearances only masks the unfair and often corrupt acts found in the hidden transcript of teachers at the local level (Scott, 1990).

A middle school teacher illuminated the local impact: "There's not a lot of material out there…you know, for Common Core[1] and preparing for these state tests. And no one to help you; all material has to be bought from the vendor. It's all a conspiracy."

It is a conspiracy, perhaps, or at the very least, multiple collusions that are beginning to be disclosed. Morgan Polikoff, an assistant professor of education at the University of Southern California, and William Schmidt, the codirector of the education policy center at Michigan State University, have found that in an effort to increase their share of a $9 billion annual market, textbook publishers promote the sale of material aligned with the Common Core State Standards; however, Polikoff and Schmidt's extensive research revealed that many textbooks were identical to the old, prestandard ones. Schmidt "dismissed most purveyors of such claims as 'snake oil salesmen' who have done little more than slap shiny new stickers on the same books they've been selling for years" (Herold & Molnar, 2014, para. 6).

Despite these revelations regarding the Common Core State Standards, teachers are still expected to align their units, lessons, and instructional activities to them. Additionally, teachers are expected to prepare their students for state-standardized exams that are aligned to the Common Core State Standards, exams that will impact teachers' yearly evaluations or measurements.

Unfolding: Definitions and Disillusionment

Our challenge is to make sure every child in America is learning from an effective teacher—no matter what it takes.

–U.S. SECRETARY OF EDUCATION, ARNE DUNCAN, 2009

Teachers matter. So instead of bashing them, or defending the status quo, let's offer schools a deal. Give them the resources to keep good teachers on the job, and reward the best ones.

–President of the United States, Barack Obama, 2012

Effective and *good:* These terms are widespread in dialogue around and about teachers. Do the terms differ or are they synonymous? What is an effective teacher? What is a good teacher? When the latter question was asked of students, the responses shared commonalities:

They like to have fun—first grader
Someone who respects their students and is funny—eighth grader
A person who is nice and understands you—third grader
They care for students like their parents would care—seventh grader
Someone who makes learning fun. Does things, does activities, not just paper quizzes—fourth grader
They're always available when you need help—ninth grader
Somebody kind, helpful, funny, amazing, all the things Mrs. G. is—fifth grader
Someone strict, but not too strict—11th grader
Someone who wants every student to succeed—a person who helps those who try—12th grader

Perhaps the most profound response came from a kindergarten student: "What is a good teacher?" "Love."

But love isn't something evaluated by test scores; in fact, it is something the new evaluation models are eroding: a love for teaching, which encompasses the love teachers have for their students, their subject matter, and learning—their students' learning as well as their own. A teacher's full day of work, which begins in the very early morning and spans well into the evening, now consists of regimented teaching within a narrow curriculum, using vendor-purchased material aligned to the Common Core State Standards, and beneath the pall of punitive accountability measures. This erosion of love has had a detrimental impact on the profession, and teachers are leaving, dejected, disillusioned, and exhausted, mentally, physically, and emotionally.

The Internet is teeming with news stories, letters, videos, and blogs from once-dedicated professionals that have made the decision to leave what they once loved. Gerald J. Conti is one of those professionals. After 27 years of teaching, he submitted a resignation letter to his superintendent and board of education. He also posted the letter on Facebook so that he could share with his current and former students his decision to retire early. His letter, eloquent and heartbreaking, went viral:

> "Data driven" education seeks only conformity, standardization, testing and a zombie-like adherence to the shallow and generic Common Core, along with a lockstep of oversimplified so-called Essential Learnings. Creativity, academic freedom, teacher autonomy, experimentation and innovation are being stifled…. My profession is being demeaned by a pervasive atmosphere of distrust, dictating that teachers cannot be permitted to develop and administer their own quizzes and tests (now titled as generic "assessments") or grade their own students' examinations. The development of plans, choice of lessons and the materials to be employed are increasingly expected to be common to all teachers in a given subject. This approach not only strangles creativity, it smothers the development of critical thinking in our students and assumes a one-size-fits-all mentality more appropriate to the assembly line than to the classroom. Teacher planning time has also now been so greatly eroded by a constant need to "prove up" our worth to the tyranny of APPR[2] (through the submission of plans, materials and "artifacts" from our teaching) that there is little time for us to carefully critique student work, engage in informal intellectual discussions with our students and colleagues, or conduct research and seek personal improvement through independent study…. After writing all of this I realize that I am not leaving my profession, in truth, it has left me. It no longer exists. (Conti, 2013)

A 15-year teaching veteran, Ellie Rubenstein posted her resignation in a YouTube video:

> I have experienced the depressing, gradual downfall and misdirection of education that has slowly eaten away at my love of teaching. The emphasis in education has shifted from fostering academic and personal growth in both students and teachers, to demanding uniformity and conformity. Raising students' test scores on standardized

tests is now the only goal, and in order to achieve it the creativity, flexibility and spontaneity that creates authentic learning environments have been eliminated.... Everything I loved about teaching is extinct. (Rubenstein, 2013)

A middle school teacher I work with, who is a 14-year veteran, further explained the damaging effect of the current educational climate on not only herself but her students as well:

> As a teacher of students with disabilities, I find the changes with common core and the new evaluation system for teachers particularly unfair for my students. I am forced to teach several grade levels beyond their capabilities. I have students who read on a kindergarten level and I teach 7th grade mathematics. This environment of teaching to a test sets my kids up the most to constantly feel like failures. They are often frustrated and I become frustrated because my livelihood is dependent on how well they achieve on a state exam that is nearly impossible for them to succeed at. I am an experienced teacher and do my best to accommodate content but am not allowed to modify anything. My lessons are formatted a specific way and the opinions of the teachers are not respected. I spend hours and hours trying to reach my students on a 7th grade level when they are simply not ready for it.

As a result of this harrowing experience, this teacher says she is "burnt out and ready to move on" to a new profession.

However, despite the research that has found an association between teacher attrition and demoralization and test-based accountability efforts (Baker et al., 2010), the stories from these teachers, and countless others, rarely surface in the public transcript; yet the loss is compounded when so many of the teachers leaving the profession are veteran teachers, who take with them years of experience and wisdom. A study by the National Commission on Teaching and America's Future (2010) found that "educator retirement robs schools of many effective teachers with just the skills and experience that schools desperately need" (p. 12). However, the misfortune in this is that because of the climate of standardization and penalizing accountability measures, veteran teachers are leaving prior to retirement.

In addition to creative and dedicated teachers reaching unmatched levels of frustration, we must also consider their students, who face a school day of rote memorization, test prep, and standardized curriculum.

A teacher new to the profession expounded on this:

> ...Everything is now about tests. Students will literally sit for hours on end taking assessments just [to] reach a certain benchmark score. Everything is based on numbers. Perhaps I do not have enough experience to really have an opinion since the new

APPR process has been in effect since I began teaching, but it is very uncomfortable. Veteran teachers have lost their love of teaching, which is so sad to see and hear. I think the process of APPR evaluation is very stressful and uncomfortable. I do not enjoy it and do not believe that it is an effective way to evaluate an outstanding teacher from an ineffective teacher. There are so many flaws in the system and it does not reflect a teacher's effectiveness.

The uniformity, conformity, and underlying frustration have also eroded what teachers and students work hard to create: a positive classroom community based on a safe, engaging environment, with mutual respect, creativity, risk taking, exploration of new ideas, and a love of learning. Unfortunately, the accountability requirements have instead created a different definition of classroom communities. Positive classroom communities

> have come to mean places where students arrive at school ready to learn; work diligently to master academic standards (particularly math and reading); go home and accurately complete homework; and return to school the next day eager to learn more. Often, teachers are so focused on ensuring that students pass achievement tests that they have little or no time to address students' social and emotional needs. (Allred, 2008, para. 2)

This standardized, sterile shift from a positive classroom community is pervasive in the schools I work in and has proven detrimental to the well-being of teachers I work with as well as their students. However, it was never more palpable than when my own child experienced a "new" positive classroom community. My daughter's first-grade teacher was defined by administrators as "good at getting the kids reading and writing on level." The teacher touted herself as "strict," and one of her colleagues, a push-in reading intervention teacher, warned me that students in her first-grade class needed "thick skin." Developing thick skin is not a typical goal one hopes five- and six-year-olds achieve, and thick skin was not what my daughter developed. Instead, she developed a dislike for school. Her days were long and tedious, filled with worksheets, workbooks, inflexible rules, and memorization and repetition. Gone were my daughter's smile, the humming of new songs learned, the retelling of stories her teacher told, the excitement of discovering something or someone new, the eager, intrinsically motivated attitude, and the positive image of herself as a student. She was reading and writing above grade level when she entered first grade but soon began to label herself as "not good at writing." Her teacher's antidote was to assign more and more worksheets and graphic organizers, implementing a one-size-fits-all approach as "extra help."

How could a child's love of learning change so dramatically in several months? "This isn't kindergarten anymore; this is first grade," I was sternly told by her teacher. She further elaborated, telling me that some of the activities my daughter would be doing would "get her ready for college." A critical look at teacher dispositions aside, it was evident that this first-grade teacher did not take the national agenda lightly; developing a "rigorous" curriculum and preparing her students to be "career and college ready" was to come at any cost. This resulted in a narrow view of achievement, meeting standards by means of repetitiveness and memorization, with total disregard to the social and emotional development needs of a child. Ironically, I recently learned that my daughter's first-grade teacher completed a degree in school building leadership and was hired as an elementary school administrator, which she called an ideal path to "positively influence student growth."

Sadly, my personal account is not unique. There are stories from friends and colleagues about the devastating consequences their children are experiencing. In local newspapers and in online forums, comparable stories are shared. A recent comment posted to Diane Ravitch's blog aptly referenced a "psychological plague":

> My husband and I have struggled with the demons of Common Core this year, watching our 9 year old son sink into what looks like depression…. This is indeed a "psychological plague" that is taking my child's spirit, and I think there are millions of other children out there experiencing similar emotional distress from CC…. I can sense the teacher feels pressured too, and is concerned about his test scores. ("Albany Mom," 2014; Ravitch, 2014).

Thankfully for my family, the year following first grade, and those subsequent, my daughter's teachers revived her love of learning through creative and passionate approaches within positive, collaborative classroom environments, despite the constraints and the standardization imposed on them. Her classroom experiences mirrored those I frequently encounter, those of the teachers with whom I work. But despite the dedication and tenacity of these teachers, their respectful, caring, and synergistic classroom communities are not immune to the erosion caused by standardization and punitive accountability measures.

When speaking with a group fourth graders, I discovered the detrimental effect of standardized testing and teacher evaluation on classroom community through the eyes of students. One 9-year-old year anxiously explained, "I want to do good on the test because I don't want Mrs. K. to get fired." "Why would she get fired?" I ask. She continued, "We asked her what the test was for and she said it was to see how we're doing and how she's doing. Then Marco asked her, 'If we do bad does that mean you're a bad teacher?' She laughed and said, 'Well something like that but it doesn't matter anyway. All anyone is going to see is how wonderful you all are. You have nothing to worry about.'" With a heavy sigh she continued, "But, I am worried. I like Mrs. K."

The in-service teachers I work with tell a similar story:

> The kids know this is high stakes. They're stressed. I'm stressed. And I think parents ease their kids' stress by saying, "Don't worry about the test, it's only to test how good your teacher is." Problem is we're a tight group here. They're a great bunch of kids and we all work well together. Of course they're upset if they think I'm going to be rated poorly because of how they do on the test.

Teachers are well aware that their classroom communities and exceptional relationships with students are eroding into an alienating environment, but regrettably, they are compelled to continue along the same destructive path, and in some instances forced to, due to the pressure for their students to do well on tests—tests that are tied to their performance evaluations. Instead of creating creative, dynamic classroom communities, they create pedagogies of silence and control, pushing students to regurgitate information (Carr & Portfilio, 2011).

Uncovering Flaws

As we are well aware, when evaluating teacher performance, student achievement is taken into account, and in most instances, this is accomplished through a value-added model. "Value-added, or growth, models track individual students' test scores from year to year, which advocates say can help isolate the effect of the instruction that students receive during one school year from their academic backgrounds and prior education experiences" (Sparks, 2011, para. 4).

But advocates of value-added models are overlooking several inherent flaws. At the most basic level, the statistical models used for the measures are not designed to evaluate teachers, and furthermore, policymakers have failed to take into consideration system error rates when designing and implementing value-added models as teacher performance measurement systems (Baker et al., 2010; Di Carlo, 2010; Schochet & Chiang, 2010; Sparks, 2011). Moreover, annual test scores simply do not give a full picture of student growth.

In reality, there is a great deal missing from the value-added model picture. For example, how do we evaluate teachers of students with attendance issues?

What consideration is given to out-of-school factors such as inadequate access to health care, home academic support, and poverty-related stress? What about food insecurity, which refers to "USDA's measure of lack of access, at times, to enough food for an active, healthy life for all household members; limited or uncertain availability of nutritionally adequate foods"? (CityHarvest, 2014, para. 1). These factors, among others, negatively and profoundly impact the in-school achievement of students.

And yet even more is missing from the evaluation picture. What about the fact that there are teachers in classroom across the nation working with a large contingent of English language learners or special education students? Despite the claim from some states (such as New York) that their value-added models take into consideration student characteristics such as poverty level, disability status, and English language learner status, research has found that even after controlling for student characteristics, there are "significant correlations between teacher ratings and students' race/ethnicity, income, language background, and parent education" (Darling-Hammond et al., 2012, p. 10).

Additionally, teachers working with students classified as "gifted and talented" are often penalized under the new value-added evaluation systems because their students continually score the highest on state tests, thus showing that their teachers didn't "add value." A frustrated teacher explained:

> My gifted kids scored well last year. And again this year. But that's through hard work. I mean, I work really hard, and so do they...sometimes after school too. But on paper the same high test scores means they didn't show any growth. On paper that shows I'm an ineffective teacher. The whole thing is so depressing.

Another missing piece of the value-added model picture that is slowly appearing in the public transcript is the evaluation of teachers based on the standardized test scores of students they do not teach and/or subjects they do not teach. Since standardized tests are only given in math and English, schools have to determine a way to give all teachers a value-added score.

A Florida teacher best expressed the situation in a firsthand account:

> I am National Board certified, have 2 masters degrees (only 1 is in education), 20+ years of experience, and was named a Teacher of the Year by three different programs in my district. Now my Title I school is graded "F" after they hiked the cut scores yet again last year and I will be following you to the unemployment office in another year or two. Should be interesting to see how they plan to staff the school after they have fired the roughly 85% of us who work in "failing" schools around the state.

> My VAM came from 4th and 5th graders' scores—students I have never taught be-
> cause I moved to this school a couple of years ago, and I teach 1st grade. (Ravitch,
> 2014, "Chris in Florida").

In April 2013, seven teachers with the National Education Association and the Florida Education Association filed a federal lawsuit challenging the fairness of their evaluation systems. Several months later

> state legislature passed a bill making it illegal to evaluate teachers on standardized
> test scores of students they never taught…the bill still allows teachers to be evaluated
> on students they may have in one class, but in a different subject. That means a social
> studies teacher can be graded on the reading test scores of his/her students. (Strauss,
> 2014, para. 9)

In this instance, the Florida teachers achieved a victory on one level but a disheartening loss on another. These teachers took action, resulting in action from the state, but the state legislation only solved one part of the problem, which still leaves teachers vulnerable to inequitable practices.

In the public transcript, stories of lawsuits related to evaluation and accountability are surfacing. Controversies in Illinois, Colorado, Florida, Indiana, Louisiana, New York, and Washington, DC, have made the news, and more stories, from more states, are making daily headlines, as flaws in the system are revealed and the storm of disagreement rages on.

Stopping the Madness

Because of the ongoing state and federal push to implement unfair and flawed teacher evaluation practices, the teaching profession is being destroyed on many levels. As discussed earlier, the fallout from these unjust practices is a procession of teachers leaving the profession, leading to a continual turnover of teachers, which keeps "the teaching force young and inexperienced, afraid and compliant. This is only one of many ways that teaching is being turned from a vocation to a job—and a low-paid, temporary one at that" (Nunez, 2012, para. 13).

Teachers, afraid and compliant, are the target of power, docile bodies that are subjected, used, transformed, and improved (Foucault, 1995). But isn't that the goal, to reduce teaching to an act of acquiescence, with scripted curriculum and teaching to the test, under punitive evaluation methods, all in the name of our children having "an effective teacher, no matter what it takes"—complete with educational resources that have been reduced to stacks of practice exams as the formula for keeping "good teachers on the job"?

The neoliberal school reform is focused on measurements that debase the relationship between schooling and educating critically engaged citizens. "The reform movement is also determined to underfund and disinvest resources for public schooling so that public education can be completely divorced from any democratic notion of governance, teaching and learning" (Giroux, 2013, para. 2).

Staunch supporters of national standardization and value-added teacher evaluation, such as Bill and Melinda Gates, remind us that these "new methods" are necessary given "the failures of America's education system" (Gates & Gates, n.d.). But if we have learned anything from a "Nation At Risk," and the follow-up Sandia Report, it is that truth is buried deep and a steady stream of messages have clouded our common sense, sweeping us up in the tide that is moving the public to private.

But there is also a tide of struggle, filled with hope and determination. Freire's (2005) words contextualize this struggle:

> People, as beings "in a situation," find themselves rooted in temporal-spatial conditions which mark them and which they also mark. They will tend to reflect on their own "situationality" to the extent that they are challenged by it to act upon it. Human beings *are* because they *are in* a situation. And they *will be more* the more they not only critically reflect upon their existence but critically act upon it. (p. 109)

Teachers are acting, and parents of students are acting, but there are also principals acting. In 2013, two New York State principals wrote an "Open Letter of Concern Regarding New York State's APPR Legislation for the Evaluation of Teachers and Principals," declaring:

> We cannot, however, stand by while untested practices are put in place without any meaningful discussion or proven research…. In a very clear manner, this letter states why everyone who cares about schools should be concerned about New York's APPR Legislation. The letter also articulates a better path forward for our schools and students. ("An Open Letter of Concern," 2013)

Since the letter was written, more than 1,550 principals and 6,500 educators and concerned citizens have signed a petition in support of these efforts to stop harmful educational practices. These signatories are not only from New York State but from states across the nation.

And just as the open letter "articulates a better path forward for our schools and students," a New York City high school principal not only suggests a distinct and feasible plan but discusses one he has already put into action:

> There are directives that are at the principal's discretion but I speak to all teachers before doing anything. The structure [teacher evaluation] is utterly flawed but there's also a lot of victimization going on. You ask another principal, "Why did you do that?" and they say, "Because I have to." They're just falling into the role of power, replicating power. But do they? We have to approach the process as a community, lessen the fear, change it from punitive to how it can help us be better teachers. We need open dialogue. We need to create a culture of response.

At the state level, rumblings of resistance and response can also be heard, such as in New York:

> In synchronized statements, Democratic leaders of the State Assembly joined Republicans in the State Senate to propose that the tests, which are aligned with the new curriculum standards known as the Common Core, be excluded, for now, from the state's new teacher evaluation system, which Gov. Andrew M. Cuomo signed into law in 2012. (Baker, 2014 para. 2)

However, New York is not alone. Legislators across the country, from both political parties, have set into motion bills to amend, delay, or repeal the Common Core State Standards—the national standards that coincide with teacher evaluations reforms, which rely on student performance on state tests (Bidwell, 2014).

Beyond action at the state level, federal action and response are critical. Pasi Sahlberg (2012), an educator, scholar, and policy advisor in Finland, who has studied education systems and reforms around the world, explained that although Finland has been the "go-to place for education reformers all around the world," the United States cannot learn any lessons from his country's successful school system unless they first address three particular issues: the funding of schools, the well-being of children, and the view of education as a human right (para. 5–6). He additionally made note of the importance of school autonomy and teacher professionalism, which are often marked as two dominant factors of Finland's educational success:

> The school is the main author of curricula. And the teacher is the sole authority monitoring the progress of students. In Finland, there is a strong sense of trust in schools and teachers to carry out these responsibilities. There is no external inspection of schools or standardized testing of all pupils in Finland. (para. 6–7)

Unfortunately, "sense of trust," "no external inspection," and "no standardized testing" are concepts unfamiliar to teachers in America. Yet they are central to the work of American teachers, and with the help of their advocates, the fight has begun to bring these concepts into their professional lives.

Support is essential; we need to work together to uncover truths and challenge top-down policies that erode the love inherent in the profession and eradicate the push for privatization and standardization. "The public sector and its public schools are precious assets of democracy which no private unit can equal or replace" (Shor, 2010). We need to work from a union standpoint that acknowledges that "teacher evaluation in most school districts is not the catalyst for professional growth" (American Federation of Teachers, n.d.).

When organizing as a community and becoming a force of opposition to oppression from a dominant power, we must follow a critical pedagogy tradition: recognizing the political construction of knowledge, approaching evaluation as an interpretative process, and understanding the harm of decontextualization (Kincheloe, 2008). And in a critical pedagogy tradition, we must hold dear the fundamental belief that "to know how to teach is to create possibilities for the construction and production of knowledge rather than to be engaged simply in a game of transferring knowledge" (Freire, 1998, p. 49).

We must continue to uncover multiple layers of injustices within the teacher evaluation system, make meaning out of the madness, and in solidarity, create a system of equity and opportunity for our teachers and also for their students.

Notes

1. At present, 44 states, the District of Columbia, four territories, and the Department of Defense Education Activity (DoDEA) have adopted the Common Core State Standards. The Common Core is a set of academic standards in mathematics and English language arts. The quick adoption of common standards can be attributed in part to the Race to the Top competition. States that adopted the standards by August 2, 2010, won points toward a share of $3.4 billion (Lewin, 2010).
2. In 2000, the New York State Board of Regents developed a new, required evaluation system called the Annual Professional Performance Review, or APPR, which is one component of the federal Race to the Top reform. It is a state-governed process for assessing teachers' and leaders' effectiveness.

References

American Federation of Teachers. (n.d.). Teacher development and evaluation. Retrieved from http://www.aft.org/issues/teaching/evaluation.cfm

Albany Mom. (2014, March 23). Mother: My son hates school, how can I help him? [Web log post]. Retrieved from http://dianeravitch.net/?s=albany+mom

Allred, C. G. (2008). Seven strategies for building positive classrooms. *The Positive Classroom, 66*, 1. Retrieved from http://www.ascd.org/publications/educational-leadership/sept08/vol66/num01/Seven-Strategies-for-Building-Positive-Classrooms.aspx

An Open Letter of Concern Regarding New York State's APPR Legislation for the Evaluation of Teachers and Principals. (2013, October 3). Retrieved from http://www.newyorkprincipals.org/home

Au, W. (2008). Unequal by design: High-stakes testing and the standardization of inequality. New York, NY: Routledge.

Baker, A. (2014, February 4). A call to ignore exam results when evaluating educators. *The New York Times*. Retrieved from http://www.nytimes.com/2014/02/05/nyregion/a-call-to-ignore-exam-results-when-evaluating-educators.html

Baker, E. L., Barton, P. E., Darling-Hammond, L., Haertel, E., Ladd, H. J. F., Linn, R. L., Ravitch, D., ...Shepard, L. A. (2010). Problems with the use of student test scores to evaluate teachers. *Economic Policy Institute*. Retrieved from http://www.epi.org/publication/bp278/

Bidwell, A. (March 6, 2014). The politics of Common Core. *US News*. Retrieved from http://www.usnews.com/news/special-reports/a-guide-to-common-core/articles/2014/03/06/the-politics-of-common-core

Bracey, G. W. (2008). Disastrous legacy: Aftermath of A Nation At Risk. *Dissent, 55*(4), 80–83.

Carr, P. R., & Portfilio, B.J. (2011). Audaciously espousing hope within a torrent of hegemonic neoliberalism. In P. R. Carr & B. J. Portfilio (Eds.), *The phenomenon of Obama and the agenda for education: Can hope audaciously trump neoliberalism?* (pp. xxi–xlvi). Charlotte, NC: Information Age.

CityHarvest. (2014). Food insecurity. Retrieved from http://www.cityharvest.org/hunger-in-nyc/food-insecurity

Conti, G. J. (2013, April 2). Gerald Conti's retirement letter. Retrieved from http://www.scribd.com/doc/133658678/Gerald-Gerald-Conti%E2%80%99s-retirement-letterConti-Letter

Council for Exceptional Children Policy Insider. (2013, August 14). Maine makes 40! States continue to receive ESEA waivers [Web log post]. Retrieved from http://www.policyinsider.org/2013/08/maine-makes-40-states-continue-to-receive-esea-waivers-.html

Darling-Hammond, L., Amrein-Beardsley, A., Haertel, E., & Rothstein, J. (2012). Evaluating teacher evaluation. *Kappan, 93*, 8–15.

Di Carlo, M. (2010, December 7). The war on error. Shanker blog: The voice of the Albert Shanker Institute [Web log post]. Retrieved from http://shankerblog.org/?p=1383

Duncan, A. (2009). Partners in reform. *U.S. Department of Education*. Retrieved from http://www2.ed.gov/news/speeches/2009/07/07022009.html

Duncan, A. (2012). Change is hard. *U.S. Department of Education*. Retrieved from http://www.ed.gov/news/speeches/change-hard

Foucault, M. (1995). *Discipline and punish: The birth of the prison*. New York, NY: Random House.

Freire, P. (1998). *Pedagogy of freedom: Ethics, democracy and civic courage*. Lanham, MD: Rowman & Littlefield.

Freire, P. (2005). *Pedagogy of the oppressed* (M. B. Raos, Trans., 30th anniversary ed.). New York, NY: Continuum International.

Gates, B., & Gates, M. (n.d.) Letter from Bill and Melinda Gates. Retrieved from http://www.gatesfoundation.org/Who-We-Are/General-Information/Letter-from-Bill-and-Melinda-Gates

Giroux. H. A. (2013, August 13). When schools become dead zones of the imagination: A critical pedagogy manifesto. *Truthout*. Retrieved from http://www.truth-out.org/opinion/item/18133-when-schools-become-dead-zones-of-the-imagination-a-critical-pedagogy-manifesto

Graham, E. (2013). "A Nation At Risk" turns 30: Where did it take us? *NEA Today*. Retrieved from http://neatoday.org/2013/04/25/a-nation-at-risk-turns-30-where-did-it-take-us/

Harvey, D. (2005). *A brief history of neoliberalism*. Oxford, UK: Oxford University Press.

Herold, B., & Molnar. M. (2014). Research questions common core claims by publishers. *Education Week*. Retrieved from http://www.edweek.org/ew/articles/2014/03/05/23textbooks_ep.h33.html

Kincheloe, J. L. (2005). The curriculum and the classroom. In J. L. Kincheloe (Ed.), *Classroom teaching: An introduction* (pp. 85–103). New York, NY: Peter Lang.

Kincheloe, J. L. (2008). *Knowledge and critical pedagogy: An introduction*. London, UK: Springer.

Lewin, T. (2010, July 21). Many states adopt national standards for their schools. *The New York Times*. Retrieved from http://www.nytimes.com/2010/07/21/education/21standards.html?_r=0

McAdoo, M. (2013). Teacher evaluation: Complex new system unveiled. *New York Teacher*. Retrieved from http://www.uft.org/news-stories/complex-new-system-unveiled

Mitchell, K. (2012). *Federal mandates on local education: Costs and consequences—Yes, it's a race, but is it in the right direction?* (CRREO Discussion Brief No. 8). New Paltz, NY: State University of New York at New Paltz Center for Research, Regional Education and Outreach. Retrieved from http://www.newpaltz.edu/crreo/brief_8_education.pdf

National Commission on Teaching and America's Future. (2010). Who will teach? Experience matters. Retrieved from http://nctaf.org/wp-content/uploads/2012/01/NCTAF-Who-Will-Teach-Experience-Matters-2010-Report.pdf

Nunez, I. (2012, September 12). Standardized test scores are worst way to evaluate teachers. *Chicago Sun Times*. Retrieved from http://www.suntimes.com/news/otherviews/15107882-452/standardized-test-scores-are-worst-way-to-evaluate-teachers.html

NYSUT. (2012). Teacher evaluation: Frequently asked questions. Retrieved from http://www.nysut.org/resources/all-listing/2012/march/teacher-evaluation-frequently-asked-questions

Obama, B. (2012). Remarks by the president in State of the Union Address. Retrieved from http://www.whitehouse.gov/the-press-office/2012/01/24/remarks-president-state-union-address

Paton, D. (2014). The myth behind public school failure. *YES! Magazine*. Retrieved from http://www.yesmagazine.org/issues/education-uprising/the-myth-behind-public-school-failure

Ravitch, D. (2014, March 23) From one teacher to another: VAM is junk science [Web log post]. Retrieved from http://wp.me/p2odLa-7tG

Robinson, K. (October, 2010). Changing education paradigms [Video]. (1:31–1:39). Retrieved from http://www.ted.com/talks/ken_robinson_changing_education_paradigms.html

Rubenstein, E. [Iquityoucantfireme]. (2013, May 21). *In pursuit of happiness* [Video file]. Retrieved from https://www.youtube.com/watch?v=uH9vxq1iJVM&feature=youtu.be

Sahlberg, P. (2012, April 17). What the U.S. can't learn from Finland [Web log post]. Retrieved from http://pasisahlberg.com/text/

Schochet, P. Z., & Chiang, H. S. (2010). *Error rates in measuring teacher and school performance based on student test score gains* (NCEE 2010–4004). Washington, DC: National Center for Education Evaluation and Regional Assistance, Institute of Education Sciences, U.S. Department of Education. Retrieved from http://ies.ed.gov/ncee/pubs/20104004/pdf/20104004.pdf

Scott, J. C. (1990). *Domination and the arts of resistance: Hidden transcripts*. New Haven, CT: Yale University Press.

Shor, I. (2009). Critical pedagogy is too big to fail. *Journal of Basic Writing, 28*(2), 6–27. Retrieved from http://files.eric.ed.gov/fulltext/EJ877253.pdf

Shor, I. (2010, October 4). Ira Shor is not "waiting for…" [Web log post]. Retrieved from http://www.notwaitingforsuperman.org/Articles/20101004-IraShor

Sparks, S. D. (2011, November 15). "Value-Added" formulas strain collaboration. *Education Week*. Retrieved from http://www.edweek.org/ew/articles/2011/11/16/12collab-changes.h31.html

Strauss, V. (2014, February 25). The most meaningless teacher evaluation exercise ever? *The Washington Post*. Retrieved from http://www.washingtonpost.com/blogs/answer-sheet/wp/2014/02/25/the-most-meaningless-teacher-evaluation-exercise-ever/

Tobin, K. (2011). Global reproduction and transformation of science education. *Cultural Studies of Science Education, 6*: 127–142. doi:10.1007/s11422-010-9293-3

U.S. Department of Education. (2012). *ESEA Flexibility Review Guidance*. Retrieved from https://www.ed.gov/sites/default/files/review-guidance.doc

U.S. Department of Education. (2014). *ESEA Flexibility*. Retrieved from http://www2.ed.gov/policy/elsec/guid/esea-flexibility/index.html

U.S. National Commission on Excellence in Education. (1983). A Nation At Risk: The imperative for educational reform: A report to the Nation and the secretary of education, United States Department of Education. Washington, D.C.: The Commission.

Whitehouse.gov. (n.d.). *Reforming No Child Left Behind*. Retrieved from http://www.whitehouse.gov/issues/education/k-12/reforming-no-child-left-behind

SECTION 2
DIS/CONNECTING PRACTICE

$\cdot\ 5\ \cdot$

ON THE RAMPARTS: EDTPA AND THE FIGHT TO RECLAIM OUR BELOVED PROFESSION

Elizabeth A. Bloom, Barbara Regenspan, and Jennifer McDowall

This chapter represents a conversation among three people, Jennifer, Barbara, and Elizabeth, all of whom are deeply immersed in, and impacted by, the new teacher certification test known as the edTPA.

Jennifer completed her student teaching in secondary English in the fall 2013 semester as part of the Master of Arts teaching program in which she is enrolled at Colgate University. Barbara is a teacher educator and Jennifer's advisor at Colgate. She also served as Jennifer's student teaching supervisor during her field placement. Elizabeth is a teacher educator at Hartwick College who supervises students in the field. Although we all live and work in New York State, we know from our colleagues at conferences, on discussion boards and blogs, and from scholarly reportage, that our experiences are widely shared by those whose state departments of education have opted to use the edTPA for determining initial teacher certification.

Collectively, the three of us staged this conversation to reflect on our remarkably complementary negative individual experiences with the edTPA, including Jennifer's accounting of her inability to use the most compelling examples of her own ingenious curriculum planning and enactment in her edTPA submission, Barbara's recounting of how she felt about trading a measure of her integrity in to edTPA by eliminating the most sophisticated curriculum of her student teaching seminar, and Elizabeth's reporting on the failing score of an otherwise successful student teacher in her program.

Our focus is on how the edTPA undermines the core values of our historically successful teacher education programs, whose philosophical and practical commitments have been defined by (a) a value system inextricably linked to social, economic, and environmental justice as praxis; (b) attention to the building of an array of thoughtful and specific interpersonal relationships as central to the growth of practicing teachers; and (c) support for development of enlivening curriculum inspired by the theoretical perspectives of Dewey, Greene, Giroux, and many other progressive scholars of the social foundations of education.

Elizabeth: Teacher education represents an essential piece of the larger picture of corporate education reform, and those engaged in preparing new teachers for the field now face the same extreme "accountability" obsession that plagues the public schools. Starting in September 2013, college students seeking New York State teaching certification must undergo a new high-stakes test, called the edTPA. Twenty-eight other states, as well as the District of Columbia, have signed on to this complicated protocol, which covers 26 certification areas. The edTPA requires that teacher certification candidates videotape a series of three to five original, interconnected lessons while they student teach. Videotaping is followed by a written document that can stretch to 35 pages and rationalizes their pedagogical decisions as correlated with student work samples, including, but not limited to, video content. The test costs applicants $300, to be paid directly to Pearson, a multibillion dollar publishing conglomerate located in the United Kingdom, and it must be passed for certification. For those who fail one or more sections, individual parts can be retaken for $100 apiece.

Although the edTPA was developed and is owned by the highly regarded Stanford Center for Assessment, Learning and Equity (SCALE), it chose Pearson as its "operational partner." Pearson's role is substantial, providing "…web-based services, including information, registration, an edTPA submission platform, and an edTPA scoring platform. The corporation is responsible for scoring of edTPA submissions and for reporting results; it handles recruitment and qualification of scorers" (edTPA, 2014, FAQ 18).

Whether intended by its creators, SCALE's choice of Pearson as a partner has effectively aligned it with the educational industrial complex's efforts to privatize public schools, end teacher tenure, destroy teachers' unions, and dismantle professional teacher preparation programs. SCALE, with all of its academic prestige, may maintain ownership of the edTPA, but the fact remains that Pearson profits handsomely from it (Madeloni & Gorlewski, 2013). Our state governments have colluded with this enterprise by outsourcing licensure decisions to Pearson even though it is a distant corporate entity, far from the Stanford campus, staffed by anonymous temporary workers, whose fundamental purpose is to enrich its stockholders.

> Barbara: The edTPA represents a pitiful distraction from growing poverty, including the decline of the middle class, and related, the rapid concentration of unconscionable levels of wealth in the hands of the very few, who are increasingly dedicated to defunding the public sphere, including public education. We in teacher education live the conceptual divides that obstruct deserved public focus on continual cuts of public school budgets along with parallel cuts in food stamps, even as teachers are held accountable for the effects of poverty and its related ills on the learning capacities of young people. We watch public schools and teachers become everybody's scapegoats, while a mixed chorus of would-be rescuers, some of them formerly respected teacher educators, jump on the intensified "accountability" bandwagon and enrich themselves with the proceeds.

Yet few in the limelight demand accountability of the billionaire privatizers, even as it becomes apparent, for instance, that charter schools, with few exceptions, as the film *Waiting for "Superman"* (Birtel, 2010) paradoxically clarifies, perform no better than the public schools they replace, and they often perform worse, as revealed by the 2013 National Charter School Study (CREDO, 2013). With global economic competitiveness the most loudly articulated motivation for the reforms, we confound young people with the mixed message that schooling will prepare them to be fully rounded and successful adults, while our hypocrisy seeps into every lesson plan that prioritizes test preparation.

Naomi Klein educates us, not only about the theft of the public resources so desperately needed to reverse social and environmental nonsustainability; she alerts us to the creation of the alternative economy of disaster capitalism, whereby the immediate and narcissistic interests of the uber-rich, who now control these resources, will be better served by the disasters caused by intentional lack of investment in the public sphere, including public education (Klein, 2007). With the aphorism "too big to fail" imprinted in the public mind, and never, in my experience, interrogated in public school curriculum except in the increasingly beleaguered Coalition of Essential Schools (whose viability is threatened by the same neoliberal reforms that eviscerate their unique curriculum), students correctly understand that dishonesty, including theft of public wealth, is currently protected if you are rich enough. Thus we find public reinforcement for the reality nobody has successfully illuminated except in individual testimonies of ex-Wall Streeters sporadically appearing in *The New York Times*: Addiction to extreme wealth is a debilitating new social disease that *does*, in fact, trickle down to the general public (Polk, 2014), including the potential college students we will fail to attract to teacher education programs, especially at private colleges like ours (where we are paradoxically positioned by our greater resources to have a transformative impact on our students through the very core values named earlier). We know from our students that their parents increasingly announce that they will not pay exorbitant tuition so that their children, and our potential students, can become (lowly) teachers.

A realistic, although cynical sounding question that emerges as a logical consequence of this line of reasoning is whether the public school students of our surviving teacher candidates will have a shot at economic security, or will they function as the reserve army of labor, the increasing class of "losers" who will serve to reinforce the passivity of the many in the service of the accretion of wealth by the few? Will this starkly depleted query about the terms of individual survival replace my own motivation for working as a teacher educator: Maxine Greene's compelling (Deweyan) rallying cries for education directed by a conception of the public good—her call for commitment to address the unfulfilled promise of expanded (and always messy) democracy tied to social and environmental sustainability?

In the meantime, the rush to hold teachers accountable is enacted so irrationally that the "effects" of the newest round of neoliberal reforms on student learning (and teacher job security) are evaluated before classroom teachers have any clarity about the content and intentions of these reforms. The job security of these teachers on whom we rely to guide our students in their classrooms is already dependent on their adherence to its prescriptions. The exception to teacher uncertainty about what adherence means is, ironically, evidenced in the cases where superintendents and/or principals interpret the intentions of the Common Core State Standards by requiring the use of (corporate-manufactured) learning modules; these, of course, disrupt years of thoughtful curriculum development by the most effective teachers and the teaching teams on which many of them successfully collaborate, often with our very best student teachers.

For myself personally, the immediate result has occurred this year—the loss to our very small certification program of three of my most effective cooperating teachers. All of them have claimed their own vulnerability in the face of the newly required Annual Professional Performance Review (APPR), which ties their job security to their students' scores on tests aligned to the Common Core State Standards. These three teachers are manipulated in other ways as well: all conceive of themselves as what the testing protocol terms "highly effective," and to be labeled otherwise would be deeply demoralizing—and so they comply with the demands to protect, ironically, their integrity. They also expressed embarrassment that they could not guarantee their ability to model for my student teachers precisely what we so appreciated about their work: the curriculum of intellectual depth they spiraled from the responses of *their* students and the attention to the needs of their most vulnerable learners that they had, in the past, sought to make explicit for mine. These wonderful teachers literally feared creating a breach in the successful relationship we have developed during years of collaboration in the education of differently gifted and challenged student teachers in the Colgate program. There is a parallel here with the fear of classroom teachers adapting to the reforms they see as jeopardizing their relationships with the individual young people in their classrooms, and especially with the most vulnerable of them, as they are coerced into delivering curriculum in which they cannot feel invested. Further complications to this picture involve the choice of the "reformers" to behave as though the budget cuts were not happening. As I was working with Jennifer and Elizabeth on the plan for this chapter, I learned that an especially talented cooperating teacher is now, due to a recent round of budget cuts, the only English teacher in her entire high school, and her teaching load is clearly illegal. Her reluctantly delivered message to me was this: She will not have the time to invest in support of a student teacher in the coming years.

Yet the front page of the fall 2013 American Federation of Teachers quarterly journal argues for "Letting the Text Take Center Stage" in the context of its elaboration: "How the Common Core State Standards Will Transform English Language Arts Instruction" (Shanahan, 2013). The article is sponsored by the powerful teachers' union, yet it advocates the magical thinking inherent in the application of top-down standardization demands, deferential acceptance that failure to achieve adequate test results on grade-level texts in the current curriculum will be "cured" by amping up to teach more demanding texts, more quickly, and with fewer resources. Guided by such magical thinking, the teacher harnessing these Common Core mandates will somehow stem the flow of disengagement in the classroom and will shepherd the now ignited student appetites toward increasingly sophisticated literacy. "Is the writer planning on visiting the classrooms of this now fourth cooperating teacher lost to us?" I ask the glossy printed page. I want to understand how any new text will take center stage in the theater of this beleaguered teacher's overcrowded English classes populated by the distracted young people I have watched her successfully engage in the past. The genuine magic she has accomplished represents the opposite of the magical thinking of the article's author. This cooperating teacher uses carefully selected brief news articles and sometimes paragraphs from scholarly literature to target a theme, or concept, or comparison with any aspect of the core text her students are studying. Such use of what I have named "intertexts" in my own writing is guided by knowledge of the past and likely future challenges to her students presented by the core texts (Regenspan, 2002). Intertexts also help her target passages in the larger work for close study and inspire writing assignments that require mining the texts for literary elements, transferable to her students' own writing. Alongside use of media literacy lessons in which projected images serve similar functions, intertexts support her to illuminate thematic connections and motivate many of her students to read the entire core text to engage in genuine critical literacy. We have accreted a wealth of such pedagogical strategies in our program, many of them developed by former students in collaboration with their cooperating teachers.

<table>
<tr><td>Jennifer:</td><td>My decision to teach is a midlife one; it comes with a commitment to leave behind the acquiescence to corporate values that troubled earlier decades of my working life, values held in sharp contrast to my concurrent commitment to art making. It may sound corny, but this desire to teach, embraced haltingly, is largely about improving the quality of my participation in the world. Now a master of arts in teaching student at Colgate University, and with teenage children of my own, I came to my student teaching experience determined to achieve the highest and best use of this formative moment in my own education, to test the potential of certain pedagogies to overcome the numbing consequence of overtesting and understimulation that I see in my own children's experiences of school. This is nothing more than what the best practitioners before me have done and continue to do, even as they succumb to onerous bureaucratic protocols and testing criteria that require them to overhaul proven curricula. Reflecting on my student teaching experience in an attempt to fulfill the requirements of my edTPA submission, I find I must likewise toss aside any of my own experiences that may seem illusory to a reviewer and may</td></tr>
</table>

> appear to edTPA as "coloring outside the lines," regardless of tenable, authentic successes. I must collude with a manipulation of my genuine experiences to express them within the constraints of a manufactured assessment tool poorly aligned with the value system that informed my student teaching.

My student teaching placement was in secondary English language arts in a generally prosperous and overwhelmingly White, lakeside community, where traditional academic standards were high and resources generally abundant. In two 10th-grade classes, I would be teaching Steinbeck's classic novella, *Of Mice and Men*; I galvanized all my social-justice-focused educational theory behind the formulation of a unit plan that would provoke student empathy for the trapped lives of the characters in this story—that would engage students in a humanizing appreciation of the American historical landscape of the 1930s and that would prepare them to recognize not only the complexities of the real world that this fiction amplified but specifically the beauty of the ways in which Steinbeck's writing acknowledged and deepened these complexities. To "read" Steinbeck's work, these students must come to the task open and awake. Reading is not passive; it is a creative act. It is the making of meaning, and it requires willingness of spirit, self-awareness, and dedication. I wanted to begin the unit in a way that would startle my students awake and signal the obligation of engagement of self that our work together would demand.

The rhythm and procedural preoccupations of school can constitute a depersonalizing institutional black hole, in which teachers lecture on topics far removed from students' lived realities, bells and buzzers signal movement, and students sleepwalk from class to class. This characterization of school was clearly symbolized by the volumes of *Mice and Men* that I would be distributing—hard bound in institutional green with a simple Times Roman title in black, with yellowed pages and the scrawled names of previous readers on the inside cover. How could I signal to my students that something new would happen when they opened the pages of this book—a symbol of the experience we were to embark on together? Over the course of two frenzied days, I downloaded and printed out on my little ink-jet printer at home 26 different covers of past editions of Steinbeck's work, and I jacketed each book so that it was a completely individualized copy. I tied the books up with ribbon—a gift—and to each ribbon I attached an envelope with the student's name that contained a question, unique to the bearer, about the context we would need to understand to read *Of Mice and Men* from an informed perspective. Answers to these questions later produced a PowerPoint presentation on the historical background of the book that the students delivered to each other. As these books were distributed, a hum filled the room, with students comparing and contrasting their volumes. I asked them to predict aspects of the story based on the cover art, and students who had never written a line in class before were moved to take pen to paper. This was one of the very fulfilling and moving moments of my student teaching experience. I felt that I had honored my students with my own transparent effort and this was an effective modeling for them; my caring catalyzed their caring. This was true of many of my student teaching experiences—emotional or psychological transactions that framed some learning, like shared energy, but always very personal, for them and for me. This is something that edTPA will never hear about from me. In fact, it is only one of what I consider to be the many highlights of my student teaching—the proving moments that won over my students and my cooperating teacher, impressed my education professors, and convinced me that I could be a successful teacher; I recognize that they have no place within the edTPA framework. The hired hand who has never met me, who reviews my videotapes and lesson plans and my 30 pages of self-analysis, will not be experiencing what is, in my estimation, the best of my student teaching work. In fact, this person will be seeing very little from me that was authentic to my student teaching experience.

Anyone reading my narrative here will recognize that a book jacket is not a lesson plan; but it is a gesture toward creating a culture of engagement in the classroom, functioning as one of the "intertexts" Barbara describes. Such gestures are not the concerns of the edTPA process which, instead, appears to privilege a benchmarking of the lowest common denominators of teaching practice, such as the promotion of weakly contextualized "academic language" above empathy for the human condition, or recognition of how symbols work to move us in ways that literalness cannot, or any of the multitude of aspirational attitudes toward literature that we seek to engender in the English language arts classroom. For the edTPA as an evaluative tool to be broadly applicable and comparable across all disciplines, it must hinge on the common, predictable, uninspired aspects of teaching, because how could it account for the extraordinary moments, the creative, innovative interactions that unlock some shared experience in the classroom and awaken the student who had his head down on the desk?

Linda Darling-Hammond and Maria E. Hyler (2013), both academic leaders at Stanford and instrumental in the development of the edTPA, advocate for its nationwide acceptance. They express their convictions that the edTPA will advance the level of professionalism in teaching in an article featured in *Rethinking Schools* titled, "The Role of Performance Assessment in Developing Teaching as a Profession." Their argument seems to be this: Standardized assessment for prospective teachers is valuable because *professions* require demonstrable acquisition of specific *testable* skills, a precedent being, for instance, the bar exam as a qualifier of emerging attorneys. In apparent contradiction, they assert that existing standardized testing for teachers is inadequate, in their estimation, because these tests are, well, not good: They claim that these tests trivialize teaching rather than force beginning teachers to confront the process of developing effective practice . Darling-Hammond and Hyler contend that the edTPA offers an important "alternative": "By evaluating teaching authentically, they [assessments developed by teachers, i.e. the edTPA] represent the complexity of teaching and offer standards that can define an expert profession" (2013, para. 13). So, in summary, standardized teacher readiness testing not designed by Darling-Hammond and Hyler is inadequate and inauthentic, at least in part because it does not "engage teachers in the development of effective practice" (2013, para.12). I read this as meaning that the edTPA intends to *prescribe* "effective" teacher training, to inflict on candidate teachers and teacher educators the most limiting type of practice—to teach to the test—and this is precisely what is happening as forced compliance with the edTPA permeates the teacher training pedagogies. This narrowing and instrumentalizing of our work has a history in the narrowing of the work of the classroom teacher, as Elizabeth reveals.

Elizabeth: I teach foundational courses to student teachers at Hartwick, so I must understand the historical context of the present—the sequence of events that have culminated in what some of us conceive as the occupation of teacher education by market forces in the form of the edTPA. I experience the current transformation of teacher education as parallel to that which has unfolded in K-12 education over a longer time period. Well-funded for-profit private entities established organizations in coalition with politicians and their associated think tanks. As with most such constellations of investment, the goal of profit making empowers a system that has additional intentions, some of them at least initially associated with a conception of the public good. Yet the promotion of greater standardization to insure continuity in the education of the least successful learners has always represented a relinquishment of the challenges of both ending poverty and developing public schools that would fully engage as active citizens the members of the community in which they were situated. We must remind ourselves, in the current climate where expanding democracy has been equated with expanding the profitability of capitalism in the interests of the few, that eliminating poverty and encouraging full citizen participation in civic and political culture *are* the challenges of making real democracy work; they also parallel education in the classroom, according to John Dewey, whose educational philosophy grounds the current Finnish miracle. Yet these goals have been soundly rejected by the increasingly wealthy financiers of the corporate reform agenda, along with their henchmen in the political realm, whose children attend private schools and are typically being raised in gated communities. It is widely known, for example, that while New York State Education Commissioner John King mandates that schools put their proverbial noses to the testing and accountability grindstone, his own children attend an elite Montessori school where students are immersed in a rich curriculum of self-direction and experiential learning.

The blueprint for absolute replacement of public education with corporate reform initiatives has been under development since 2000, when the Thomas B. Fordham Institute created the National Council on Teacher Quality (NCTQ). The NCTQ was established to promote alternative paths to certification that would bypass schools of education (Au, 2013), some of them sources of the continually replicated research that confirms the direct correlation between parent income and school achievement and especially the correlation between poverty and low school achievement.

NCTQ's influence was authenticated by its partnership with *U.S. News & World Report's* internationally recognized ranking of teacher education programs. Its board includes such corporate reform luminaries as Michelle Rhee and Joel Klein, both outspoken proponents of linking student test scores to teacher evaluation. The NCTQ also endorses the parallel practices of using teacher candidates' test scores to evaluate teacher education programs and the scores of the students of newly certified teachers to evaluate the teacher preparation programs from which they graduated. The stranglehold of standardization and accountability is now complete; every level of the education system becomes dependent on successful test preparation. In 2013, *The Washington Post* reported that the London-based investment bank IBS estimated the global education market at 4.4 trillion and climbing (Strauss, 2013). The demand for a steady diet of cash to feed the beast that has become the global education industrial complex expands unabated. At the same time, "local" budget cuts that eliminate teachers, art, music, and inquiry-oriented environmental science become normalized.

The power of the interdependent complex of players on the entire political structure, as well as the mainstream media, has been strengthened by characterizing the battle for our education system as pitting greedy self-interested teachers (i.e., teachers' unions) against altruistic reformer billionaires like Bill Gates and Rupert Murdoch, among others (Sirota, 2013). And of course, all of these powerfully funded partnerships in the manufacture of oppositional sound bites have had the effect of further eroding democracy. Those who champion corporate education reform manipulate the same legal framework to privatize education as that constructed by the Supreme Court decision in *Citizens United* (January 2010), which other extreme antidemocratic activists have successfully deployed to destroy labor unions and dismantle publicly funded social programs (Barkan, 2012).

The narrative around the implementation of the edTPA also follows the same arc of capitulation that occurred in K-12 education. Like the leadership in teachers' unions, we in colleges of education have generally betrayed our students by failing to loudly challenge the fundamental premises on which the need for the edTPA was built in the first place—i.e., our education system is broken and that state of affairs is compounded by schools of education, staffed by indolent tenured professors, who turn out mediocre legions of unprepared and underprepared new teachers. We have treated the arrival of the testing and accountability movement in the academy as inevitable and have shown a remarkable ability to adapt to the new job descriptions most of us find appalling. Neoliberal forces have been entirely successful in universalizing market freedoms and market ethics as a near total replacement for the state's role in providing social goods like public education (Harvey, 2005). By and large, teacher educators have stood dumbly by as this process has unfolded.

In my experience attending workshops and conferences, such as the 2013 meeting of the New York State Association of Teacher Educators in Saratoga, New York, teacher educators mostly confined the expression of their anguish and outrage to hushed conversation in hallways and scribbled notes on passed napkins. Like our counterparts in K-12 education, we have been soft, compliant, and afraid, and we have failed to exercise our right and obligation to dissent even as our commissioner of education has taken the floor at such events to make shaming speeches in response to our modestly worded challenges.

Regret for our failure to act with force and decisiveness now emerges, as the more precise nature of the costs exacted from ourselves and our students becomes calculable. In the two institutions we represent, Colgate University and Hartwick College, teacher education is profoundly personal.

Relationships between faculty and students are nurtured and negotiated over an extensive period of time and culminate in the complex, nuanced decisions around student teaching and credentialing. A most important third party, the cooperating teacher, brings her experience and expertise to this relationship at the commencement of student teaching; together, the three parties share in navigating the art of teaching in a specific classroom, with particular young people in a unique community context. Each student teacher, whether timid and anxious or confident and eager, brings a quality of combined hope and anxiety to this experience that is palpable to college supervisors and cooperating teachers who are tuned in to these students' particularities. With intense effort and robust support, the teacher candidate's vision of her own hoped-for competence may be realized. The ultimate and typically relative success or failure of each individual student teacher depends on many factors. Before the imposition of the edTPA, the final decision to credential was always determined in relationship, between people who know one another in the lived context in which the student teaching experience takes place.

Now, the very language of practice that we are compelled to adopt in our teacher education courses serves to distance us from lived relational experience; children become "focus learners" and a lesson becomes a "learning segment." The imposition of this ill-defined proprietary jargon is just one way in which edTPA traps teacher candidates and teacher education programs into compliance. Only the acceptance of a new language, and with it the concomitant acculturation to new and proprietary norms, can assure success; edTPA's language must assert itself into teacher training curricula if teacher candidates are to become adept performers of the edTPA protocols. Perhaps the feelings of demoralization on the part of teachers and teacher educators like us, a common reaction to the mandates of the edTPA, indicate some level of awareness of a kind of death of ourselves, our students, and their students.

Mark Garrison (2013) likened the implementation of this constellation of reforms to an acceptance of "a factory model of education premised on humans as things to be sold on the world market. As is factory production, such education is, indeed, rigorous (inflexible, rigid, likened to a corpse)" (para. 1). Giroux (2013) identified the use of the edTPA as part and parcel of the proletarianization of teacher work, reducing teachers to specialized technicians who manage and implement curriculum-adopted bureaucracies rather than developed or critically appropriated lessons designed to fit particular pedagogical concerns.

Jennifer: I have been nurtured by such emphasis on relationship as described by Elizabeth, and this has effected a gradual fine-tuning of my practices as a teacher during student teaching. During the three-way conferences that followed Barbara's observations, she, my cooperating teacher, and I discussed in depth the reception of the lesson by not only the range of students in the room but by the specific individuals in the room, many of whom required and deserved a variation on the modes of teaching I was employing. The classroom, then, when it functioned well, was operating on multiple levels in a complexly vectored geometry of meaning-making that engaged learners individually, personally, and truthfully. Success was measured by actions of single students in single moments; never in our conferences did we tally up an average of test scores and use this to qualify the usefulness of a lesson.

The requirement to satisfy my anonymous edTPA auditor creates a total paradigm shift. Populating the Internet are videos that take teacher candidates step-by-step through edTPA language and rubrics; they direct the use of them as guidance for lesson planning. The value of the correlation has nothing to do with intent to provide a better framework for student engagement, or better lesson content with regard to developing critical thinking in students, or any goals reinforcing our unknowable human obligations to one another (Readings, 2002). Rather, the focus is instrumental—always on a requirement to pass the assessment by meeting the demands of edTPA itself.

As teacher educators find themselves distanced from the engaged pedagogy (hooks, 1994) that has exemplified their best modeling for us, their students, I am left questioning just what could be "authentic" about the edTPA. My personal experience of the process is that my professors and cooperating teacher initially assured me that I should concentrate on testing my own developing teacher belief paradigms during my student teaching placement and that the edTPA would take care of itself. They attempted to reassure me that with my strong theoretical framework, the rudimentary accomplishments, of which the edTPA required evidence, would be present in my teaching in abundance. I did this; I fulfilled my student teaching juggling only the often complementary but occasionally competing agendas of my professors, my cooperating teacher, my placement school, my students, and myself. I developed a complicated lesson planning template that attended to all of these constituents. It began with the Common Core State Standards addressed in the lesson. It articulated the provoking essential questions specific to the text that the school administrators wanted displayed on the blackboard each day. It identified formative and summative assessments, student activities, academic vocabulary, "bell ringers," and "exit tickets," as well as educational theory supporting the lesson that was more instrumental than I was accustomed to, given the Dewey-inspired philosophical perspective of my teacher education program. I also attached to my lesson plans a list of questions that were essential to me, questions that in some part grew out of the Colgate teacher education claims and in some part grew from a particular student teaching seminar devoted to consideration of Maxine Greene's classic 1982 article, "Public Education and the Public Space":

What are the opportunities in this lesson to address:

1. *Meta-cognitive strategies for life-long learning*
2. *Love of learning, enjoyment*
3. *Self-initiated inquiry*
4. *Recognition of empowering aspects of language/reading/writing mastery*
5. *Complexity and tensions, disconfirming evidence*
6. *Inter-connectedness, multi-disciplinarity*
7. *Ways that students can be the experts*
8. *Acknowledgement of how the class community has created new knowledge*
9. *Ways to permeate the school/community/family boundary*
10. *Scaffolding on background knowledge*
11. *Demonstration of the value of this lesson: how does it make the world a better place*
12. *Creativity: how has this lesson made something new happen*

By comparison, edTPA provides the following instruction to substantiate adequate lesson planning:

Using your preparation program's lesson plan format as a guide, …Be sure to address all lesson plan components described in your edTPA handbook while making sure that each submitted plan is no more than four pages in length. If you are using a lesson plan model that extends beyond that limit, you will need to condense them or excerpt the necessary components listed here:

- State-adopted or Common Core Standards
- Lesson objectives associated with the standard
- Formal and informal assessments
- Instructional strategies and learning tasks
- Instructional resources and materials ("Making Good Choices," 2013, pp. 6–7)

I came to understand that successful submission to the edTPA process is dependent on just that, "submission," using the edTPA assessment as the defining guide in thinking about what teaching means and identifying how it is I would teach, using the edTPA template for lesson planning, using the edTPA rubric to determine the content of each lesson and making sure that I am continually asking the students to "produce" so that I have student work that demonstrates the success of my teaching. I find this exploitative and suffocating. As a student teacher, I was encouraged to practice the construction of meaningful formative assessments that shift the emphasis in the classroom from teaching to learning. edTPA encumbers the student teaching process with the demand that candidates stockpile artifacts, sample student work that demonstrates effective teaching, not effective learning. This is a perversion of the "authentic" assessment that edTPA claims it fosters. So, if I am not prepared to ensure that student work accomplishes a demonstration of my teaching skills, then I need to make sure that my 30 pages of written explanation to the edTPA bridge this authenticity gap. This places an emphasis squarely on my writing skills, despite the edTPA's contention that this is not the case: "While the rubrics do not address the quality of your writing, you should be mindful that your written work reflects your thinking and your professionalism" ("Making Good Choices," 2013, p. 5).

I am counting on my written argument "carrying" me through the edTPA process, even though I must write in a voice of acquiescence, because the alternative is the video, and this aspect of the assessment is riddled with factors that are beyond my control.

As a media-saturated culture, we are startlingly naïve to the ways in which moving images can be manipulated and are manipulating. They project a sense of being in the moment that is completely misleading. Video flattens the emotionality and energy in the room; it reduces the action to a linear visual and aural narrative when, in fact, there are many narratives happening concurrently. I noticed in an early taping how a student in the foreground of the shot reaching into her book bag to take out a sweatshirt, and another student drinking water from a water bottle, punctuated the lesson in odd and unnatural places, distracted from the actions of students who were in the background of the shot but who were thoroughly engaged in the activities of the lesson at those moments. Viewing the tapes later, I realized the impact of an odd camera angle: Such knowledge is obvious to students of film who have been educated to be conscious of how "dutch" angles are used to communicate confusion and something off kilter or foreboding about a scene. The videotaped "truth" is constricted by the breath of the shot; what is happening just beyond the range of the camera? I found that videotaped moments created a sense of discordance for the viewer that were not truthful to the experience in the classroom and, for that reason, I sought to carefully craft the video-tapings: arranging the chairs, making requests of student behavior during the tapings, positioning myself in a particular relationship to the camera. These "staged" videos, choices about props and setting and delivery, not to mention content, manufactured a relationship between me and the students that was more pleasing to the camera but was far less productive and engaging than our genuine exchanges. We experienced markedly that the presence of the camera altered the energy in the room—much has been observed and written about this—and this is not an insignificant change, particularly when the attention of students can hang so delicately on a persuasive or creative moment of teaching, or the teacher's personal enthusiasm, or a warm and welcoming fleeting expression.

These perversions of filming are less than adequate assessments tools. A cooperating teacher in the classroom experiences every moment of student teaching as an authentic witness. Shouldn't this analysis be privileged over that of a disengaged viewer of the videotape, with no background to inform the viewing and no appreciation of the specific persons in the room? How is an edTPA assessor meant to recognize the accomplishment of a student who asks a question that for the first time reveals an achievement in depth of analysis or a student who moves beyond a cynical or derisive view of the work to a real appreciation? Such quiet triumphs are precisely the moments that are celebrated by cooperating teacher and student teacher alike.

Further, the edTPA demand of sequential lessons is severely limiting in terms of the genuine progression of learning in the classroom, which is not sequential, is not linear, and tends, in my limited experience, to accumulate. How can I tie in the revelatory consequences of my lessons that did not surface in the predictable structure of a particular class or a particular assessment? When we were studying Joseph Campbell's mono-myth and his 12-point structure of the heroic journey, we found it useful to reference Jung's idea of archetypes. Jung is difficult and archetypes are fundamentally conceptual. To their credit, my students didn't want to parrot these ideas; they wanted to grapple with them and revisit them in different contexts until they felt they understood their implications for human complexity. One student, Brian, would drop into my study halls and ask questions; he would pass me in the hall and pose examples of archetypes, asking if I agreed with his interpretations. He and his classmates had passionate discussions, challenging each other to deeper understanding. These conversations lasted longer than my unit plan on *Frankenstein* for which Campbell's journey served as intertext. How could I represent this learning, which I felt was a hugely satisfying and exemplary kind of "student work," within the context of the edTPA? This is where I turn to the circular edTPA graphic representation of the learning process and lament its inward perspective—its closing down of the potential future inquiry that won't *count* but evidences the growth that matters to myself and my professors. I am reminded of the proliferation in ancient Celtic art of the serpent eating its tail, which, in one powerful interpretation, speaks to a fear of darkness and the unknown, of what exists beyond the explored forest.

Barbara: Do the fears that characterized ancient society also characterize our own? Are we afraid that an actual depth of awakened student curiosity could make the elephants in the room visible and reveal the nonsustainability of the very culture we feed with our compliance? Jennifer's own lesson planning goals for her students remind us of the focus of the Eriksonian model of human development, whose emphasis on integrity is so resonant with Dewey's prizing of the social imagination of young people fueling the curriculum. The three-way conference following observations of her lessons have similarly ignited the social imagination of myself and of Jennifer's cooperating teacher. We are reminded of what education is for. In contrast, the edTPA, with what Elizabeth describes as its "mechanical efficiency presenting a conceit of objectivity," appears empty. Related, Elizabeth points out that although SCALE claims on its website that the role of direct observation of students will not be diminished by the edTPA, the observation of students becomes unavoidably distorted through the distancing lens of its requirements. A specific required "academic" vocabulary imposes on both our students, and the cooperating teachers who are expected to adopt it as well, an additional challenge to the development of the flexible communicative skills so lyrically exemplified in Jennifer's delicate work of relating to a collectivity of specific individuals with intentionality. Indeed, it is precisely the partially intuitive nature of this communicative challenge in teaching that has always quite reasonably discouraged many otherwise confident and knowledgeable young people from deciding to do this work. Here again, the notion that a new vocabulary can be prescribed for instantaneous usage reinforces the impression that the edTPA developers were intellectually careless and/or lacking knowledge about both language acquisition and the challenge of adapting one's language to an array of individual receptivities. All of this contextualizes the cynicism experienced by the three of us as we consider Elizabeth's presentation of a particular student's edTPA failure.

Elizabeth: Daniel was a shy 18-year-old when he entered Hartwick College; he blushed easily and frequently made self-deprecating remarks. He was kind and generous towards his peers, dependable and conscientious in his courses. Aspiring to become an art teacher, he frequently contributed compelling drawings to group projects. Coming from a fairly privileged suburban background, he was one of those students for whom consciousness raising around issues of class and race was particularly transformative.

The conversion from neophyte to licensed professional occurs, not only in the relation between faculty members and students, but also in community. Maxine Greene (1982) instructed us that if we are to remake society, we must come together as human beings who are alive to each other. As part of a successful small group project in one of my own courses during his sophomore year, Daniel was a leader among his peers in designing and enacting social reconstructionist lessons for third graders over six weeks in a local elementary school. This experience took place in Ken Snider's classroom. Ken, my teacher partner in this and similar endeavors for the past eight years, manifests his own fierce intellectuality in a curriculum that models commitment to the pursuit of social justice and critical arts-focused pedagogies. His classroom is rich with color, music, and languages that seek to connect his students to the enlivening vision of a democratic global human community. Portraits of Gandhi and Bob Marley, banners in Hebrew and Arabic, emblazon his walls.

Inspired by Ken's modeling and Julia Weber Gordon's (Weber, 1946) lyrical account of her teaching in a one-room school in rural New Jersey during the years immediately preceding World War II, Daniel and his classmates designed a unit on water ecology that employed Sobel's place based pedagogy.(Sobel, 2005). They began their study by examining the local ecosystem, which led to the children's collection of frog eggs, followed by a lecture from a local biologist specializing in amphibians. They created a mural illustrating pond life and its potential vulnerabilities. They studied issues of scarcity, potability, and water overuse on the global, regional, and local level. Students tracked their own family's water usage and brainstormed ways to reduce waste; they used this information to create posters to educate their peers in the school. They observed all components of the local water system, whose observation included field trips to the reservoir, the water treatment plant, and the discharge point in the river that flows through town. Finally, the children investigated local commercial sources of pollution and wrote letters to appropriate businesspeople and legislators, calling for an end to specific problematic practices. The water ecology unit provided evidence for my students of the imaginative curricular possibilities in commitment to service in the interest of the public good. The study developed based on the response of the children in negotiation with their teacher to each of its previous initiatives, confirming, through the delighted engagement in critical literacy of these third graders, the value of the Deweyan concept of education as the process of individual growth nurturing and being nurtured by democratic community life.

Daniel was so moved by this experience that he committed to becoming an elementary classroom teacher, viewing his own potential to use his expertise in graphic arts to promote the very use of literacies he so admired in Ken's classroom. Then, after a required minipracticum at a residential school for children with profound disabilities, he decided to add special education to his certification. Although I was not his student teaching supervisor, I maintained my relationship with Daniel as he navigated the most important stage in his preservice teaching career: a first student teaching placement in the special education resource room of a small rural school characterized by the high poverty of its families. Over the seven weeks of this placement, Daniel's connections with his students and his growth and performance so pleased his cooperating teacher and principal that they asked him to consider applying for an opening position in the upcoming school year. A one-on-one teaching session with a child during his placement not only encouraged him to apply for the teaching position but it simultaneously earned him a failing score on his edTPA submission.

Daniel explained to me that he chose to work with a fourth grade student for his edTPA submission whose individualized education program (IEP) indicated a math fluency level of first grade specifically because he believed his work with her revealed his special talent for making deep connections with individual struggling learners. In his initial lesson, Daniel began by viewing an instructional video with this child on the subject of adding numbers greater than 10. (The video itself was produced by Pearson, which was an unusually strategic decision on his part.) Daniel encouraged his student to use manipulatives he made available to concretize the mathematical concepts in a series of word problems, gradually offering less and less scaffolding. In the videotape he submitted, Daniel believed that he captured his student's eventual ability to use the manipulatives independently and finally to successfully tackle problems without them. He indicated in his written material how he had shaped his approach to this student around what he knew about her from conversations with her teachers and his own direct experience in previous encounters with her: She had a negative attitude toward math in general and felt discouraged with her lack of progress in comparison to her peers. Daniel used his knowledge about how girls in particular can develop a genuine phobia toward math that impedes their ability to engage with the mathematical problems placed in front of them. He decided to utilize his illustration skills to approach his student as the young NASCAR fan he had learned she was. Creating a "moving" racecar that tracked her incremental progress on individual problems, Daniel sought to address the obstacle in the way of her engagement. He related having written the following:

> During the time that I was implementing these lesson objectives, my "focus learner's" attentiveness and motivation towards the specific math problems increased, and she was able to complete 15 addition problems with sums greater than ten in 5 minutes. She had been unable to do any of this before.

Daniel completed the process of videotaping and writing to the edTPA's specifications, uploaded his documents to the Pearson platform, paid his $300, and then moved on to his next student teaching placement. Several weeks later, he learned his fate. Daniel failed with a 19 out of a possible 75 points. Among other indicators, he had "earned" 1 of 5 possible points for his work addressing Rubric 2: *"Planning Challenge and Support for the Focus Learner."* The feedback from an anonymous scorer included a single score summary sheet and three pages of canned commentary:

> *There is little to no evidence of planned supports; OR there is a severe mismatch between the focus learner's chronological age or development level and the ways in which the candidate uses instructional strategies, supports, or materials; OR learning tasks and supported strategies do NOT align to lesson objectives and/or do NOT reflect required modifications and accommodations to the IEP.*

The statement offered three distinctly different possibilities for his low score, so Daniel was left guessing. He lamented as he reviewed this feedback, "I only wanted to know what I did wrong so I could correct my error next time. Everything I've done has been reduced to a single sheet of numbers and I don't even understand what they mean."

Disturbingly, Daniel's distress included consideration that he had not cheated, whereas he knew others had. He reported a fellow teacher candidate "schooling" her students to raise their right hands if they knew the answer to his questions, and the left if they did not, thereby creating the illusion of full class engagement and understanding. The temptation to manipulate the outcome of such a high-stakes test is represented on the NCTQ's own blog. An August 2012 post entitled "edTPA: Slow This Train Down" (Greenberg & Walsh, 2012) challenges the validity of the edTPA as a measure of teacher quality for a number of reasons. The test does not provide a full picture of the candidate's grasp of content as he or she chooses the topic for the videotaped lessons—an area of inquiry or text about which they are particularly confident. Further, the student can rehearse the video segments as many times as necessary, create an ideal group of students, or engage in any number of other ways to game the system. A consideration not aired on the blog is the reality that candidates who fail may retake the edTPA as many times as they like, given that they have the financial resources. The interpretation is certainly invited that the entire protocol fails to screen out inadequate teachers, but rather, rewards both instrumental test preparation and access to financial resources (Greenberg & Walsh, 2012).

Further, while the incentive for teacher candidates is to cheat, the incentive for the scorer is to rush. The trained scorers with whom I have talked reported that to do justice to the challenge of evaluating a candidate's work, the process takes five to seven hours; Pearson pays $75 per test scored. We can only speculate about the scoring of Daniel's test, and we do not intend to rule out the possibility that the anonymous Pearson evaluator found weaknesses in Daniel's work that I did not. Yet for all of the supposed objectivity claimed by SCALE and its allies, no large-scale independent research has tested its validity. The rush to judge our candidates has indeed trumped the requirement for such research.

The damage wrought by the edTPA extends to our college classrooms as well. Despite years of experience indicating that the student teaching seminar was best used as an opportunity to process the feedback of cooperating teachers and supervisors in a supportive atmosphere of equally vulnerable peers, Daniel's student teaching seminar instructor, a beloved veteran teacher and teacher educator, felt compelled to construct this year's seminar around the need of his students to pass the edTPA. To do so, he was forced to displace attention from the developmental process that unfolds during student teaching. This is the process in which dialogue, supported by the study of educational philosophy and pedogogical methods, responds to the ever-deepening challenges visible to our teacher candidates. Those challenges become visible through the mentoring of their cooperating teachers punctuated by our observation visits. One could argue that Daniel had been deprived of the thoughtful support on which we had prided ourselves. He characterized his seminar as "very stressful and devoted 80% to test preparation."

Barbara: In contrast with the avowed programmatic integrity that we described in our introduction, I close our chapter with a reflection on how I, this past academic semester, eliminated curriculum that specifically privileged the pursuit of social justice through revisioned historical accounts, facilitation of deepened relationships between historiographers at Colgate and my students, and the liveliest social reconstructionist curriculum we had collectively developed for use in high school classrooms. I did this in favor of making the time available to support my students to strategize toward their individual presentation of evidence for their edTPA portfolios, whose evidence, we agreed within our seminar accompanying student teaching, was necessarily and artificially biased toward less substantive educational concerns.

What I displaced from my own student teaching seminar to accommodate relatively modest attention to the edTPA were precisely my highest level of "pedagogical concerns of depth" mentioned by Giroux. In previous years, I had organized hour-long sessions between history and English faculty at Colgate who were generously willing to share their own research related to specific historical and textual challenges facing my student teachers in their own current classroom teaching. This year I eliminated such meetings. The emphasis of those meetings on contemporary historiography, with its immediate appeal to young people genuinely curious about how knowledge is made, and its tendency to challenge Eurocentrism, was lost to the English and social studies candidates.

This year, we considered instead, outside of any historical or textual context, what assignment might instantaneously generate a student product that would prove each a winning teacher according to edTPA rubrics. To accommodate this parochial need of my teacher-candidates, I distanced myself from my own motivation, one shared by Elizabeth and Jennifer: pursuit of what Maxine Greene (1982) named "grace unrealized," attention to the potential for greater humanity and attention to deeper and more imaginative engagement. Greene's query is far more relevant now than it was in 1982 when she delivered it in her presidential address for the American Educational Research Association: "If it were not for images of possibility, it would be difficult to describe what is lacking" (p. 4). I fear that we have entered a haunted reality in which it is, in fact, more and more difficult to make generally visible the images of possibility like those on Ken Sider's walls that have informed our work and the work of our students. Celia Oyler, professor of education at Teachers College, Columbia University, an outspoken critic of the corporatization of education, captured both the personal pain we experience in the requirement of the edTPA that we now adopt "teaching to the test" methodologies to support our students to "succeed," as well as we our determination to resist (Klonsky, 2012).

> Elizabeth: We began this chapter with a declaration of our core values and an explication of their expression in the teacher education programs and schools in which we are immersed: We live with social, economic, and environmental justice as praxis in our classrooms; we commit to deep and thoughtful relationships among teacher educators, teachers, and teacher candidates; and we instantiate the work of our beloved philosophers—heroes such as Dewey, Eisner, and Greene—in the curriculum we develop in our own classrooms and that which we nurture in our students. We have read and written, observed and experienced our way to these conclusions; we trust with deep certainty that they are good ones.

We invite readers to consider the models in which we are currently engaged in New York State to resist the edTPA and other elements of the neoliberal "accountability" agenda. There is a flourishing online world of activists, muckrakers, and support networks from which to gain information and find community. In New York, readers can begin by accessing oa4pe.wordpress.com, atthechalkface.com, MarkGarrison.net, and fairtest.org, among many others; or they can engage with grassroots activist organizations, such as NYS Allies for Public Education, United Opt Out National, and New York City Organization of Radical Educators (NYCORE), whose advocacy has begun to see substantive success. Parents have been emboldened to opt their children out of the tests, and teachers have found the courage to speak out. As in 16 other states, New York's lawmakers have introduced legislation to halt the corporate reform agenda in response to citizen activism. Alabama, Florida, Georgia, Indiana, Iowa, Kansas, Kentucky, Louisiana, Maine, Maryland, Massachusetts, New Hampshire, New Jersey, New York, Ohio, Oklahoma, and Wisconsin are all in the process of trying to withdraw from the Common Core State Standards ("Education Week," 2013).

Ann Schulte (2012), education professor and activist at California State University, inspired by Barbara Madeloni and others, issued this prescient warning in 2012: "…unless 'we put our bodies upon the gears of the machine[,]' we will be relegated to the role of the technicians who maintain it" (para. 14). As we write, we sense the gears of the machine straining under the weight of those courageous enough, alive enough, and angry enough to heed this warning. Our despair turns to invigoration as the traditional boundaries among teachers, teacher educators, aspiring teachers, and parents melt away.

We gather together in living rooms, classrooms, high school auditoriums, and in front of state departments of education to share our outrage and demand a return to sanity. Finally, there is joy in solidarity.

References

Au, W. (2013). *What's a nice test like you doing in a place like this?* Retrieved from http://www.rethinkingschools.org/archive/27_04/27_04_au.shtml

Barkan, J. (2012). *Hired guns on Astroturf: How to buy and sell school reform.* Retrieved from http://www.dissentmagazine.org/article/hired-guns-on-astroturfhow-to-buy-and-sell-school-reform

Birtel, M., Chilcott, L., Hindmarch, E. (Producers), & Guggenheim, D. (Director). (2010). *Waiting for "Superman"* [Motion picture]. United States.

CREDO (2013). The National Charter School Study. Retrieved from http://credo.stanford.edu/documents/NCSS%202013%20Final%20Draft.pdf

Darling-Hammond, L., & Hyler, M. E. (2013). *The role of performance assessment in developing teaching as a profession.* Retrieved from http://www.rethinkingschools.org/archive/27_04/27_04_darling-hammond_hyler.shtml

edTPA. (2014). Retrieved from http://edtpa.aacte.org

Education Week: Exit strategy: State lawmakers consider dropping Common Core. (2013). Retrieved from http://www.edweek.org/ew/section/multimedia/anti-cc-bill.html

Garrison, M. (2013). *The political significance of the king's math.* Retrieved from http://www.markgarrison.net/archives/2146

Giroux, H. (2013). *Teachers as transformatory intellectuals.* Retrieved from http://www.sef.org.pk/old/Educate/education/Teachers%20as%20Transformatory%20Intellectuals%20by%20Henry%20Giroux.pdf

Greenberg, J., & Walsh, K. (2012, August 27). edTPA: Slow this train down [web log post]. Retrieved from http://www.nctq.org/commentary/viewStory.do?id=32495

Greene, M. (1982). Public education and the public space. *Educational Researcher, 11*(6), 4–9.

Harvey, D. (2005). *A brief history of neoliberalism.* Oxford, UK: Oxford University Press.

Higgins, J. (2013, June 13). *Test scores and magical thinking.* Retrieved from http://thestoryofteaching.com/2013/06/13/test-scores-and-magical-thinking/

hooks, b. (1994). *Teaching to transgress: Education as the practice of freedom.* New York, NY: Routledge.

Klein, N. (2007). *The shock doctrine: The rise of disaster capitalism.* New York, NY: Metropolitan Books.

Klonsky. F. (2013, May). *Cynthia Oyler and Merryl Tisch.* Retrieved from https://preaprez.wordpress.com/2013/05/17/celia-oyler-and-merryl-tisch/

Madeloni, B., & Gorlewski, J. (2013, June). *Radical imagination, not standardization: Critical teacher education and the edTPA.* Retrieved from http://www.tcrecord.org/content.asp?contentid=17163

Making good choices: A support guide for edTPA candidates. (2013). Retrieved from http://www.edtpa.com/Content/Docs/edTPAMGC.pdf

Polk, S. (2014, January 18). For the love of money. *The New York Times*. Retrieved from http://www.nytimes.com/2014/01/19/opinion/sunday/for-the-love-of-money.html

Regenspan, B. (2002). *Parallel practices: Social justice-focused teacher education and the elementary school classroom*. New York, NY: Peter Lang.

Schulte, A. (2012, December 14). Anne Schulte: Teacher performance assessment isn't the answer. *Education Week Teacher: Living in Dialogue Teacher Blogs*. Retrieved from http://blogs.edweek.org/teachers/living-in-dialogue/2012/12/ann_schulte_teacher_performanc.html

Shanahan, T. (2013). *Letting the text take center stage: How the Common Core State Standards will transform English language arts instruction*. Retrieved from http://www.aft.org/pdfs/americaneducator/fall2013/Shanahan.pdf

Sirota, D. (2013, March 11) *Getting rich off of school children*. Retrieved from http://www.salon.com/2013/03/11/getting_rich_off_of_schoolchildren/

Sobel, D. (2005). *Place-based education: Connecting classrooms & communities* (2nd ed.). Great Barrington, MA: Orion Society.

Strauss, V. (2013, February 9). *Global education market reaches 4.4 trillion—and growing*. Retrieved from http://www.washingtonpost.com/blogs/answer-sheet/wp/2013/02/09/global-education-market-reaches-4-4-trillion-and-is-growing/

Weber, J. (1946). *My country school diary. An adventure in creative teaching, etc.* New York, NY: Harper & Bros.

· 6 ·

CRASH [DIS-]COURSE: A CRITICAL VIEW OF TEACHING, TESTING, AND THE TIMES

Pamela Althea Joyce, Joy Barnes-Johnson, and Joanne M. Carris

In March 2010, the Obama Administration proposed revisions to the Elementary and Secondary Education Act (ESEA), also known as No Child Left Behind (NCLB; No Child Left Behind Act of 2001), called "A Blueprint for Reform" (U.S. Department of Education, 2010). A major part of this blueprint was a focus on universal standards for language and mathematics education and college-readiness programs. From this legislative push, a renewed interest emerged in the work done at the state level, with the nation's governors and education officials in the development of what have come to be called the Common Core State Standards (National Governors Association Center for Best Practices and Council of Chief State School Officers, 2010). However, the Common Core State Standards were actually written

> …under the aegis of several D.C.-based organizations: the National Governors Association, the Council of Chief State School Officers, and Achieve. The development process was led behind closed doors by a small organization called Student Achievement Partners, which David Coleman headed. The writing group of 27 contained few educators, but a significant number of representatives of the testing industry. (Ravitch, 2014, para. 15)

The Common Core State Standards (CCSS) were designed to balance our education system. Developed as a potential means for creating a universal standard of basic education in the United States, the CCSS provide literacy and numeracy skill minimums for teachers to use when developing educational programs for children, thus creating the standard for "high quality education." To date, 45 states, the District of Columbia, four territories, and the Department of Defense Education Activity have adopted the CCSS. Standardized tests, including state and national assessments of college and career readiness, are being developed based on the CCSS. Are we truly ready for this?

The answer is no, especially when teacher evaluation becomes a part of the student assessment process, with students' scores affixed with ratings of effective teaching. As Darling-Hammond, Amrein-Beardsley, Haertel, and Rothstein (2012) argued, standardized tests are unstable measures of teacher effectiveness. When used to identify an individual teacher's "effectiveness," ratings of teachers vary tremendously from one state test to the next, from one year to the next, and even from one class to another. Darling-Hammond et al. additionally pointed out that what students learn is not solely a result of one teacher's instruction in that content area. For example, some students may delve into the material further on their own, with or without the use of personal media and technology, and some may find support and/or assistance from a tutor, parent, or friend. How, then, can value accurately be assigned or attributed to a single teacher? The standards-based reform effort proposes just that: Teachers can, in fact, contribute to changes in student performance, thereby affecting that performance on CCSS assessments.

Critical Lens on Tests and Testing

The use of standardized test results as a consideration for teacher evaluation becomes all the more troubling when considering the intrinsic flaws of these tests from a critical theoretical perspective. Critical theory is a sociological framework used to critique society and social systems generally in light of dynamics created by class, race, and ethnicity. From a critical perspective, standardized exams are culturally and class biased; they do not account for disproportionate funding between schools in economically impoverished areas and those in more affluent neighborhoods; they do not consider the varying socioeducational and socioemotional forces impacting student learning gains among particular student populations (such as low-income students) that can lead to lower scores in comparison to those of their peers; and, instead, they establish conditions that make it seem plausible to narrow the curriculum to material covered on exams (Madaus & Clarke, 2001; Noguera, 2003).

> A critical social theory is concerned in particular with issues of power and justice and the ways that the economy, matters of race, class, and gender, ideologies, discourses, education, religion and other social institutions, and cultural dynamics interact to construct a social system. (Kincheloe, 2004, p. 281)

There are tacit as well as overt relationships among those who exercise power within the education system. These powers help construct incremental triage approaches to the issue of academic achievement.

The compelling work of Muller, Riegle-Crumb, Schiller, Wilkinson, and Frank (2010) drew critical attention to another problem associated with student achievement and performance:

> The underrepresentation of minority students in advanced math classes is an indicator that opportunities to learn within the school are bounded by race and ethnicity, and this likely extends beyond math classes to how academic efforts and achievements are rewarded. Beyond the individual academic abilities and background of minority students, the existence of a limited opportunity structure is likely to shape their future educational efforts and experiences, perhaps by giving African American and Latino students little reason to expect that they can get ahead and be academically successful. Additionally, to the extent that the prevailing academic opportunity structure is racially stratified, teachers and other school personnel may also discourage the achievement of minority students, either overtly or more subtly. In short, an institutionalized system of constrained opportunities for minority students at the beginning of high school is likely to influence their subsequent achievement, regardless of their own degree of academic promise. (pp. 1042–1043)

Looking through this critical lens, all stakeholders in the school experience have to be considered part of both the problems and the solutions with regard to student achievement. Not only teachers and their students, but administrators, parents, guardians, families, and student support networks within and outside of the school play a role in defining the discourse.

Tate (2013) recently articulated three types of factors that influence student achievement that deserve consideration here: distal, propensity, and opportunity factors.

Distal factors, also called antecedent factors (Byrnes & Wasik, 2009), describe any set of risk factors that represents an underlying vulnerability for a particular condition or event. Things like gender, ethnicity, socioeconomic status, prior achievement, family values, expectations, and experiences are all distal factors. *Propensity* factors are any factors that relate to the ability or willingness to learn content once it has been exposed or presented in a particular context. Prerequisite skills, preexisting knowledge, domain-specific understanding, and self-regulation sit squarely within the realm of motivation of the learner and may not be directly attributable to the efforts of a teacher. Finally, *opportunity* factors, which are factors that relate to school stakeholders' curriculum choices—like coursework, school climate, and teacher variables—seem the only viable set of factors for consideration in any evaluation system, with only limited application. Few studies have explored this important relationship, which is a critical component of the discourse about supports for achievement. Perhaps reimagining the narrative about achievement to include these critical factors could shed necessary light and provide additional perspective on the problem.

Darling-Hammond et al. (2012) further highlighted that, while some teaching evaluation models claim to control for previous test scores and student demographics, these statistical techniques do not, in fact, have sufficient flexibility to be altered for different student populations. Therefore, teachers who teach student populations that, due to a variety of socioeducational and sociopolitical influences, historically score lower on standardized exams, are at a disadvantage when compared to teachers who have a less diverse student population. These historically marginalized populations—students with special needs and those from low-income backgrounds (Chapman & Lestch, 2013)—are persistently low performing when standardized tests are used to measure student learning across a range of studies. To level the playing field for students, schooling systems must move away from using a single standardized test as the sole criterion for determining important decisions such as student assessments coupled with teacher evaluations. This position is one shared by many, including the New York Civil Liberties Union (2012).

Standardized achievement tests and other psychometric assessments are not objective. Standardized testing can be viewed as a specific tool or "technology of power" used to advance the domination of the ruling class (Foucault, 1977), as many standardized tests reinforce and perpetuate the ruling group's values and narratives. Morris (2004) additionally highlighted the way in which the construction of any instrument for measuring human activity embodies the ideologies and subjectivities of those who develop it. As such, psychometric assessments are by nature flawed; they are not objective, neutral measures but rather valorize the perspectives of psychometricians, who have consistently been members of the dominant group. As power relations underscore institutionalized knowledge, those in positions of power decide what knowledge is deemed relevant and, therefore, what will be included as the "official knowledge" on standardized tests. Standardized tests reproduce the ruling group's perspectives and culturally bound narratives, while ignoring those of subordinate groups, or worse, viewing subordinate groups' perspectives and narratives as inferior. In reflecting the discourse of the ruling class, standardized testing guarantees the preservation and continuation of its ideology, thereby maintaining the status quo. With an emphasis on standardized tests to be used for teacher evaluation, the purpose of education becomes antidemocratic, as the curriculum priority shifts to a focus on teaching to tests. In a test-driven economy of school curricula, the knowledge and values of the dominant culture are reproduced and perpetuated, preserving the current social order. In the current social order, education policymakers favor the use of standardized achievement tests, claiming they are an objective measure of student progress and, therefore, teacher effectiveness.

However, Brady (2011) stated the following:

> Standardized tests are created by and for the dominant culture. They will, then, reflect that culture. Even the sequence in which words appear in a sentence can make a difference in the ability of a test-taker reared in a subculture to guess what the dominant-culture writer of the test item was thinking. To be fair and useful, writer and reader must be culturally aligned. (para. 15)

Support: The Great Potential Equalizer

An inherent problem exists when applying a single set of evaluation standards to teachers and students in a system with an imbalance of funding resources. Comparing underfunded schools to well-resourced schools exposes a prevalent crisis situation in our system. Epstein (2011) explained the idea of underfunding by proposing that because of unequal school funding models, low-income students attend schools that often receive fewer resources per pupil than students in affluent school districts. Since a percentage of school funding—beyond what the federal and state governments provide—comes from local property taxes, school districts in wealthier neighborhoods receive more funding than those in poorer areas. The Education Trust (2006) report,

"Funding Gaps 2006," concluded that states and localities on average spent $908 less per pupil in districts with the most students of color and $825 less per pupil in districts with the most low-income students, in comparison to expenditures in the wealthiest and Whitest districts (Education Trust, 2006, p. 6). While in recent years some states have moved to remedy this imbalance by providing more state funding to districts rather than relying on local taxes, the legacy of this inequity persists.

In addition to factors of economic support, those related to academic support must also be taken into consideration. Despite efforts to statistically control for prior test scores as well as student and school dissimilarities that are considered to affect achievement, it is simply unjust to compare results between high-need populations and other mainstream cultural groups. Some students come from communities that are able to support academic development, while many of the students from high-need populations are not exposed to this type of support. This point becomes abundantly clear when a community is defined by the support of family and teachers—teachers with varying styles and abilities for teaching their subjects. Thus enters the consideration of "good teaching" as well as the consideration of reform efforts.

In describing what "good teaching" is most likely to be, Haberman (1991) described indirect activities that ultimately create the conditions not only for strong teaching but for improved learning: reflection. Instruction that is rich in opportunities for 1) student technology engagement; 2) critical interrogation of social dynamics like equity, fairness, justice, and human difference; 3) real-world experience that takes students out of traditional classroom contexts and encourages them to serve as reporters and role players; 4) involvement in heterogeneous groups, and inclusion of elements of autonomy and choice of activities is fundamental to transformative pedagogy. These elements approach "good teaching." We argue that these elements approximate the kinds of support necessary for academic development. Although Haberman acknowledged that "good teaching is not a sufficient basis for reform.… these suggestions can begin to create an alternative to the pedagogy of poverty" (p. 294). A "pedagogy of poverty" refers to a teacher-centered approach, with traditional and regimented methods that lack metacognitive experiences, aimed at controlling students rather than educating them (Haberman, 1991).

In a sense, reform has become an expected norm in the schooling system. As more scholars work to describe what is happening in schools, the differences between traditional habits of teaching and contemporary teaching strategies of reform, like those proposed by Haberman, have become more evident.

In a study by Byrnes and Wasik (2009), they compared reform-only teachers to traditional teachers and what they called "balanced teachers," who incorporated both reform-consistent and traditional teaching practices. In their analysis, reform-only teachers were identified by the high frequency of student exposure to relevant mathematical content and activities advocated by the National Council of Teachers of Mathematics (e.g., use of manipulatives, explanations of answers). Traditional teachers were characterized by their high frequency use of traditional methods like blackboard drills. Balanced teachers incorporated both styles consistently. What they found raises interesting questions about the role of support. The impact of the teacher with regard to mathematics achievement was not significant, and neither was the students' approach to mathematics learning. The greatest influences on mathematics achievement could be mapped to antecedent factors—family support.

Byrnes and Wasik (2009) wrote the following:

> …it is not that disadvantaged children lack access to the kinds of content and instructional styles that affluent children are exposed to (the traditional opportunity thesis); it is that they have access but their environment is so distinct from their home lives that they do not benefit. (p. 180)

Children raised in families that are not, for myriad of reasons, able to support their child's academic process, including time helping with homework, are not developing mathematics competency. Similarly, Roscigno (2000) described a framework that considers characteristics within Black and Latino families that impact achievement directly. Teasing out economic strata and educational attainment levels, for example, allows for deeper analysis of math and reading achievement. "Family stratification shapes levels of achievement for African-Americans and Hispanics relative to Whites" (p. 280). In fact, Roscigno described an analysis of parental structure, family structure, and income as "critical to an understanding of the achievement gap" (p. 267).

In the same light, how then can we account for family structures that are "intact" but transient because of social problems like homelessness? The plight of homeless children is a significant one for consideration in this discussion. Residential instability promotes the persistence of, and helps widen, the achievement gap among homeless children; "addressing achievement disparities in urban school districts may be virtually impossible without addressing mobility related to poverty" (Masten, 2012, p. 364). Homelessness is not a part of curriculum. Homelessness is not taken into consideration when a student is taking a standardized test. Homelessness is an issue that is not factored into student achievement; therefore, grades supposedly do not reflect these personal problems. However, in addition to a student's own perseverance and diligence, teachers' high expectations for these students can absolutely foster school success, but it is not necessarily always achievement and improvement that can be measured on state standardized tests (Carris, 2011). These realities further support Baker et al.'s (2010) assertion:

> The nonrandom assignment of students to classrooms and schools—and the wide variation in students' experiences at home and at school—mean that teachers cannot be accurately judged against one another by their students' test scores, even when efforts are made to control for student characteristics in statistical models. (p. 3)

While the dissimilarities in students and schools affecting standardized test performance undoubtedly indicate the inappropriateness of standardized test scores as a measure for teacher evaluations, such an evaluation structure seems to serve as a means for perpetuating the "official knowledge." Equally problematic, this furthering of the "official knowledge" through a reliance on standardized testing additionally narrows the curricula, inhibits critical thinking, and ignores the multiple dimensions in ways of knowing beyond cognitive, mechanical approaches. With high-stakes standardized tests, schools and teachers are forced to restrict curricula to the information tested to avoid penalties. Schools often limit exploration of knowledge and subject matter not covered on standardized exams to dedicate as much time as possible to test-taking strategies and preparation for English language arts and mathematics exams (Haberman, 1991). English, math, and test-taking skills become the focus of the school day, and subjects not tested every year through standardized exams, such as social studies, science, and art, are not given as much time or consideration. While English language arts and math are certainly crucial subjects for students to study, other areas must be taught to provide students with a balanced education, resulting in well-rounded individuals.

Metacognitive Experiences Versus Noncritical Thinking

Curriculum geared to standardized tests inhibits any potential for critical analysis and creative investigation of knowledge. Haberman (1991) described well the pedagogical conditions of impoverished schools, which are characterized by blackline masters and verification exercises, with students and teachers having few opportunities to construct knowledge or derive meaning from schooling experiences. In this environment, problem solving and process-based thinking, in which students are encouraged to connect seemingly unrelated information to the interrelational nature of knowledge, are inhibited. Teachings and instruction centered on standardized exams and assessments do not engage and foster students' abilities to question and create meaning through interpretation of complex information. Opportunities to infer, position oneself within the material being learned and the world itself, or identify interconnections and multidimensions of reality are limited. Instruction centered on high-stakes exams teaches students to uncritically memorize preselected, disjointed information to succeed. An unintended consequence associated with this one-dimensional approach to teaching and its evaluation is the decreased potential for meaningful process-oriented education, grounded in critical questioning and problem solving. On the contrary, multidimensional pedagogy does not just foster cognitive growth, but rather, it enables intellectual, emotional, and spiritual development. Multidimensional teaching encourages holistic growth as students critically engage with learning. The alternative, to uncritically examine and memorize preselected information that can be identified on a bubble sheet and scored by a machine, is not acceptable. Teacher evaluations rooted exclusively in students' performance on standardized tests neglect diverse components of knowing and learning. As teachers are forced to "teach to the test," value in instruction and knowledge is placed solely on cognition—a culturally bound narrative—at the expense of critical, affective, intuitive, and experiential elements. Through high-stakes hyper-standardization and curriculum narrowing, diverse ways of knowing are simultaneously disregarded and devalued.

Recasting and Revisioning: Teaching Worth Supporting

Teaching is as much an art as it is a science. Teaching is a cogenerative process (Tobin, 2012) that produces authentic learning when all sociocultural perspectives are embraced. Members form learning communities that can construct meaning and develop new understandings in a dialogic environment. The goal of the learning community is not to "fix" anyone but rather that all stakeholders work together to achieve something. Taking this dynamic into consideration, it appears as if the need for a scapegoat is the direct result of a "fix-it" attitude, which flaunts benchmark procedures that are "one-size-fits-all" and negates the urgency of developing intellectually well-rounded students. Those in power promote the idea that student improvements lie under the auspices of teachers, and implementation of a more stringent teacher evaluation program is what is needed. Enveloped in these circumstances, teachers are left holding the bulk of responsibility for student achievement, and policymakers avoid identifying flaws in the education system. The result is a blame-shifting mentality, where teachers are solely responsible for student failure. The premise is that students will achieve proficiency on state tests through the efforts of each teacher with which they come in contact. As stated earlier, student learning is not exclusively the product of one teacher's instruction; there are a multitude of external factors that also contribute not only to what students learn but to the learning process, in both negative and positive ways. Whether considered institutional or individual, these external factors are real (Byrne & Wasik, 2009; Mueller et al., 2010; Tate, 2013).

Teachers share information with students and are responsible for a portion but not all of student academic growth. Lev Vygotsky (1978) posited the cognitive theory of the zone of proximal development (ZPD), in which the "teacher," through a sequence of steps, scaffolds learning to accomplish a particular activity. His theory involves intellectually raising students from a lower level of performance to a higher platform of self-advocacy, self-emancipation, and self-accomplishment, where the teacher plays a significant supportive role in the learning process. Through scaffolding efforts, teachers implement a graduated learning process that fosters interconnections with students and assists them in meeting their learning goals. With teacher assistance, student ownership of the learning process and students' critical voices have the potential to emerge under scaffolding situations. However, for meaningful scaffolding to occur in the classroom, critical educators must go beyond "grade-level" set curriculum by constructing generative themes (Freire, 2004), which incorporate students' lived experiences in classroom instruction. Generative themes connect literacy directly to students' lives and promote individual empowerment and culturally responsive teaching practices (Villegas & Lucas, 2002). Freire, Villegas, and Lucas noted the importance and key responsibility of the classroom teacher to the student: to promote student empowerment and acknowledge students' cultural backgrounds as significant contributors in the learning process. In essence, teachers are challenged to bring the outside into their classrooms, acknowledging that learning does not take place in a vacuum and that numerous influences contribute to student achievement. There is an array of learning experiences outside the scope of the classroom, beyond the expertise of the teacher, that affects academic ability, and awareness of these variables aids in student achievement.

Learning as Community: Situated Learning

Sociocognitivists Lave and Wenger (1991) offered yet another consideration for enhancing student achievement beyond the classroom. They encourage expanding the role of responsibility for learning from the teacher/student dyad to an apprenticeship relationship resting more on participatory student action occurring outside of the classroom setting. As such, they proposed the theory of situated learning, which locates learning squarely in the processes of coparticipation, to be considered not as an individual experience but to include the participation of someone who acts as a teacher with the ability and expertise to share knowledge (Lave & Wenger, 1991). This is a theory in which a framework of participation and learning occurs as individuals co-participate in an event, gaining access to modes of behavior appropriate for a learning environment, not otherwise available to them in a classroom setting. In the co-participation learning scenario, students eventually develop skills and enhance their levels of performance in specific areas. In this way, students gradually learn the performance skills needed to participate in society and are eventually able to transport these skills to various settings, subsequently making learning portable. In essence, situated learning can provide well-rounded benefits to students as well as offer a more diverse community of practice, where legitimate peripheral participation can lead to democratic experiences for all students, with an opening for access to power through an expansion of the learning environment. Hence, situated learning embraces the acknowledgement that teaching also occurs outside of school walls and the awareness that "teachers" appear everywhere in a fluid life, embracing learning possibilities in all walks of life. With a learning environment so inclusive and far-reaching, a critical theoretical mind-set questions how the responsibility of student achievement can rest solely on one teacher or even a small group of teachers.

Closing Thoughts

Grounding teacher evaluations in students' performance on standardized tests diverts attention away from the real ills of the education system, while focusing blame on teachers. Presently, the American tactic for "fixing" existing educational problems is deeply disconcerting and brings into question the common sense, or lack thereof, of the imposing importance of standardized testing. The idea of holding a substantial part of teacher evaluation contingent on student achievement as defined by test scores, under the ever-changing sanctions of education policymakers, is also questionable. Kincheloe (2000) defined this state of mechanistic practices as "cognitive illness," unsettling mindless behavior, which has been demonstrated over and over in past decades with evidence of ineffective policymaking decisions and minimal statistical improvement of specific student populations. Enveloped by this illness, policymakers fail to recognize what already exists, what is salvageable and effective in the school system. Instead of positive school reform, preserving some of the good and incorporating some of the new ideas, policymakers continue to point the finger of blame at one group, teachers, and thus reproduce failed methods of improvement in the system.

A closer look at the present reality in the school system reveals the need to critically act on a diverse spectrum of possibilities to initiate new ideas, and couple existing ones, to enact critical change. Recovering from societal "cognitive illness" caused by fragmented thought requires openness to change, to transform the societal mind-set to a higher level of critical consciousness (Kincheloe, 2000). If this shift does not occur, how do we (a) recover, (b) move away from positivistic remedies, and (c) advance toward critical praxis? How then can we institute reforms that are "characterized as informed action that demand curricular and instructional strategies that produce not only better learning climates but a better society as well" (Kincheloe, 2004, p. 70)? Long-term goals for a better society are at the crux of a strong educational system and the underpinning of the answers to these critical questions. Multiple voices, blended in democracy, achieving positive results, are tantamount to ensure development of the best schooling system.

The Nigerian proverb, "it takes a whole village to raise a child," is pertinent for the successful comeback of our school system, as a variety of voices are relevant for the positive growth of education. Educators and noneducators alike are part of the village and, therefore, should be committed to providing the necessary tools for all students to reach their highest potential, allowing our youth to be in a position to replenish society in the future (Joyce, 2008). The question emerges: Is American society heading in a direction that promotes an umbrella effect of teaching that is all-encompassing and able to produce student achievement results from collaborative efforts based on an awareness of an expansive learning environment?

To date, the system has not been able to enter into a mindful conversation or adapt assertive action for transformative change to ensure achievement for all students. As Giroux (1997) pointed out, rather than comprehending the world holistically as a network of interconnections, the American people are taught to approach problems as if they exist, in isolation, detached from the social and political forces that give them meaning (p. 13). It is this aspect of isolation that keeps education surface oriented, and thus, assists the system in perpetuating education's most damaging legacy: a constricted vision of teaching, learning, and knowledge, which leaves students unable to achieve to their maximum potential.

Employing the interconnectedness of critical theories and alternative schooling practices, teacher evaluation and student achievement can occur under a more inclusive environment that allows teachers to incorporate instruction that addresses students' diverse needs, embraces meaningful teachings that facilitate higher order thinking, and promotes achievement for all students. Sewell (1992) advised, "If enough people, or even a few people who are powerful enough, act in innovative ways, their action may have the consequence of transforming the very structure that gave them the capacity to act" (p. 4). The bottom line is that people need to act to initiate change, and with action, change will create a pathway. Critical action, when applied to the American school system, can facilitate change and innovations with the force of collective power behind it. Action can circumvent the idea of stagnation in structure and "build the possibility of change into the concept of structure" (p. 3). The open mind of collective power can jar the steadfast ineffective structure of our existing school system and bring about equitable evaluations of our teachers and fair student assessment practices. The challenge begins within the system and involves assistance from the "village."

References

Baker, E., Barton, P., Darling-Hammond, L., Haertel, E., Ladd, H., Linn, R.,…Shepard, L. (2010). *Problems with the use of student test scores to evaluate teachers* (Briefing Paper No. 278).

Washington, DC: Economic Policy Institute. Retrieved from http://www.epi.org/publi
cation/bp278/

Brady, M. (2011, April 4). Unanswered questions about standardized tests [Web log post]. Retrieved from http://www.washingtonpost.com/blogs/answer-sheet/post/unanswered-ques
tions-about-standardized-tests/2011/04/26/AFNRPlmE_blog.html

Byrnes, J. P., & Wasik, B. A. (2009). Factors predictive of mathematics achievement in kindergarten, first and third grades: An opportunity—Propensity analysis. *Contemporary Educational Psychology, 34*(2), 167–183.

Carris, J. (2011). *Ghosts of no child left behind*. New York, NY: Peter Lang.

Chapman, B., & Lestch, C. (2013, August 11). EXCLUSIVE: Achievement gap widens for
students after city's new standardized tests. *New York Daily News*. Retrieved from http://
www.nydailynews.com/new-york/education/achievement-gap-widens-city-new-standard
ized-tests-article-1.1423531

Darling-Hammond, L., Amrein-Beardsley, A., Haertel, E., & Rothstein, J. (2012, March 1).
Evaluating teacher evaluation. *Phi Delta Kappan*. Retrieved from http://www.edweek.org/
ew/articles/2012/03/01/kappan_hammond.html

Education Trust. (2006). *Funding gaps 2006*. Washington DC: Author. Retrieved from http://
www.edtrust.org/dc/press-room/press-release/the-education-trust-releases-funding-
gaps-2006.

Epstein, D. (2011). *Measuring inequity in school funding*. Washington, DC: Center for American Progress. Retrieved from http://www.americanprogress.org/issues/education/report/
2011/08/03/10122/measuring-inequity-in-school-funding/

Foucault, M. (1977). *Discipline and punish: The birth of the prison*. New York, NY: Random
House.

Freire, P. (2004). *Pedagogy of the oppressed*. New York, NY: Continuum.

Fry, R. A. (2008). *The role of schools in the English language learner achievement gap*. Washington,
DC: Pew Hispanic Center.

Giroux, H. (1997). *Pedagogy and the politics of hope: Theory, culture, and schooling*. Boulder, CO:
Westview Press.

Haberman, M. (1991). The pedagogy of poverty versus good teaching. *Phi Delta Kappan, 73*(4),
290–294.

Joyce, P. (2008). *School hazard zone: Beyond the silence/finding a voice*. New York, NY: Peter Lang.

Kincheloe, J. (2000). *Toil and trouble*. New York, NY: Peter Lang.

Kincheloe, J. (2004). *Critical pedagogy*. New York, NY: Peter Lang.

Lave, J., & Wenger, E. (1991). *Situated learning: Legitimate peripheral participation*. Cambridge,
UK: Cambridge University Press.

Madaus, G. F., & Clarke, M. (2001). *The adverse impact of high stakes testing on minority students:
Evidence from 100 years of test data*. Retrieved from http://eric.ed.gov/?id=ED450183

Masten, A. S. (2012). Risk and resilience in the educational success of homeless and highly mo-
bile children: Introduction to the special section. *Educational Researcher, 41*(9), 363–365.

Morris, M. (2004). The eighth one: Naturalistic intelligence. In J. Kincheloe (Ed.), *Multiple
intelligences reconsidered* (pp. 159–176). New York: Peter Lang.

Muller, C., Riegle-Crumb, C., Schiller, K. S., Wilkinson, L., & Frank, K. A. (2010). Race and academic achievement in racially diverse high schools: Opportunity and stratification. *Teachers College Record (1970)*, *112*(4), 1038.

National Governors Association Center for Best Practices and Council of Chief State School Officers. (2010). *Common Core State Standards*. Retrieved from http://www.corestandards. org/the-standards

New York Civil Liberties Union. (2012, June 27). *High stakes tests harm students and teachers, undermine equity in New York's schools*. Retrieved from http://www.nyclu.org/news/high-stakes-tests-harm-students-and-teachers-undermine-equity-new-yorks-schools

No Child Left Behind Act of 2001, Pub. L. 107–110, 115 Stat. 1425 (2002, January 8). Retrieved from http://www2.ed.gov/policy/elsec/leg/esea02/107-110.pdf

Noguera, P. (2003). *City schools and the American dream: Reclaiming the promise of public education*. New York, NY: Teachers College Press.

Ravitch, D. (2014, January 18). *My speech about Common Core to MLA* [Web log post]. Retrieved from http://dianeravitch.net/?s=mla+speech

Roscigno, V. J. (2000). Family/school inequality and African-American/Hispanic achievement. *Social Problems*, *47*, 266–290.

Sewell, W. H. (1992). A theory of structure: Duality, agency and transformation. *American Journal of Sociology*, *98*, 1–29.

Tate, W. (2013, April 8). Keynote address presented at the annual meeting of the National Association for Research in Science Teaching, Rio Grande, Puerto Rico.

Tobin, K. (2012). Sociocultural perspectives on science education. In *Second International handbook of science education* (pp. 3–17). Springer Netherlands.

United States Department of Education. (2010). *A blueprint for reform: The reauthorization of the elementary and secondary education act*. Alexandria, VA: Education Publications Center. Retrieved from http://www2.ed.gov/policy/elsec/leg/blueprint/blueprint.pdf

Villegas, A., & Lucas, T. (2002). *Educating culturally responsive teachers: A coherent approach*. Albany: State University of New York Press.

Vygotsky, L. S. (1978). *Mind in society: The development of higher psychological processes* (M. Cole, V. John-Steiner, S. Scribner, & U. E. Souberman, Trans. and Eds.). Cambridge, MA: Harvard University Press.

· 7 ·

REMEMBRANCES OF THINGS PAST: TEACHER EVALUATION, HIGH STAKES TESTING, AND THE MARGINALIZATION OF SOCIAL STUDIES AND HISTORY INSTRUCTION

Lynda Kennedy

In recent decades, there has been a move to hold teachers and their teaching practice accountable, at least in part, for the academic gains of students on a limited number of standardized tests. Since the No Child Left Behind Act (NCLB) of 2001, which mandated that all students be held to the same standards in reading and math, and which threatened the loss of federal funding if adequate progress was not made in these areas, other subject disciplines such as social studies and history have found themselves marginalized. Conversely, with the release of the Common Core State Standards in 2010, there seems to be a call to develop just the sort of skills that are built by a solid social studies or history curriculum—such as close reading of a variety of nonfiction texts, including primary sources, and an analysis of perspective—not to mention calling for a reintroduction of content-rich reading in the lower grades, building schema for secondary social studies and history work. Unfortunately, the tests that are accompanying the new standards have become even more high-stakes, with not only student promotion but school rating and even teacher career advancement (or termination) tied to their outcomes. What does this mean for teachers who see it as their role to introduce their students to a historical perspective of our current circumstance, to develop in them an understanding of what it means to be a citizen of this country and the world, and to foster critical thinkers who understand history not as a series of facts but as events that can be interpreted from a variety of subjective understandings? How do these high-stakes tests confine and curtail the curriculum and impact quality teaching as seen through that expansive lens rather than the lens of content delivery?

A History of "Quality" Teaching

Evaluation of teacher practice in any discipline requires a solid definition of the phrase "quality teacher." Unfortunately, as Marilyn Cochran-Smith (2005) stated, "In short, everybody likes teacher quality and wants more of it. The problem is there is no consensus about what it is" (p. 6). Historically, there hasn't been anything approaching consensus on this matter. For much of the time, content knowledge and even pedagogical knowledge were not considered as important to teaching so much as being a certain type of person, possessing certain qualities. In a journal she kept while attending the first state-run normal school (teacher training school) in the United States, Mary Swift noted the qualities the school administration proposed teachers should have. These qualities included health, a good reputation, a well-balanced mind, an interest in children, patience and self-control, along with a high sense of moral responsibility and accountability (Hoffman, 1981).

In 19th-century America, when public schools were conceived as panacea for certain social problems (immigration, poverty, the spread of disease), quality teachers were believed to need some of the same dispositions found in a nurse or social worker—or a mother. Schools and the teachers in them were asked to solve the problems of society, or more specifically, to ensure that the students did not become problems *for* society. Schools were called on to provide suitable controlling mechanisms for the immigrant "problem" of the late 19th and early 20th century, when citizenship and other aspects of the social studies curriculum began to replace history classes. Special English classes for new arrivals were given, and teacher outreach to immigrant families was encouraged. Teachers in turn-of-the-century schools in New York taught not only children but their immigrant parents in evening classes (Hoffman, 1981). Even giving instruction on cleanliness as a deterrent to disease fell under the auspices of schools and teachers.

After World War II and with the beginning of the Cold War, the focus of education shifted to preparing students to contribute to U.S. global competitiveness. Fears of Soviet technological advancement—embodied by Sputnik—prompted policies promoting science and foreign language as essential elements of the school curricula. The 1983 National Commission on Excellence in Education publication, "A Nation At Risk," blatantly drew the line from education to the failing U.S. economy, stating that America's "position in the world" was no longer secure and we would need to protect our "competitive edge" through education reform (p. 6). This theme was reemphasized in No Child Left Behind (NCLB) Act, where the relationship of student achievement to the national economic growth was specifically highlighted. NCLB stated the following: "Satisfying the demand for highly skilled workers is the key to maintaining competitiveness and prosperity in the global community" (U.S. Department of Education, 2004, p. 5).

The current phrase being used by politicians and educational reformers reflecting this theme is "college and career ready." Indeed, the U.S. Department of Education, under President Obama, released a publication entitled "College and Career Ready Standards and Assessments." In his foreword, President Obama wrote the following: "A generation ago, we led all nations in college completion, but today, 10 countries have passed us…. And the countries that out educate us today, will out-compete us tomorrow" (U.S. Department of Education, 2010, Introduction). The implication is that schools have been failing to turn out a competent workforce, therefore threatening national economic growth and global competitiveness. For "schools," one could easily read "teachers," and teachers have been given the burden of ensuring our country's competitiveness and the blame for its failure.

Connecting ineffective teaching to student failure and thereby to the country's failure has led to decades of an increasingly frantic call to "fix" the profession and a struggle to find the secret ingredient for developing an effective teaching force. As Darling-Hammond and Berry (1988) indicated, from 1983 to 1985, more than 700 pieces of legislation were enacted to improve the quality of teachers, and the struggle to find a new measure of quality began. In policy statements issued under NCLB, subject matter competence is emphasized as the hallmark of teacher quality (Cochran-Smith, 2005), and competence was assumed by the attainment of credentials—either university degrees or tests passed. Reports covering quality teacher preparation under NCLB also tended to use academic credentials along with certification as the primary marker of "quality" (Schiller, 2004). Occasionally, demonstrated pedagogical competence has been included along with credentialing and subject matter mastery as a quality marker.

Defining quality teaching when it comes to social studies and history (history integrated with other humanities subjects, such as civics) teaching has been as difficult as defining quality teaching in general. Even outlining what subject knowledge the teachers needed proved problematic. What/whose history should/can be included in a tightly paced curriculum? Influencing the choice of historical content—*what* we want our teachers to teach – is the *why* of social studies/history teaching. If the *why* is to promote a deep understanding of the historical context and continuum that contribute to our own geopolitical context, the content and assessments of teaching will be very different than if the *why* is purely about building an accepted national narrative. Content will be different yet again if the *why* is simply to prepare students to pass a test. Nationwide, the conversation around the *what* and *why* of history instruction has as many outcomes as there are school systems. The argument becomes as basic as defining the difference between social studies and history and as complicated as identifying measures of success.

As the evaluation of schools, and now individual teachers, has become increasingly reliant on the performance students have on English language arts and math tests, there has been a significant decline in social studies/history instruction in the elementary grades (Fichetta & Heafnera, 2012). In many states, there is also a lack of emphasis in the upper grades. Only roughly half the states have required history assessments, and less than half of these assessments are used to make decisions that could be considered high-stakes (Au, 2009). This has an impact on teacher training, with credentials no longer seen as a guarantee of quality social studies or history teaching, especially in the elementary grades. Preservice programs at the elementary level barely give a nod to social studies, often just requiring one course on social studies *methods* (how to develop and teach a social studies curriculum) and no history *content* courses, leaving in-service teachers ill equipped to make thoughtful choices about content, even if they are given the time.

The current emphasis on math and English language arts over social studies or history would have taken education reformers at the turn of the last century by surprise. The teaching of history in the 19th and early 20th century was seen as essential to the moral training of students. "The study was seen to provide, if not a laboratory of ethics, at least an observatory in which the consequences of various human actions could be watched from a safe distance and the appropriate lessons drawn" (Diorio, 1985, p. 74). In 1893, the

National Education Association's Committee of Ten issued its report on the secondary level curriculum. The committee's subcommittee on history, civil government, and political economy recommended that all students take four years of secondary level history, as it "broadened and cultivated the mind, counteracted a narrow and provincial spirit, prepared students for intellectual enjoyment in after years, and assisted them to exercise a salutary influence upon the affairs of their country" (Bradley Commission, 1988, p. 1). In 1916, the Committee on Social Studies, a subcommittee of the Commission on the Reorganization of Secondary Education, put out its final report entitled, "The Social Studies in Secondary Education." Concerned with social order and issues of citizenship, the committee recommended courses with titles such as "Problems in American Democracy," which would include discussions of health, recreation, education, charities, and other social issues, encouraging an active, engaged citizenry (Lybarger, 1983, p. 463).

In spite of the seeming correlation, we cannot squarely blame the rise of standardized tests for the decline in the centrality of the history and/or civics-focused social studies curriculum. "Progressives" of the mid-twentieth century, concerned with efficiency and usefulness of education, dismissed much of traditional history as having no practical use in student's lives and therefore as not important in the modern curriculum (Nash, Crabtree, & Dunn, 2000). It was felt that history could be studied by the relatively few students who were bound for college, but the majority would not need it, or, as some thought, were not capable of learning it (Ravitch, 2000). By 1987, 15% of students in the United States did not study U.S. States history in high school, and 60% no longer took classes in world history or Western civilization (Bradley Commission, 1988).

Students who did attend schools with social studies and/or history classes were likely to encounter a wide variety of approaches to teaching history, depending on what textbooks they used or what political trends existed. Even if we ignore extremists on both sides of the issue, with oversimplified versions of a happy Euro-centric history ruined by multiculturalism such as is depicted in Gingrich's (1995) *To Renew America* on one side, and the call during the 1960s and 1970s for separate ethnically and gender-specific history instruction on the other (Moreau, 2003; Zimmerman, 2002), we are still left with a plethora of traditions in U.S. history teaching to choose from and many potential "great ideas" to explore in a relatively short period of time. Content choices have to be made, and in the states where there are standardized social studies/history tests, the content the teachers include is necessarily shaped by the need to align to the assessments. As Wineburg (2004) wrote in his overview of the historical expectations of student knowledge in U.S. history, "We cannot insist that every student know when World War II began and who our allies were while giving tests that ask about the battles of Saratoga and Oriskany" (p. 1412).

Pedagogical Approaches to Teaching History— Looking for "Quality"

Clearly there is more to understanding history than the mere memorization of facts, but fact recall is the most easily assessed element and therefore tends to permeate the teaching of history. As Kincheloe (2001) stated, students in a fact-driven situation "become fact collectors, not knowledge workers who can conduct research and interpret data" (p. 50). He went on to say that the teachers of these students become more like factory foremen and become deskilled and isolated from the spirit of their work. When John Goodlad (1984) and his colleagues were researching schools, they found that isolated facts—names, dates, places—were all that were being taught and tested, in spite of teachers' self-reports of providing a wider variety of experiences for their students. In recent decades, there has been a movement to encourage a history education that engages students to think like historians, conduct research and view history as being less about facts than about informed interpretation (Levstik & Barton, 2005; Wineburg, 2001). The recommendations of the 1988 Bradley Commission on History in Schools for history instruction included a thematic approach, rather than the presentation of facts devoid of context, and it also suggested the use of original sources, as the study of history should include the exploration of contexts and the exercising of "critical judgment based on evidence" (p. 7). Even the New York City "K-8 Scope and Sequence for Social Studies" (New York City Department of Education, 2008–2009) emphasized thinking skills such as "handling diversity of interpretations" (p. iii) and included "essential questions" that group factual information conceptually, such as "How does a nation balance its own needs with the needs of the world?" (p. 31). The inclusion of primary source interpretation, with document-based and constructed-response questions in the curriculum and on tests, allows students to do the work of historians and construct their own knowledge, once again redefining the idea of quality instruction.

Teachers who are encouraged to use primary sources and a more interpretive approach must find a way to be comfortable with guiding the interpretations, while leaving room for differences. They also must be comfortable knowing that allowing an exploration of history that is not predigested may lead to some strong feelings on the part of students, such as the elementary school child who, after studying the earliest European encounters with people in the Americas, declared, "I think Columbus went to Hell" (Levstik, & Barton, 2005, p. 61). Teachers must be ready to assist the student who is not making connections, for, as Carlton Bell noted in 1917, some students are easily able to work with primary sources and synthesize information in a logical way, while others end up with a bunch of disconnected facts (see also Wineburg, 2004). An approach to history that encompasses the skills of "doing" history requires teachers to have a firm grasp of those skills—the skills of the historian—as well as a depth of content knowledge that enables them to guide their students to a nuanced understanding of the past. This view of quality history teaching also requires the teacher to have time in the pace of the curriculum to allow for real discovery, discussion, and debriefing—time not easily found if the subject is not prioritized. The skills developed by such an approach are also not as easily measured by a standard, majority multiple-choice test, which is better geared toward measuring fact recall.

The national or state standards for social studies and history can provide some guidance for establishing a working idea of "quality" history teaching, but these have also come under fire. The National Standards for History received tremendous criticism from those who thought they were too negative and neglected "important" history, such as the Wright brothers (Nash et al., 2000), while including other events, such as the founding of the National Organization for Women, deemed unimportant by the likes of Lynne Cheney (1994). The state standards didn't fare much better. In 1998, the Thomas B. Fordham Foundation issued a report written by David Warren Saxe, in which Saxe and a panel made up of two professors of history and two professors of education reviewed state social studies/history standards and graded them. New York State received an "F," which the panel coded as meaning "useless." Saxe and the panel objected to standards that were outlined using a social studies framework (such as New York's). They also objected to any evidence of "presentism" and gave as a negative example the New York standards' inclusion of language encouraging multiple perspectives and a value perspective when learning history that involves slavery and totalitarianism. The panel explained its actions: "Applications of present-day sensibilities to the past may easily confuse and divert students from understanding people and their times" (Saxe, 1998, p. 18).

Clearly, there is a lack of a shared vision and a wide variety of ideologies surrounding quality social studies/history instruction regarding the best way to "develop" quality history/social studies teachers and measure their effectiveness. Although we cannot completely blame the current educational policy climate for the absence of social studies and history in many grades, their already inconsistent place in the school curriculum has made these subjects particularly vulnerable in the era of high-stakes testing and a value-added approach to teacher evaluation.

Still Searching

The connection of teacher performance to student attainment as measured on standard assessments has become the central point of much of the current public discourse. With Race to the Top funding being provided under the administration of President Barack Obama requiring a clear avenue for teacher assessment (U.S. Department of Education, 2009), states have been struggling to find a new way to measure quality teaching—now generally categorized as teacher *effectiveness*. In New York City, where using student tests scores as a measure of effectiveness was vehemently challenged by the teachers' union and many other educational thinkers, a new approach to teacher evaluation was only just recently approved. After much negotiation, 20% to 25% of a teacher evaluation will be based on student performance on state tests (Joseph, 2013). Student test performance will also continue to be a factor in school "report cards." This initiative follows a year when New York City teacher's names, along with ratings largely based on a value-added model of student performance, were made public (Santos & Gebeloff, 2012), so the stakes for these tests and the feelings of stress around them remain incredibly high.

Complicating this pursuit of a measurement of effective teaching is the dissonance between two of the major public discussion and policy strands in education reform. On the one hand, teachers are told that they are to prepare critical thinkers who are "college and career ready," who show facility with 21st-century skills such as creativity, problem solving, and collaboration. On the other hand, research shows that teachers have been pushed by the punitive use of the current assessments into skill and drill approaches that "focus on rote memorization and lower-order thinking as the tests themselves are usually structured to assess breadth of often shallow, fragmented bits of knowledge (Au, 2009, p. 46).

In New York City, this dissonance is exemplified by the reliance on both the standardized assessments as a marker of teacher proficiency and the use of the "Framework for Teaching" developed by Charlotte Danielson (2011). These are two of the major elements of the new teacher evaluation system. Danielson's Framework, adapted for New York, contains thoughtful descriptions of teacher competencies, along with clear operationalized examples of what these look like in practice. The three major categories that the competencies are divided into are "Planning and Preparation," "The Classroom Environment," and "Instruction" (Danielson, 2011). Under "Instruction," Danielson tackles assessment:

> Assessment of student learning plays an important role in instruction; no longer does it signal the *end* of instruction; it is now recognized to be an integral part *of* instruction. While assessment *of* learning has always been and will continue to be an important aspect of teaching (it's important for teachers to know whether students have learned what they intend)[,] assessment *for* learning has increasingly come to play an important role in classroom practice. And in order to assess student learning for the purposes of instruction, teachers must have their finger on "the pulse" of a lesson, monitoring student understanding and, where appropriate, offering feedback to students. (p. 22)

This view of assessment is in direct contrast to the use of high-stakes tests, which in many states are generally not even graded and returned until after the school year is over and are therefore useless for the purpose of informing instruction (Simon, 2012).

Other descriptions of highly effective teaching contained in the Framework are also hard to imagine in the culture that has been created by high-stakes standardized testing. If a high school history teacher in New York City is to be evaluated partly by using Danielson's Framework, there would most likely be a disconnect among the elements of quality teaching outlined by Danielson, the reality of school structures, and the elements valued by state student assessments. For example, the Framework gives an unsatisfactory marker as, "The teacher says, 'The district gave me this entire curriculum to teach, so I just have to keep moving'" (Danielson, 2011, p. 23).

The ideal practice outlined in the Framework is that the teacher would not move on with new material until student understanding is assured. A reality for many teachers, however, is that there is pressure to keep moving. The "New York City High School Scope and Sequence for Global History &

Geography, American History, Economics and Participation in Government" (2010), for instance, has U.S. history teachers covering the history of our country, from first European contact with native cultures to the present day, in one school year. Students are required to show knowledge of dates and events along that expanse as part of the state assessments. In schools that keep a tight pacing schedule, trying to teach the content of each unit in the scope and sequence, there is little time for the teacher to provide experiences that build a critical understanding of history, historical thinking skills, or historical perspective.

In the first decades of the 21st century, there was an increased acceptance of standardized testing. Due to the introduction of NCLB, between 2002 and 2008 annual state spending on standardized tests rose from $423 million to almost $1.1 billion (Vu, 2008). As we move into the second decade of the 21st century, the pendulum may finally be swinging back from viewing standardized tests as the best way to assess student achievement. Even educational historian Diane Ravitch (2006), formerly a champion of NCLB initiatives, has expressed frustration with the current focus on standardized test performance as evidence of a "quality" education, reminding us that "a full education is one that prepares students not only to pass tests, but also to read, write, think, speak and participate in society" (p. 58). Parent groups across the country, frustrated by the loss of instructional time to test preparation and delivery, are organizing to opt their children out of the testing, with help from groups such as Fair Test, Time Out From Testing, and Change the Stakes. In addition, the use of these tests to assess teacher effectiveness is being called into question by growing research. One of the largest research projects was a multimillion dollar study founded by the Bill & Melinda Gates Foundation entitled "Measures of Effective Teaching" (MET). This was a three-year study that worked with 3,000 volunteer teachers to examine how a set of measures can reliably examine effective teaching. Various tools for measuring teacher effectiveness were used, including classroom observation instruments, student surveys, and student gains on assessments. The study was reviewed by the National Education Policy Center, which is housed at the University of Colorado, Boulder, and whose mission is to produce and disseminate peer-reviewed research to inform education policy decisions. The authors of the review wrote, "While the MET project has brought unprecedented vigor to teacher evaluation research, its results do not settle disagreements about what makes an effective teacher and offers [sic] little guidance about how to design real-world teacher evaluation systems" (Rothstein & Mathis, 2013, summary). These trends and findings, combined with the full introduction of the Common Core State Standards, with their emphasis on reading and writing in the disciplines and the use of informational texts in the younger grades, as well as specific recommendations for social studies/history in Grades 6–12, would seem to offer hope for the lessening of the stakes associated with state assessments in just two subject areas. There is hope, perhaps, for the corresponding widening of the curriculum to move social studies and history back into a more central position. However, the momentum of assessment development and value-added teacher evaluations has yet to slow down, and this has complicated how the Common Core State Standards are being received.

Although often conflated with standardized tests, the Common Core State Standards can be seen to have the potential for widening what has become a very narrow curriculum, particularly in the elementary years. As previously stated, initially much of the reaction to the Common Core State Standards from the social studies and history teaching professional communities was positive, as the new standards seemed to honor skills central to good social studies and history teaching, such as "analyze the relationship of a primary and secondary source on the same topic" (Common Core State Standards, 2012). The draft of the New York State Common Core Standards for social studies easily aligns the social studies core curriculum's conceptual understandings and social studies practices, or what can be thought of as the "essential skills or habits of mind utilized by social scientists or historians" (New York State, 2012, p. 4), with the literacy skills outlined by the Common Core State Standards. There is articulated alignment between conceptual understandings and key ideas in social studies and Common Core-aligned outcomes in English. However, the rollout of the Common Core State Standards into schools and the aligned standardized assessments have once again focused on math and English language arts. Nineteen states, including New York, have joined together into the Partnership for Assessment of Readiness for College and Careers (PARCC) for the development of English and math assessments. Even the intended method of assessment delivery has the potential to derail a return to a curriculum that includes social studies or history. According to the PARCC (2013) document, "Assessment Administration Guidance," "The expectation is that all students will take PARCC assessments on a computer" (p. 4). This includes the typing of essays. As student performance on these tests will contribute to the evaluation of their teachers and even the survival of their schools, one can easily see typing skills superseding history as a prioritized part of the learning day.

The promise of the Common Core State Standards to expand the curriculum looks like it is to be undermined by the continued practice of shrinking assessment down to tests focused on English and math, which has the added pressure of school and teacher "failure" tied to it. With such high stakes attached to assessments in these two subject areas, one can predict that the narrowing of the curriculum that began with NCLB's focus on English and math will continue (Common Core, 2012). Unless the pendulum indeed begins to reverse its arc and there is a radical change in what we value as essential student learning and what we accept as authentic assessment of effective teaching, social studies and history are likely to remain marginalized subjects for the foreseeable future.

References

Au, W. (2009). Social studies, social justice: W(h)ither the social studies in high-stakes testing? *Teacher Education Quarterly, 36*, 1, 43–58.

Bell, J. C. (1917). The historic sense. *Journal of Educational Psychology, 8,* 317–318.

Bill & Melinda Gates Foundation. (2013). Ensuring fair and reliable measures of effective teaching. Retrieved from: http://www.metproject.org/downloads/MET_Ensuring_Fair_and_Reliable_Measures_Practitioner_Brief.pdf

Bradley Commission on History in Schools. (1988). *Building a history curriculum: Guidelines for teaching history in schools.* University Heights, OH: National Council for History Education.

Cheney, L. (1994, October 20). The end of history. *The Wall Street Journal,* pp. A22, A26–A27.

Cochran-Smith, M. (2005). The new teacher education: For better or worse? *Educational Researcher, 34*(7), 3–17.

Common Core. (2012). *Learning less: Public school teachers describe a narrowing curriculum.* Retrieved from http://commoncore.org/reports

Common Core State Standards. (2012). *English language arts standards.* Retrieved from http://www.corestandards.org/ELA-Literacy/RH/6-8

Danielson, C. (2011). Framework for teaching, revised edition: NYC DOE priority competencies. Retrieved from http://www.danielsongroup.org/article.aspx?page=FfTEvaluation Instrument

Darling-Hammond, L., & Berry, B. (1988). *The evolution of teacher policy.* Santa Monica, CA: Rand.

Diorio, J. (1985). The decline of history as a tool of moral training. *Education Quarterly, 25*(1/2), 71–101.

Fichetta P. & Heafnera T. (2012). National trends in elementary instruction: Exploring the role of social studies curricula. *The Social Studies.* 103, 67–72.

Gingrich, N. (1995). *To renew America.* New York, NY: HarperCollins.

Goodlad, J. (1984). *A place called school*. New York, NY: McGraw-Hill.

Hoffman, N. (1981). *Woman's "true" profession: Voices from the history of teaching*. New York, NY: The Feminist Press.

Joseph, C. (2013, June 1). New York to evaluate teachers with new system. *The New York Times*. Retrieved from http://www.nytimes.com/2013/06/02/nyregion/new-evaluation-sys tem-for-new-york-teachers.html

Kincheloe, J. (2001). *Getting beyond the facts: Teaching social studies/social sciences in the twenty-first century*. New York, NY: Peter Lang.

Levstik, L., & Barton, K. (2005). *Doing history: Investigating with children in elementary and middle schools* (3rd ed.). Mahwah, NJ: Lawrence Erlbaum.

Lybarger, M. (1983). The origin of the modern social studies: 1900–1916. *History of Education Quarterly, 23*(4), 455–468.

Moreau, J. (2003). *School book nation: Conflicts over American history textbooks from the Civil War to the present*. Ann Arbor: University of Michigan Press.

Nash, G., Crabtree, C., & Dunn, R. (2000). *History on trial: Culture wars and the teaching of the past*. New York, NY: Vintage Books.

National Commission on Excellence in Education. (1983). *A nation at risk: The imperative for educational reform*. Washington, DC: Author.

New York City Department of Education. (2008–2009). New York City K-8 social studies scope & sequence. Retrieved from http://schools.nycenet.edu/offices/teachlearn/ss/Soc StudScopeSeq.pdf

New York City Department of Education. (2010). *New York City high school scope and sequence: Global history, geography, American history, economics, participation in government*. Retrieved from http://schools.nyc.gov/NR/rdonlyres/B60E475E-5919-40A0-A812-B5BEE8A8B9E3/86669/ HS_SS_SS_8510final1.pdf

New York State. (2012). New York State Common Core K-8 social studies framework. Retrieved from http://www.engageny.org/sites/default/files/resource/attachments/ss-framework-k-8.pdf

Partnership for Assessment of Readiness for College and Careers (PARCC). (2013, March). PARCC assessment administration guidance version 1.0. Retrieved from http://www. parcconline.org/sites/parcc/files/PARCC%20Assessment%20Administration%20Guid ance_FINAL_0.pdf

Ravitch D. (2000). *Left back: A century of battles over school reform*. New York, NY: Simon & Schuster.

Ravitch, D. (2006). National standards: 50 Standards for 50 states is a formula for incoherence and obfuscation. *Education Week, 25*(17), 54, 56, 58. Retrieved from http://www.edweek. org/ew/articles/2006/01/05/17ravitch.h25.html

Rothstein, J., & Mathis, W. (2013). *Review of two culminating reports from the MET project*. Boulder, CO: National Education Policy Center. Retrieved from http://nepc.colorado.edu/ thinktank/review-MET-final-2013

Santos, F., & Gebeloff, R. (2012, February 24). Teacher quality widely diffused, ratings indicate. *The New York Times*. Retrieved from http://www.nytimes.com/2012/02/25/education/ teacher-quality-widely-diffused-nyc-ratings-indicate.html?pagewanted=all

Saxe, D. W. (1998). *State history standards: An appraisal of history standards in 37 states and the District of Columbia.* Washington, DC: Thomas B. Fordham Foundation.

Schiller, R. (2004). From the highly qualified teacher to the highly proficient teacher. In National Evaluation Systems, Inc. *What is a qualified, capable teacher?* (43–48).Amherst, MA: Pearson.

Simon, S. (2012, June 12). *Parents protest surge in standardized testing.* Retrieved from http://www.reuters.com/article/2012/06/12/us-usa-education-testing-idUSBRE85B0EO20120612

U.S. Department of Education. (2004). *A guide to education and No Child Left Behind.* Retrieved from http://www2.ed.gov/nclb/overview/intro/guide/guide.pdf

U.S. Department of Education. (2009). Race to the top executive summary. Retrieved from http://www2.ed.gov/programs/racetothetop/executive-summary.pdf

U.S. Department of Education (2010). College and career ready standards and assessments. Retrieved from http://www2.ed.gov/policy/elsec/leg/blueprint/faq/college-career.pdf

Vu, P. (2008, January 17). *Do state tests make the grade?* Retrieved from http://www.pewtrusts.org/en/research-and-analysis/reports/2008/01/17/do-state-tests-make-the-grade

Wineburg, S. (2004). Crazy for history. *The Journal of American History,* 90, 4. 1401–1414.

Zimmerman, J. (2002). *Whose America? Culture wars in the public schools.* Cambridge, MA: Harvard University Press.

SECTION 3
ENVISIONING CHANGE

$\cdot$ 8 $\cdot$

CURRICULAR RELEVANCE: STUDENTS' NEEDS AND TEACHERS' PRACTICE

Anne Beitlers and Pedro Noguera

In this chapter, we explore what schools can do to improve the academic preparation of Black and Latino males by focusing specifically on the issue of teacher effectiveness. With the adoption of the provisions of Race to the Top (RTTT), several states have enacted new policies for evaluating teachers in the hope that by weeding out ineffective teachers, the quality of teaching will improve and student achievement will increase (Darling-Hammond, 2011; "Race to the Top Program Executive Summary," 2009). There is, however, considerable debate over whether teacher evaluation systems, especially those that are tied to student achievement on standardized tests, will be an effective mechanism for improving teaching and achievement, or for that matter, evaluating teacher effectiveness (Darling-Hammond, 2011). Given the debate, there is a need for more research on teaching to learn what teachers understand about meeting the learning needs of their students and how this in turn influences their practice. This is particularly important for Black and Latino male students whose educational needs have been poorly served in many schools throughout the country. By understanding the factors that contribute to teacher effectiveness for Black and Latino males, we will be in a better position to determine whether current education policies will lead to the improvements that are so desperately needed for this vulnerable population.

A growing number of policymakers have come to the conclusion that finding ways to improve the effectiveness of teachers is key to closing the achievement gap ("Race to the Top Program Executive Summary," 2009). Disparities in student outcomes are particularly prominent between Black and Latino males and their White, Asian, and female counterparts (Holzman, Jackson, Beaudry, Dexter, & Watson, 2012). Although this is not a new issue, it is a problem that is drawing increased attention and alarm because of the social and economic consequences that result from such high rates of failure. A recent study released by the Schott Foundation, entitled "The Urgency of Now" (Holzman et al., 2012), documented that despite a concerted effort to reduce dropout rates and increase graduation rates over the last few years, progress for Black males remains slow at best. In fact, the report found that "at the current pace of progress…it would take nearly 50 years for Black males to secure the same high school graduation rates as their White male peers" (Holzman et al., 2012, p. 7).

This gap is evident across many levels of educational attainment. In every state, Black and Latina females earn more high school and college diplomas than males. Higher percentages of White and Asian male students earn a greater number of degrees at all levels, and dropout rates for Black and Latino males are considerably higher than for other students (National Center for Education Statistics [NCES], 2010; Noguera & Hurtado, 2012; Orfield, Losen, Wald, & Swanson, 2004). High dropout rates and low college enrollment are only part of the problem. Black and Latino males are generally less successful than other groups of students in most educational settings (Darling-Hammond, 2006; Holzman, et al., 2012). High unemployment and high incarceration rates are just some of the negative societal impacts that are closely tied to high levels of educational failure among Black and Latino males (Darling-Hammond, 2006; Nicholson-Crotty, Birchmeier, & Valentine, 2009; Noguera, Hurtado, & Fergus, 2012; Smith, 2009; Torres & Fergus, 2012).

To effectively meet the learning needs of their Black and Latino male students, teachers must incorporate teaching methods that will improve academic performance. Increasing relevance in curriculum and pedagogical practice has long been recommended as a method for increasing academic engagement for all students, but it is especially crucial for Black and Latino males (Heath, 2009; Ladson-Billings, 2009; Thompson, 2004; Villegas & Lucas, 2002). After a brief review of literature on curricular relevance and a description of the study from which data were selected, this chapter will examine how teachers in three all-male schools that serve low-income Black and Latino students frame relevance as a need for their students and then reveal the discrepancy between this reported need and teachers' practice. Data from our study will show that although teachers were knowledgeable about the importance of curricular relevance, relevance was not widespread in the observed schools.

Relevance Reviewed

Several notable studies have suggested that by increasing the degree of curricular relevance, student performance will improve. Such findings have been generated in the research literature on culturally responsive pedagogy (Gay, 2000; Ladson-Billings, 2009; Thompson, 2004; Villegas & Lucas, 2002), literacy methods (Alvermann, 2002; Heath, 2009; National Institute for Literacy [NIL], 2007; Tatum, 2008), the effective teaching of boys (King & Gurian, 2006; Ladson-Billings; 2011; Tatum, 2008), and even the definition of academic rigor (Matusevich, O'Connor, & Hargett, 2009). In these bodies of literature, relevance has been described as encompassing three major categories: (a) creating a personal connection between the curriculum and students' interests; (b) creating connections among students' culture, "funds of knowledge," and the curriculum; and (c) assigning students tasks and projects that are perceived as authentic due to their "real-world" connection—their relation to the lived experiences of students. These three categories will be used to outline this review of literature and later will tie directly to what teachers in the study said about students' need for curricular relevance.

Connections to Personal Interests

To begin, scholars such as Boykin and Noguera (2011) have found that relevance in curriculum can be achieved when teachers are able to develop a personal connection between curriculum and students. Similarly, other scholars have found that when teachers enact changes to enhance curricular relevance, teachers are able to "use…knowledge about students' lives to design instruction that builds on what they already know while stretching them beyond the familiar" (Villegas & Lucas, 2002, p. 21). Research has shown that personal connections activate schemata and encourage students to engage in the construction of knowledge. Additionally, they serve as a bridge to new knowledge, concepts, and information (Thompson, 2004; Villegas & Lucas, 2002).

In contrast to the banking method of teaching, in which the teacher covers material prescribed by the state or district curriculum and students are expected to absorb it (Freire, 2009; Kohn, 2011), curricular relevance has been advocated as a way to encourage active engagement and greater student buy-in and ensure enhanced learning (Boykin & Noguera 2011). Banking methods continue to be used widely in urban schools (Haberman, 1991; Kohn, 2011), despite evidence that such methods often result in boredom, disengagement, and a shallow understanding of material and concepts (Kohn, 2011). Although didactic teaching and other banking methods might make it easier for teachers to achieve a closer alignment between state-level tests and the lesson plans teachers utilize, reliance on such teacher-centered methods often results in students who fail to fully grasp concepts and are ultimately less successful (Au, 2007; Villegas & Lucas, 2002). Moreover, according to research, simply memorizing and regurgitating disconnected facts leads to disengagement, something that is of particular concern for Black and Latino male students (Cammarota, 2004; Villegas & Lucas, 2002). A lack of curricular relevance and an inability on the part of teachers to make personal connections between their students' lives and the curriculum contribute to higher levels of academic failure and an exacerbation of the achievement gap between urban and affluent students, who generally have access to higher quality curriculum that allows for deeper processing of knowledge (Darling-Hammond, 2006).

In addition to supporting students in the co-construction of knowledge with their teachers, relevance in instruction and the curriculum has been found to increase student motivation (NIL, 2007; Villegas & Lucas, 2002). Researchers such as Tatum (2008) and Ladson-Billings (2011) have found that this is especially true for efforts to improve the literacy of Black and Latino males (Ladson-Billings, 2011; Tatum, 2008). When teachers are able to connect knowledge of students' hobbies, activities, and experiences out of school to the curriculum, motivation and engagement increase considerably (Cohen, Garcia, Apfel, & Master; 2006; Heath, 2009). Conversely, not doing so can lead to students feeling bored and disconnected from school (Villegas & Lucas, 2002).

One way to ensure connections between students' personal interests and curriculum is through choice. Several studies have found that when students, and especially Black and Latino males, are allowed to choose their own topics in reading and writing, their academic performance is more likely to improve (King & Gurian, 2006, NIL, 2007; Reed, Schallert, Beth, & Woodruff, 2004). The opportunity to choose has been found to motivate and engage students at a higher level, boost confidence, and encourage a willingness to engage in problem solving (Cordova & Lepper, 1996). Increasing engagement and motivation for learning in the school context is particularly key for Black and Latino students who may not have personal experience or exposure to school being an avenue to successful adulthood and do not always believe that school is the right path for them (Villegas & Lucas, 2002).

Connections to Culture

Curricular relevance can be achieved by affirming students' cultural identity through curriculum (Ladson-Billings, 1995, 2009) or infusing knowledge of students' culture into the curriculum (Gay, 2000; Ladson-Billings, 2009; Moje & Hinchman, 2004; Thompson, 2004). Tatum (2008) advocated especially for making cultural connections to texts when reading with Black males, although students in general benefit from connections to texts that have cultural similarities to them (Moje, Overby, Tysvaer, & Morris, 2008). Moje et al. (2008) suggested that culture does not refer only to race, ethnicity, age, class, or gender but also to people who respond to struggle in similar ways, which is an important consideration when choosing classroom texts, illustrative examples, or anecdotes. Furthermore, it is essential not to make generalizations about students' culture. Boykin and Noguera (2011) warned that there are wide variations within groups, and teachers need to understand their students beyond skin color, socioeconomic status, or language. Instead, they should consider patterns of values, priorities, behaviors, and relationships, including relationships with institutions (Boykin & Noguera, 2011). Fully understanding students' culture assists teachers in selecting texts and designing curriculum that will engage students, boost confidence in reading (Tatum, 2008), and improve performance (Cohen et al., 2006).

Just as personal connections serve as a bridge to new knowledge, content, and concepts, so can culture (Lee, 2005; Moje & Hinchman, 2004). Lee (2005) used cultural modeling as a means to improve literacy skills with her Black students. In particular, she bridged her students' knowledge of signifying to new understandings about literature and literary devices. Her students who were exposed to cultural modeling showed extensive gains in literacy skills and their ability to solve problems. Her strategy was effective because bridging new knowledge with culture activates prior knowledge, which in turn assists students in deep processing and knowledge production (Villegas & Lucas, 2002). Creating such opportunities for Black and Latino males to link their culture to new knowledge and thoroughly process information is a pivotal approach to ending their history of underachievement (Boykin & Noguera, 2011).

Connections to the Real World

In addition to providing relevance by making explicit connections between the curriculum and students' personal interests and their lived cultural experiences, scholars also recommend designing curriculum that is authentic in its real-world applicability (Heath, 2009; Matusevich et al., 2009). King and Gurian (2006) proposed that boys need opportunities for authentic audiences and real-life rewards. Such opportunities might include publishing or sharing writing at an event outside of school, like an open-mic event at a café, or science competitions. Heath (2009) similarly found strong engagement when school projects allowed students to investigate their communities. Furthermore, real-world applicability encourages intrinsic motivation as students see the connection between school learning and problems they confront in their communities (Heath, 2009). Cohen et al. (2006) found that motivation is a critical component of instruction, especially when students are asked to take risks, because it increases engagement and performance, especially with Black students.

Ample evidence points to the importance of relevance in curriculum (Gay, 2000; Heath, 2009; Ladson-Billings, 2009; Tatum, 2008; Thompson, 2004; Villegas & Lucas, 2002). Making connections among students' interests, culture, and the real/authentic world is advisable for all students but critical for Black and Latino males who too often have experienced poor instruction void of such opportunities and therefore have checked out of school (Haberman, 1991; Ladson-Billings, 2011; Tatum, 2008). In addition to boosting motivation and engagement, relevant connections allow for deeper processing of information through the activation of prior knowledge, which positively influences performance (Boykin & Noguera, 2011; Villegas & Lucas, 2002). Improved performance, in turn, is crucial to narrowing the achievement gap between Black and Latino students and their counterparts (Darling-Hammond, 2006).

The Study

Between 2006 and 2009, the Metropolitan Center for Urban Education at New York University collected data in seven all-male schools located in four different urban locations to describe the experiences of Black and Latino males within these schools. The study collected data from myriad sources including teachers. This chapter draws from a smaller study that used teacher interview, focus group interview, and classroom observation data from three of the original seven schools to answer the following questions:

1. What do teachers interviewed in the study perceive as the instructional needs of their students?
2. What instructional practices were characteristic as reported in the teacher interview, focus group, and classroom observation data?
3. Did variation occur between reported instructional needs and observed practice? If so, in what areas?

Cross- and within-case qualitative data analysis were used to examine the relationship between what teachers said students needed instructionally and teachers' practice and the discrepancies that occurred between reported needs and practice. Five main steps were taken during analysis: (a) Interview transcripts were read and coded, (b) information was sorted by code within each school, (c) "incidences" in classroom observations were tallied and charted, (d) data were analyzed in each case, and (e) data were analyzed across the three cases.

Data Sources

Teachers and their approach to providing relevance in their curriculum are the focus of this chapter; therefore, the data being examined centered on teachers' perceptions of students' need for relevance and their approaches to including relevance in their curriculum. Drawing from 13 teacher interviews, 6 teacher focus group interviews, and 49 classroom observations, data from three of the schools in the original study were analyzed to determine how teachers define the instructional needs of their students and to contextualize the practice exhibited by teachers in the classroom.

Teacher and observational data were obtained from three schools. All were all-male schools located in large, U.S. cities. They schools served low-income students and were what Darling-Hammond (2006) referred to as majority minority. The first was located in a Midwestern city and opened in 2006. At the time of data collection, the school had a population of 565: 98% were Black, 15% were in special education classes, 84% qualified for free or reduced lunch, and 25% were proficient on the state English exam. The second school was located in an Atlantic Coast city and opened in 2004. At the time of data collection, the school had a population of 449: 57% were Black, 30% were Latino, 22% were in special education classes, 71% qualified for free or reduced lunch, and 52% were proficient on the state math exam. The third school was located in the same Atlantic Coast city as the second school. It opened in 2006 and had a population of 120: 96% were Black, 3% were Latino, 26% were in special education classes, 91% qualified for free or reduced lunch, 19% were proficient on the state English exam, and 11% were proficient on the state math exam.

Teachers Discuss Students' Need for Relevance

One pertinent theme to emerge from teacher interview and focus group transcripts was the need to gain awareness of students' personal interests to inform curriculum design. Teachers developed their understanding of students in two different ways. One teacher took a very direct approach and asked students what they were interested in and wanted to learn in class. Two other teachers took a more subtle approach and engaged in simple, personal conversations with students about a variety of topics that were not related to school. One teacher exemplified taking a simple approach to finding out what interests students:

> I would say I think that any good teaching you should be aware of your students and try to use [what] you can. I find myself, like, I do talk a lot about my experiences in my life, and let them do the same, when they can tap into where we're going, where we're going towards.

Another teacher was curious about specific interests like music and movies, information he reported as "trivial." Although he suggested that he was conversing with students about what "some might think [are] trivial things," he was correct in believing otherwise. Knowledge of students increases pedagogical content knowledge, or more specifically, what Ball, Thames, and Phelps (2008) referred to as knowledge of content and students. This knowledge helps teachers plan curriculum, including choosing models or exemplars and predicting where students might need further clarification (Ball et al., 2008;

Shulman, 1986). The questions and conversations described by teachers in the interview transcripts were simple, and perhaps "trivial," as one teacher suggested; however, this is a notable finding that encourages teachers to use such simple methods within their class structure to acquire the details necessary to individualize curriculum. This particular kind of curricular relevance—that is connected to students' personal experiences and interests—serves to motivate and engage students and increases student buy-in, all of which enhance student learning (Boykin & Noguera, 2011; Cohen et al., 2006). This is especially true for Black and Latino males (Ladson-Billings, 2011; Tatum, 2008).

Another theme to unfold from teacher focus groups and interviews was the need to link abstract concepts and content in curriculum to students' culture or community. One teacher provided several suggestions from her science class; she reported using "sickle cell anemia, which affects primarily Black people and…some of the things like high blood pressure and diabetes that affect Black people differently than White people." These topics are applicable to the 99% Black population at the school. This teacher not only demonstrated strong pedagogical content knowledge in her ability to make her coursework relevant to her students' community (Ball et al., 2008; Shulman, 1986), but she was also culturally responsive with her choices by creating an opportunity for students to "see themselves," or at least their community, in the curriculum (Gay, 2000; Ladson-Billings, 2009; Moll, Amanti, Neff, & Gonzalez, 1992). This finding is closely related to the previous finding that proposed infusing students' interests and experiences into curriculum, but it involves making connections on a slightly larger scale—that of community and culture. This approach is beneficial in that it creates an opportunity for students to learn about their world beyond the self, leading to critical consciousness, which is so pivotal to an emancipatory education such as critical pedagogy (Freire, 2009). Considering the example of diabetes that the aforementioned teacher shared, increased awareness of the cultural idiosyncrasies associated with the disease would engage students in learning and then ideally motivate them to take action. Of course, making community- or cultural-level associations has its limitations. Rarely are classrooms homogeneous, and caution must be applied so as to not isolate students who do not belong to the example community. In these instances, solutions such as comparing/contrasting multiple models or allowing students to investigate the issue within their own communities would resolve the limitation.

A prevalent theme that materialized in teacher interview transcripts is infusing real-world relevance to curriculum content taught out of context.

A prime example is a math teacher who engaged students using the notion of profit and loss rather than merely discussing positive and negative numbers:

> So my kids don't understand. I was teaching integers, okay, on a number line. They had no idea in the sixth grade the differences between positive and negative numbers for the most part. Not the whole class, right? That then I apply that to profit and loss when you're balancing a budget, they get it. So I think that's just a strategy, but I think that's enriching…because you're going to find profit and loss through your everyday, adult life, as opposed to negative and positive integers on a number line. So I think it's being able to take what the basic is, okay, and even if they haven't mastered it, applying it to something that happens in their real world day to day that they can understand. Because otherwise they shut off from it.

With the infused context, learning about integers became a more tangible concept for students. Students could draw from previous experiences with money and budgeting as a visual representation of the abstract mathematical term. The math teacher described this process as an "enriching strategy," since students could draw from examples of profit and loss from real life, such as living within a realistic budget—an extension of this assignment she completed with students. Thus, a second feature of infusing relevance is maximizing transference skills from one social context to another. Data drawn from the previous example and from three other teacher interviews demonstrate a second thematic strand: the role of making real-life connections to enable transference of knowledge. When students are able to apply the concept learned to life beyond the classroom, the ability to retain and transfer that learning also increases as students activate schemata (Lee, 2005; Villegas & Lucas, 2002). As such, a key finding about relevance from this research is a scaffolding approach devised through narrative interaction in participatory sets at the start of a unit. Interview transcripts demonstrate that teachers would introduce the terminology to be learned, followed by a story of how it relates to real life. Next, the teachers would ask students to come up with their personal examples. As the lessons for the unit proceeded, the personalized examples remained a grounding metaphor that students could recall whenever the abstract terminology became elusive. In this way, teachers were effective at making relevant connections to the real world to assist their students in building bridges between real life and new knowledge.

A notable finding made apparent through a closer examination of the data was that some teachers were ineffective at making explicit associations between curricular relevance and academic performance. As the data convey, teachers in the study understood the need for curricular relevance in the classroom but didn't directly report how students would benefit academically. One teacher exemplified this loose connection by suggesting that students need to be stimulated. On closer examination of the transcript, it is clear that when he used the term *stimulate*, he was referring to either motivating or engaging students. Another teacher in the study conveyed the importance of finding what makes students "tick," which also indicated engagement. Indeed, motivation and engagement are necessary components for raising student achievement (Boykin & Noguera, 2011; Cohen et al., 2006; Heath, 2009), but teachers in the study did not make such complete parallels. Data suggest that these teachers have only a superficial understanding of the advantages of curricular relevance. This finding warrants more exploration into the implications of teachers understanding what they need to do but insufficiently understanding why.

Additionally, the transcripts suggested a focus on motivation and engagement for the purpose of improved behavior. Case in point: The teacher who used the word stimulate previously stated that his students needed "instant gratification," placing emphasis on their need to be immediately fulfilled or pleased. A behavior focus is of particular concern because of its congruence with a "pedagogy of poverty" (Haberman, 1991; Kohn, 2011). Haberman first wrote of this pedagogy of poverty in 1991 in his influential article of the same title. He described the pedagogy as replete with low-level thinking activities and teacher-centered instruction in conjunction with a focus on routine and accountability to control behavior. Teachers in the study focused on engaging students, which is pertinent and leads to increased achievement (Boykin & Noguera, 2011), but the teachers stopped short of noting academic benefits such as a deep understanding of curriculum and improved problem solving through cultural connections to content, noted by Lee (2005).

Four key findings surfaced from teacher interview and focus group transcripts. First, teachers in the study discussed gaining awareness of students' personal interests and experiences through simple measures such as a quick, reciprocal conversation, and then they used the information to scaffold curriculum with relevant connections. Second, teachers similarly proposed supporting curriculum with cultural associations. Third, teachers suggested using real-life anecdotes and examples as a bridge to new learning. Last, some teachers exhibited superficial understanding of the advantages of curricular relevance that did not extend to academic benefits. Next we look at classroom observation data to determine how effective teachers in the study were at including curricular relevance in the observed classes.

The Discrepancy

Although teachers in the study reported relevance as the most prevalent theme needed by students, it was not well represented in classroom observations. In the three case study schools, 37 teachers participated in either individual interviews or focus groups (or both). Of these 37 teachers, 14 (37%) were quoted recommending relevance for their students. Furthermore, 108 quotes that involved teachers speaking of their students' instructional needs were pulled from interview and focus group transcripts. Of these, 29 (26%) involved relevancy (see Figure 8.1).

To examine classroom practice relative to curricular relevance, classroom observations were coded and tallied; then evidence of the themes that emerged, in this case, relevance, were tracked through the classroom observation data, recorded, and counted. Instruction noted in observations included discussions, questioning, reading, writing, worksheets, hands-on activities, and multimodal curriculum; these noted instructional tasks were termed incidences. In total, 365 incidences were recorded in 49 classroom observations. Unfortunately, relevance was noted in only 35 incidences (9.5%) out of the 381 total recorded. Taking a close look at the numbers—the teachers who were both interviewed and observed—relevance was noted in about half of the classes, but according to total numbers of incidences, 19 out of 173, relevant instruction was noted only 11% of the time (see Figure 8.1).

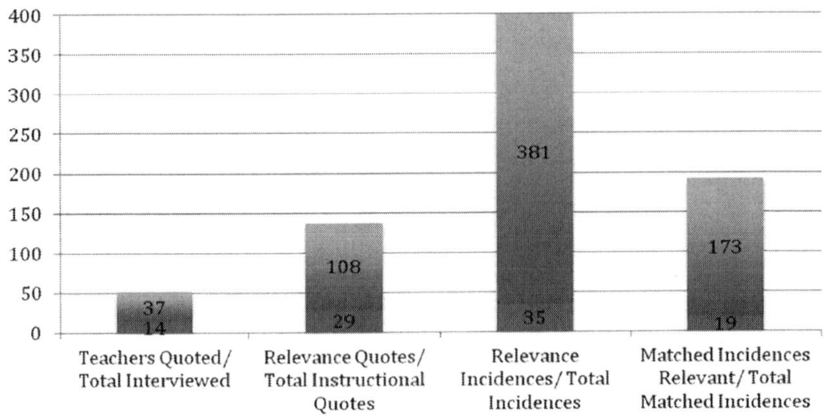

Figure 8.1. Prominence of Relevance in Interviews and Observations.

A closer examination of classroom observation data helps provide a more detailed description of instruction in the case study schools. The instruction described in classroom observations varied, as the numbers suggest. Some teachers provided examples of relevance. For instance, one teacher chose a book that engaged students in both reading and discussion, most likely due to its exploration of teenage relationships and manhood. Observations also showed teachers providing warm-up prompts that included connections to the self and the real world. One example of this involved a teacher who had students listen to a public radio story and then asked questions such as, "How does what you hear affect your life?" "How does what you hear make you feel?" "What can you 'do'?" Such questions inspire students to make personal connections, as well as consider their place in the world. Another teacher used cars in equations students were solving about the scientific concept of momentum. It is not clear if his choice to use cars in this manner was meant to engage students or make the content more applicable to the world outside his class; either way, the content was presumably more relevant to the students.

There was also a notable lack of relevance in instruction. In several classes, students were reading and responding to comprehension questions and solving equations on worksheets. Sometimes they "corrected" their responses during class time to make sure their answer was right. In these classes, there were few discussions that connected students' work to larger concepts or the world outside of school. For example, one observer noted the following:

> Most of the instruction took place over answers in the textbook and homework, a lot of factual information and questions were covered (with a side focus on explaining vocabulary words) and not much discussion was had. Even when the topic of uniforms came up and students seemed engaged and there was possibility for a good discussion, she moved on[,] which seemed to favor coverage over meaningful discussions.

This notation seemed to typify much of the observed instruction.

Teachers were also observed lecturing students. One science teacher, who said in her interview that students needed content that connected to the real world, even suppressed students from asking questions during her lecture. When one student attempted to solicit information that would have helped him and his classmates make a real-world connection to the information being disseminated, the teacher said there would be no questions. In interviews, this teacher said the following:

> In terms of the Science it is not connecting. And right now, I think part of the battle is in Science is, like, should it be content driven or should it be inquiry driven[,] where inquiry they learn by doing or content where, you know, they have to memorize it and know it. And the problem is everyone wants to do inquiry, but the state test they just took it was memorization. You know what I'm saying? So like you had to know it. So there's, like, this conflict. Like—how am I supposed to teach it for them to get it? Like I can do inquiry-based learning which they like, it's creative, they can do projects. But if that doesn't get them all the content, you know what I'm saying? Then I just don't know what the balance is right now. And right now I lean more on they need to know the content which, you know, those, those, those aren't necessarily the classes they enjoy the most.

She was clearly impacted by expectations to cover content on the state exam, and these expectations compelled her to lecture as opposed to doing an inquiry-based project or lab.

For the most part, it is not possible to determine exactly why teachers in the case study schools were not providing more relevance in the curriculum. Perhaps they lacked control over curriculum design and were unable to customize it to their students' need for relevance. In the current testing climate that emphasizes standardization, individualization is a challenge, especially if teachers need to align curriculum with specific tests (McNeil, 2003). Many urban schools are requiring teachers to focus only on content and skills that will be tested, and in some cases, teachers are required to teach a specific curriculum that determines their daily practice—this predicament was noted by the aforementioned science teacher who chose to lecture to cover more content (McNeil, 2003). In these situations, it is challenging to consider students' personal interests and culture and make curriculum authentic or applicable to the real world.

Additionally troubling to the lack of relevance in the case study schools was the emphasis on teacher-centered instruction. The classroom observation data exposed a prominence of direct instruction that emphasized a recall of knowledge and lacked critical thinking. Many incidences involved teachers asking students fact-based questions, discussions that were teacher-centered and teacher-led, and worksheets that involved fact recall or practicing skills out of context. Such curriculum is consistent with the poor quality curriculum that is prevalent in urban schools and is one cause of the persistent underachievement of low-income Black and Latino males (Darling-Hammond, 2011; Haberman, 1991). Such low quality curriculum in the case study schools speaks to a lack of teacher effectiveness that is pervasive in many urban schools, which are often characterized by a pedagogy of poverty (Darling-Hammond, 2006; Haberman, 1991; Kohn, 2011). Teachers in such schools emphasize memorization and recall of knowledge, out-of-context skill and procedure drill, and behavior management (Haberman, 1991; Kohn, 2011). Although ample research exists that such methods are ineffective, teachers in urban schools are pressured to conform to such methods, resulting in a stubborn reproduction of ineffective curriculum and poor achievement outcomes (Haberman, 1991; Kohn, 2011). This stubborn reproduction is consistent with institutional pressure from society and other factors that make it difficult for teachers or schools to fight against the status quo (Anyon, 1981; Bourdieu & Passeron, 2011; Carnoy & Levin, 1985). The aforementioned science teacher who felt pressure to lecture content on the state exam would be an example of this. This is a matter of concern in light of current policy in RTTT that will evaluate teachers in part based on students' test scores (Boser, 2012; Duncan, 2009; "Race to the Top Program Executive Summary," 2009; Weiss, 2013).

The lack of teacher effectiveness at providing relevance in the case study schools is disappointing given that the teachers understood the need for it. Furthermore, ample research supports the need for relevance in curriculum (Ladson-Billings, 2009; King & Gurian, 2006; Matusevich et al., 2009; Tatum, 2008; Villegas & Lucas, 2002). Although relevance is well-supported by research, and teachers in the study reported the need for relevance in their schools, it failed to be a predominantly observed component of teacher practice.

Teachers interviewed in the study were aware of students' needs or at least their need for relevancy in the curriculum. Their limited success at providing this need points to teachers struggling to be effective in a setting that serves low-income Black and Latino males. It would be easy to place blame on teachers here, but they should not shoulder the responsibility for improving instruction all on their own. Teachers in the study understood the importance of scaffolding curriculum with relevance, but then there was a disconnect somewhere. Perhaps some fault lies in the difficulty of translating theory into practice. Consider one of the findings from this study: some teachers were noted having only a superficial understanding of the academic benefits of curricular relevance. Their recommendations to provide relevancy primarily focused on students' needing to be engaged and motivated— more of a behavior focus than an academic one. In this case, researchers need to place more emphasis on creating ways to improve curriculum that are accessible to teachers who do not have time to read academic journals that outline research findings. Teachers need support and guidance within their already busy schedule, not as an add-on. Furthermore, if teachers understand what their students need, but those needs are not addressed in their practice, it is additionally necessary to determine what is impacting teacher effectiveness.

The Question of the Disconnect

The discrepancy between needs and practice shows that teachers in the case study schools were not effective at practicing what they said their students needed. More specifically, few observations showed evidence of teachers providing relevance in the classroom. Unfortunately, based on the available data, the reasons why teachers were not able to provide more relevance for students remain incomplete. It is possible that teachers, like the science teacher observed in the study, struggled to balance testing expectations with more meaningful work or that they did not know how to develop projects that considered both content and students' interests. In an environment where teachers are being evaluated based on student progress, they cannot ignore the significance of such exams (Darling-Hammond, 2011; "Race to the Top Program Executive Summary," 2009).

We do know that the teachers in the classroom observations were not effective at providing the curricular relevance that was reported as a need in interviews and focus groups. Although it was the most commonly reported need in interviews in the study, few incidences in classroom observations showed evidence of relevance in curriculum—only about 10%. Students were provided with limited opportunities to think critically about their world, something that is crucial to an emancipatory education outlined in critical pedagogy (Freire, 2009; Giroux, 1988; Sleeter & McLaren, 1995). On the contrary, evidence pointed to a pedagogy of poverty—low-level thinking, out-of-context work, memorization, and regurgitation—that is frequently reproduced in urban schools, although research and student achievement point to such a pedagogy's lack of effectiveness (Darling-Hammond, 2006; Haberman, 1991; Kohn, 2011).

Although it is not possible to determine with certainty from this study what is impacting teachers' ability to incorporate what they know students need into their practice, it is a concern that should not be taken lightly. Black and Latino males have suffered the effects of poor instruction for too long (Darling-Hammond, 2006, 2011; Haberman, 1991). These effects include being at the underperforming end of the achievement gap and high dropout, unemployment, and incarceration rates (Darling-Hammond, 2006).

There is no question that instruction needs to improve in struggling schools, such as many of those that serve low-income Black and Latino males, but efforts should be made to determine the best way to proceed. If teachers understand what needs to be done, like the teachers interviewed in this study, but struggle to do it, we need to determine why the struggle exists. To improve the teaching force, teaching needs to be effective (Darling-Hammond, 2011), and to do this, we need to work directly with teachers to determine how best to help them incorporate what they know students need into their practice.

Improving practice is especially crucial at a time when academic demands are increasing through the adoption of the Common Core State Standards, while teachers are simultaneously being evaluated based in part on student outcomes on state exams (Duncan, 2009; Porter, McMaken, Hwang, & Yang, 2011; "Race to the Top Program Executive Summary," 2009). To meet the needs of students who are underachieving, such as many low-income Black and Latino males, teachers will need to increase opportunities for critical thinking and cognitive demand while potentially feeling compelled to cover content on exams that is part of their teacher evaluation (Boser, 2012; Duncan, 2009; Porter et al., 2011; "Race to the Top Program Executive Summary," 2009).

As expectations increase, curricular relevance can help. Relevance supports students academically by building bridges between what students know and new content (Boykin & Noguera, 2011). Curricular relevance also encourages active engagement and greater student buy-in (Boykin & Noguera, 2011). Teachers in the study knew relevance was an important consideration in instruction for their students. Research supports their knowledge. Now it is time to create opportunities for relevance to have a prominent place in the classroom. These opportunities would include teacher development but also policy changes that align expectations of cognitive demand with valid assessments, along with teacher supports that outweigh narrow measures of accountability and effectiveness.

References

Alvermann, D. E. (2002). Effective literacy instruction for adolescents. *Journal of Literacy Research, 34*(2), 189–208.

Anyon, J. (1981). Social class and school knowledge. *Curriculum Inquiry, 11*(1), 3–42.

Au, W. (2007). High-stakes testing and curricular control: A qualitative metasynthesis. *Educational Researcher, 36*(5), 258–267.

Ball, D. L., Thames, M. H., & Phelps, G. (2008). Content knowledge for teaching: What makes it special? *Journal of Teacher Education, 59*(5), 389–407.

Boser, U. (2012). *Race to the top: What have we learned from the states so far? A state-by-state evaluation of race to the top performance.* Retrieved from http://www.americanprogress.org

Bourdieu, P., & Passeron, J. (2011). *Reproduction in education, society and culture.* Thousand Oaks, CA: Sage.

Boykin, W. A., & Noguera, P. (2011). *Creating the opportunity to learn: Moving from research to practice to close the achievement gap.* Alexandria, VA: ASCD.

Cammarota, J. (2004). The gendered and racialized pathways of Latina and Latino youth: Different struggles, different resistances in the urban context. *Anthropology & Education Quarterly, 35*(1), 53–74.

Carnoy, M., & Levin, H. (1985). *School and work in the democratic state.* Stanford, CA: Stanford University Press.

Cohen, G. L., Garcia, J., Apfel, N., & Master, A. (2006). Reducing the racial achievement gap: A social-psychological intervention. *Science, 313*(5791), 1307–1310.

Cordova, D. I., & Lepper, M. R. (1996). Intrinsic motivation and the process of learning: Beneficial effects of contextualization, personalization, and choice. *Journal of Educational Psychology, 88*(4), 715–730.

Darling-Hammond, L. (2006). Securing the right to learn: Policy and practice for powerful teaching and learning. *Educational Researcher, 35*(7), 13–24.

Darling-Hammond, L. (2011). Effective teaching as a civil right: How building instructional capacity can help close the achievement gap. *Voice in Urban Education, 31* (Fall):44–58.

Duncan, A. (2009, June 14). *States will lead the way towards reform.* Speech presented at the Governors Education Symposium, Cary, NC.

Freire, P. (2009). *Pedagogy of the oppressed.* New York, NY: Continuum.

Gay, G. (Ed.). (2000). *Culturally responsive teaching: Theory, research, and practice.* New York, NY: Teachers College Press.

Giroux, H. A. (1988). *Teachers as intellectuals: Toward a critical pedagogy of learning.* Westport, CT: Bergin & Garvey.

Haberman, M. (1991). The pedagogy of poverty versus good teaching. *Phi Delta Kappan, 73,* 290–294.

Heath, S. B. (2009). *Ways with words: Language, life, and work in communities and classrooms.* New York, NY: Cambridge University Press.

Holzman, M., Jackson, J., Beaudry, A., Dexter, E., & Watson, K. T. (2012). *The urgency of now: The Schott Foundation 50 state report on black males and public education.* Cambridge, MA: Schott Foundation.

King, K., & Gurian, M. (2006). Teaching to the minds of boys. *Educational Leadership, 64*(1), 56–58, 60–61.

Kohn, A. (2011, April 27). Poor teaching for poor children…in the name of reform. *Education Week.* Retrieved from http://www.alfiekohn.org/teaching/edweek/poor.htm

Ladson-Billings, G. (1995). Toward a theory of culturally relevant pedagogy. *American Educational Research Journal, 32*(3), 465–491.

Ladson-Billings, G. (2009). *The dreamkeepers: Successful teachers of African American children.* San Francisco, CA: Jossey-Bass.

Ladson-Billings, G. (2011). Boyz to men? Teaching to restore black boys' childhood. *Race, Ethnicity and Education, 14*(1), 7–15.

Lee, C. D. (2005). Signifying in the zone of proximal development. In C. D. Lee & P. Smagorinsky (Eds.), *Vygotskian perspectives on literacy research* (pp. 191–225). New York, NY: Cambridge University Press.

Matusevich, M. N., O'Connor, K. A., & Hargett, M. P. (2009). The nonnegotiables of academic rigor. *Gifted Child Today, 32*(4), 44–52.

McNeil, L. (2003). The educational costs of standardization. In L. Christensen & S. Karp (Eds.), *Rethinking school reform: Views from the classroom* (pp. 215–224). Milwaukee, WI: Rethinking Schools.

Moje, E., & Hinchman, K. (2004). Culturally responsive practices for youth literacy learning. In T. Jetton & J. Dole (Eds.), *Adolescent literacy research and practice* (pp. 321–350). New York, NY: Guilford Press.

Moje, E. B., Overby, M., Tysvaer, N., & Morris, K. (2008). The complex world of adolescent literacy: Myths, motivations, and mysteries. *Harvard Educational Review, 78*(1), 107–154.

Moll, L. C., Amanti, C., Neff, D., & Gonzalez, N. (1992). Funds of knowledge for teaching: Using a qualitative approach to connect homes and classrooms. *Theory into Practice, 31*(2), 132–141.

National Center for Education Statistics (NCES), U.S. Department of Education. (2010). *The condition of education 2010.* Washington, DC: Author.

National Institute for Literacy (NIL). (2007). *What content-area teachers should know about adolescent literacy.* Washington, DC: Author.

Nicholson-Crotty, S., Birchmeier, Z., & Valentine, D. (2009). Exploring the impact of school discipline on racial disproportion in the juvenile justice system. *Social Science Quarterly, 90*(4), 1003–1018.

Noguera, P., & Hurtado, A. (2012). Invisible no more: The status and experience of Latino males from multidisciplinary perspectives. In P. Noguera, A. Hurtado, & E. Fergus (Eds.), *Invisible no more: Understanding the disenfranchisement of Latino men and boys* (pp. 1–15). New York, NY: Routledge.

Noguera, P., Hurtado, A., & Fergus, E. (2012). What we have learned: The role of public policy in promoting macro- and micro-levels of intervention in response to the challenges confronting Latino men. In P. Noguera, A. Hurtado, & E. Fergus (Eds.), *Invisible no more: Understanding the disenfranchisement of Latino men and boys* (pp. 302–312). New York, NY: Routledge.

Orfield, G., Losen, D., Wald, J., & Swanson, C. B. (2004). *Losing our future: How minority youth are being left behind the graduation rate crisis.* Cambridge, MA: Harvard University.

Porter, A., McMaken, J., Hwang, J., & Yang, R. (2011). Common Core standards: The new U.S. intended curriculum. *Educational Researcher, 40*(3), 103–116.

Race to the Top Program Executive Summary. (2009). Washington, DC: U.S. Department of Education.

Reed, J. H., Schallert, D. L., Beth, A. D., & Woodruff, A. L. (2004). Motivated reader, engaged writer: The role of motivation in the literate acts of adolescents. In T. Jetton & J. Dole (Eds.), *Adolescent literacy research and practice* (pp. 251–282). New York, NY: Guilford Press.

Shulman, L. S. (1986). Those who understand: Knowledge growth in teaching. *Educational Researcher, 15*(2), 4–14.

Sleeter, C., & McLaren, P. (1995). *Multicultural education, critical pedagogy, and the politics of difference*. Albany: State University of New York Press.

Smith, C. D. (2009). Deconstructing the pipeline: Evaluating school-to-prison pipeline equal protection cases through a structural racism framework. *Fordham Urban Law Journal, 36*(5), 1009–1049.

Tatum, A. W. (2008). Toward a more anatomically complete model of literacy instruction: A focus on African American male adolescents and texts. *Harvard Educational Review, 78*(1), 155–180.

Thompson, G. L. (Ed.). (2004). *Through ebony eyes: What teachers need to know but are afraid to ask about African American students*. San Francisco, CA: Jossey-Bass.

Torres, M., & Fergus, E. (2012). Social mobility and the complex status of Latino males: Education, employment, and incarceration patterns from 2000–2009. In P. Noguera, A. Hurtado, & E. Fergus (Eds.), *Invisible no more: Understanding the disenfranchisement of Latino men and boys* (pp. 19–40). New York, NY: Routledge.

Villegas, A. M., & Lucas, T. (2002). Preparing culturally responsive teachers: Rethinking the curriculum. *Journal of Teacher Education, 53*(1), 20–32.

Weiss, E. (2013, September 12). Mismatches in race to the top limit educational improvement: Lack of time, resources, and tools to address opportunity gaps puts lofty state goals out of reach. Retrieved from http://www.epi.org/publication/race-to-the-top-goals/

· 9 ·

ALIGNING MULTIDIMENSIONAL TEACHER EVALUATION WITH PROFESSIONAL DEVELOPMENT CENTERED ON ENGLISH LANGUAGE LEARNERS

Haiwen Chu and Gloria Rodríguez Bañuelos

From the perspective of a long-standing, comprehensive teacher professional development program focused on apprenticing teachers in developing expertise over time, we critique existing teacher evaluation systems in terms of both content and process. In terms of content, we assert that existing definitions of "effective" teachers and student outcomes are narrow and misleading. In terms of process, we argue that teacher evaluation embodies and perpetuates inequitable, hierarchical power relations while providing insufficient supports for sustained and generative teacher growth. We examine three cases: federal policies concerning teacher evaluation, a specific evaluation system used widely in Texas, and an alternative system that we are developing with a specific school in Texas.

In this chapter, we explore a model of teacher expertise that is organized into six interconnected domains. These domains are vision, motivation, reflection, knowledge, practice, and context (Walqui, 2008). For each domain, we critique federal and state policies and teacher evaluation systems and suggest alternatives. Vision refers not just to beliefs about the nature of teaching and of students as capable individuals but also to images of students' potential futures. Motivation refers to the reasons and emotions that teachers bring to the work of teaching and incentives for their continued engagement and growth. Reflection in its multiple forms allows teachers to reason about the past, adapt in the present, and plan for the future. In terms of knowledge, although many forms of knowledge are relevant, we analyze what counts as forms of pedagogical knowledge in regard to student outcomes. The domain of practice, while closely connected to each of these other domains, is most directly incorporated into teacher evaluation systems through classroom observation protocols and scoring rubrics. Finally, the domain of context refers to the professional communities in which teachers work and contains our analysis of the power relations and opportunities for professional growth provided by teacher evaluation.

We explore the promise of an innovative, comprehensive system of teacher evaluation closely aligned with sustained professional development. Recent Arrivals Secondary School (RASS) in a metropolitan school district in Texas serves newly arrived immigrant students in Grades 6 through 9. As part of a transformation School Improvement Grant, RASS is engaged in whole-school change with the Quality Teaching for English Learners (QTEL) initiative at WestEd. Teachers participate in intensive professional development and instructional coaching aimed at ripening the potential of English language learners (ELLs). QTEL draws on sociocultural theories of learning and teaching to develop teacher expertise that enables the design and implementation of instruction that embodies the five principles of QTEL. These principles serve as the basis for an instrument for classroom observation that guides teachers' professional growth. These classroom observations are more focused on challenging and supporting ELLs than existing teacher evaluation systems. The new teacher evaluation system draws on these evaluations together with teacher portfolios of annotated student work.

Our analysis of federal and state policies is informed by critiques of neoliberal education "reform" as part of conservative modernization (Apple, 2006). The diffusion of the policies in No Child Left Behind (NCLB) and Race to the Top (RTTT) has had a strange career in Texas. On the one hand, the Texas accountability system of the 1990s is frequently considered to have been the model on which NCLB was built (Vasquez Heilig & Darling-Hammond, 2008), and RTTT has accelerated the targeting of teachers for punitive actions based on test scores (Mangiante, 2011). Texas, however, has not participated in either RTTT or the Common Core State Standards. In this sense, Texas provides a particularly interesting case, as it embodies an older system of accountability and academic standards that has not tied teacher evaluation to test scores. At the same time, the Texas state legislature has recently reduced the number of exams required for high school graduation.

In the late 1990s, Texas was one of the first states to implement a statewide system of teacher evaluation known as the Professional Development Appraisal System (PDAS; Texas Education Agency, 2005). Teachers are rated on a 4-point scale on 50 standards organized in eight domains (see Table 1). On each standard, teachers are rated as "exceeds expectations," "proficient," "below expectations," or "unsatisfactory." These ratings are then aggregated to generate a rating for each of the eight domains. Teachers must receive a proficient rating on each of the eight domains to continue teaching. Compared to other states with performance-based teacher evaluation systems, the PDAS has relatively low levels of data triangulation, relying on only three kinds of data: classroom observation, teacher self-report, and summative administrator evaluation (Shakman et al., 2012).

Vision: Images of ELLs and Their Futures

The domain of vision includes teachers' images of who their students currently are but also their promise. With ELLs as a specific focal group, it is particularly telling that the federal label for the group is "Limited English Proficient." This label focuses on a deficit, rather than the promise that students possess. Although some have argued that NCLB made strides in equity by forcing states and districts to attend to academic achievement, studies have also shown that increased emphasis on ELLs as a subgroup for school sanctions may have led to practices that minimize the impact on school accountability status (Vasquez Heilig & Darling-Hammond, 2008). For NCLB, ELLs are primarily framed by a deficit that needs to be overcome so that they can pass tests (Menken, 2008).

Indeed, some scholars have suggested alternative framings to "limited English proficient." While historically the term "language minority children" pointed at the demographic realities, this term is quickly becoming outdated and inaccurate in light of shifting population trends. But even such a term as "English language learner" does not capture the promise of children who begin their lives at home speaking a language other than English. For this reason, "emergent bilingual" has served to emphasize the promise that these learners have in terms of becoming bilingual, biliterate, and bicultural partic-ipants in society (Garcia & Kleifgen, 2010).

Although ELLs are both a large and rapidly growing demographic group, especially in Texas (Flores, Batalova, & Fix, 2012), most teacher evaluation systems treat ELLs as an afterthought. In many settings, programs are de-signed so that teachers called ELL specialists "push-in" to mixed classes to provide additional services to ELL students. These push-in ELL specialists are evaluated inconsistently, and there is significant variation in terms of what states require of such specialists (Holheide, Goe, Croft, & Reschly, 2010). The classroom observation protocols lack standards that focus on meeting the needs of ELLs. In Texas, although there is an additional state certification exam for English as a Second Language (ESL; Texas Education Agency, 2011), classroom observations under PDAS do not directly address the instructional needs of ELLs. The other major component of teacher evaluation systems consists of student test scores, and these scores fail to ac-count for the multiple challenges that accompany testing ELLs (e.g., Abedi, 2004; Hopkins, Thompson, Linquanti, Hakuta, & August, 2013; Solano-Flores & Trumbull, 2003).

Motivation: Reasons and Incentives

The system of accountability pioneered in Texas and disseminated through the federal NCLB act draws heavily on audit culture (Apple, 2006), which cen-ters on the bureaucratic inspection as a means of asserting control. In NCLB, these controls were put into law as school-level sanctions based on students' test scores, so the monitoring of individual teachers' classroom practices was left to the discretion of administrators. In the Texas context, Torres (2012) conducted a cross-case analysis of teachers' experiences with the PDAS using a Foucauldian lens of surveillance and discipline/punishment. These practices are detailed more in the context section.

RTTT has brought further prominence to financial incentives for teacher performance as largely defined by test scores, accelerating the trend by shift-ing the emphasis to "effective" teachers, determined by "student growth" (Mangiante, 2011). As states have applied for RTTT grants, they have mostly defined and measured growth in terms of student performance on state standardized exams. In many cases, student growth is based on value-added models that are problematic both practically and methodologically

(Darling-Hammond, Amrein-Beardsley, Haertel, & Rothstein, 2011). Despite these concerns, these scores are a large component of evaluation systems, with more than 20 states weighing student growth between 35% and 55% of a teacher's rating (Baker, Oluwole, & Green, 2013). Student test scores have been further linked to performance-based pay schemes, even though multiple studies have repeatedly failed to demonstrate an impact on student achievement (Glazerman & Seifullah, 2012; Springer et al., 2010; Springer et al., 2009).

Because teachers are also individuals with personal lives and positions within the school context, motivation cannot easily be incentivized with money. Teachers need to be invited to identify areas for growth not only for themselves but for their colleagues and the school at large. Taking on different roles within the school and providing support for colleagues may also be sources of motivation that cannot be quantified financially.

Reflection: Engaging in Reasoning

NCLB and RTTT are largely silent on teacher reflection. Although PDAS has a Teacher Self-Report component, the depth of this reflection is severely restricted in practice. Torres (2012) reported that teachers' contributions are framed as responses to the evaluation and observation reports written by administrators, which in turn are more heavily weighted within the process. Although teachers are asked to participate in discussions and conferences, the room for genuine reflection is minimal and generally highlights the imbalance within the hierarchy rather than a focus on the problems of instructional practice (Torres, 2012).

These silences on reflection leave out a powerful tool for teacher practice and growth (Walqui, 2008). Reflection provides a means for teachers to reason through their experiences and develop practical wisdom before, during, and after the act of teaching. First, teachers can engage in *anticipatory* reflection in which they predict, given where their students are, what might constrain their learning and what supports might accelerate their ability to learn. During teaching, teachers reflect "on the spot," responding contingently to students' actions and interactions to adjust instruction and guide it toward instructional goals. This kind of *active/interactive* reflection is a form of reflection in action. After a particular classroom episode, teachers can engage in *recollective* reflection, revisiting those past events to glean lessons to inform future practice. Put together, these forms of reflection become embodied as mindfulness, the accumulated wisdom of practice that allows teachers to exercise professional and practical judgment. In all cases, what students do and what they are capable of doing with the appropriate supports and invitations are always at the center of the process of reflection. To engage in these forms of reflection, teachers need time, purposefully designed and structured opportunities, and clearly defined lenses through which to look forward, at, and backward on their practice in the classroom. These notions of reflection go well beyond the usual conception of reflection, which focuses on its recollective aspect. In the sense named here, reflection extends into forms of pedagogical reasoning and thinking.

Knowledge: Uniting Content and Pedagogy

Although Walqui (2008) catalogued many interrelated forms of knowledge, including general pedagogical knowledge, pedagogical content knowledge, knowledge of students, and knowledge of self, in this section we critique subject matter knowledge as it is conceived of and evaluated by NCLB, RTTT, and PDAS. In a later section, we offer a more nuanced approach to knowledge, including how it should be experienced by students and ELLs in particular, drawing attention instead to the interplay between academic rigor and language focus.

Teacher certification and teacher education have traditionally focused primarily on the domain of subject matter knowledge or "content knowledge." NCLB mandated states to provide "highly qualified" teachers, defined by academic credentials, state certification, and subject matter knowledge. What counts as knowledge, however, is not ideologically neutral but rather is shaped by economic arguments about the skills that students need (Apple, 2006). This conception of subject matter knowledge is closely related to the emphasis on student achievement on standardized test scores. Test-based accountability that focuses on student test scores has tended to fragment knowledge and narrow the curriculum (Au, 2007). NCLB and RTTT have thus intensified the tendency for teachers to view their disciplines as rigidly defined bodies of facts that are sequential in nature (Grossman & Stodolsky, 1995).

Specific to the work of teaching, varied species of essential knowledge have been identified, such as pedagogical content knowledge (Shulman, 1986), pedagogical language knowledge (Galguera, 2011), and mathematics knowledge for teaching (Hill, Rowan, & Ball, 2005). Beyond these forms of pedagogical knowledge, teachers' knowledge of their students' lived experiences and multiple knowledge bases is also essential (Turner et al., 2012). We address these forms of knowledge in greater detail when we describe instructional coaching practices as well as the development of teacher pedagogical content knowledge through portfolios of student work.

Practice: Classroom Instruction

NCLB is largely silent on what classroom instruction should look like. RTTT likewise is relatively agnostic about the specific form of classroom evaluation within teacher evaluation. The PDAS system common across Texas provides multiple criteria for rating classroom observations. Table 1 displays the domains and standards for PDAS. Of these, only the first five domains are rated primarily through classroom observation. From the perspective of directly addressing the language needs of ELLs, only four of the PDAS standards highlight language or communication. These standards are italicized in Table 1. PDAS standards regarding professional communication with students do not provide any greater specificity than "appropriate and accurate." PDAS is not specific in that the four levels are distinguished by frequency descriptors: "Almost all of the time," "most of the time," "some of the time," and "less than half of the time." These are applied to specific statements that are the same across all levels, such as, "The teacher uses appropriate and accurate verbal and non-verbal communication with students." Further, it is sufficient for raters to checkmark their responses rather than to provide detailed, descriptive narratives and justifications for their ratings.

Table 9.1. Summary of the Eight Domains of the Professional Development Appraisal System (PDAS).

I) Active, Successful Student Participation in the Learning Process
  1. Engaged in learning
  2. Successful in learning
  3. Critical thinking or problem solving
  4. Self-directed
  5. Connects learning
II) Learner-Centered Instruction
  1. Goals and objectives
  2. Learner centered
  3. Critical thinking and problem solving
  4. Motivational strategies
  5. Alignment
  6. Pacing/sequencing
  7. Value and importance
  8. *Appropriate questioning and inquiry*
  9. Use of technology
III) Evaluation and Feedback on Student Progress
  1. Monitored and assessed
  2. Assessment and instruction are aligned
  3. Appropriate assessment
  4. Learning reinforced
  5. Constructive feedback
  6. Relearning and reevaluation
IV) Management of Student Discipline, Instructional Strategies, Time and Materials
  1. Discipline procedures
  2. Self-discipline and self-directed learning
  3. Equitable teacher-student interaction
  4. Expectations for behavior
  5. Redirects disruptive behavior
  6. Reinforces desired behavior
  7. Equitable and varied characteristics
  8. Manages time and materials
	V) Professional Communication
	  1. *Written with students*
	  2. *Verbal/nonverbal with students*
	  3. *Reluctant students*
	  4. Written with parents, staff, community members, and other professionals
	  5. Verbal/nonverbal with parents, staff, community members, and other professionals
	  6. Supportive, courteous
	VI) Professional Development
	  1. Campus/district goals
	  2. Student needs
	  3. Prior performance appraisal
	  4. Improvement of student performance
	VII) Compliance with Policies, Operating Procedures, and Requirements
	  1. Policies, procedures, and legal requirements
	  2. Verbal/written directives
	  3. Environment
	VIII) Improvement of Academic Performance of all Students on the Campus
	  1. Aligns instruction
	  2. Analyzes TAKS data
	  3. Appropriate sequence
	  4. Appropriate materials
	  5. Monitors student performance
	  6. Monitors attendance
	  7. Students in at-risk situations
	  8. Appropriate plans for intervention
	  9. Modifies and adapts

In contrast to relying entirely on administrator observations, we outline the potential offered by teacher portfolios, in particular those that incorporate student work. Although portfolios have been most closely associated with teacher preparation and certification, several studies have documented successful implementations for in-service teachers as part of whole-school change. Portfolios are a flexible structure that can be put to both formative and summative uses within a teacher evaluation system. A further distinction can be made between learning portfolios and assessment portfolios. A learning portfolio documents a teacher's journey of growth, documenting key moments of learning along the way. An assessment portfolio is generally more rigidly defined and structured as a performance that marks the end of a course or process, such as those required by the National Board for Professional Teaching Standards Certification (McNelly, 2002). In all cases, the purposes and uses of portfolios need to be broadly shared and understood by teachers and administrators.

One example of portfolios in teacher evaluation was in a district-wide effort (Attinello, Lare, & Waters, 2006). Both teachers and administrators reported several benefits in terms of how they viewed the portfolio process as accurate and comprehensive measures that are useful for professional growth and positioned to change practice and reflection. The main concern voiced by teachers and administrators was the amount of time required. A broader study of a larger number of small schools implementing teacher portfolios as part of evaluation found that they were able to better identify levels of performance in terms of assessment and professionalism not included in classroom observations (Tucker, Stronge, Gareis, & Beers, 2003). The benefits of portfolios can thus be summarized as including fairness, usefulness, feasibility, and accuracy. Each of these makes structures and criteria explicit and invites teachers to take an active role in how they choose to meet the requirements.

School-based portfolios also hold promise, when they are focused on specific issues and include purposeful samples of student work across different achievement levels (Xu, 2003). In the case of one school that developed teaching portfolios in an environment of trust, teachers from widely different experience levels were able to grow, take risks, and claim ownership over their professional learning (Xu, 2003). The shared task of writing portfolios also fostered developing and deepening professional relationships and collaboration among teachers, as well as between the principal and teachers.

Context: Power Relations and Professional Growth

One final domain of critique against federal and state teacher evaluation systems is the concentration of power and authority within the administrative hierarchy of school systems. The PDAS in particular was analyzed by Torres (2012) through a Foucauldian lens. Through hierarchical observation, teachers' practices are observed and monitored by their supervisors and peers. Over time, this regime of surveillance is turned inward, as normalizing judgments become self-monitored, where deviations from the behaviors dictated by the rules of the system can be documented and punished. Beyond the classroom observation, administrator evaluation, and teacher self-report, which are the three formal structures of the PDAS system, informal structures such as "walk-through" observations, "plexiglass peephole" observations, and peer observations were also part of the regime of surveillance. Teachers complained about the lack of transparency and clarity in the observation process.

In contrast to reproducing these hierarchies, one promising alternative for teacher evaluation is peer assistance and review (PAR). In contrast with hierarchical models for teacher evaluation, PAR systems draw on experienced teachers to become observers and raters of their peers' performances. The teachers are referred to as "consulting teachers" who are identified as excellent and released from their regular teaching duties to either mentor new teachers or provide interventions for tenured teachers who are identified as ineffective (Goldstein, 2004). These consulting teachers provide formative feedback and assistance to teachers throughout the school year. At the end of the school year, the consulting teachers are also centrally involved in panels that make summative personnel decisions about continuation of service.

While peer models advance teacher leadership and more distributed models of school-based decision making, the central role of the principal can persist due to cultural and institutional norms (Goldstein, 2004). Feelings of trust between teachers and their consulting teachers is also key, with low-performing teachers reporting less trust (Goldstein, 2005). One study found that the ratings generated by a school-based, peer-driven teacher evaluation system had a statistically significant impact on student achievement in reading (Gallagher, 2004). Although there was a positive but not statistically significant impact in mathematics, this difference was due in part to greater teacher and rater pedagogical knowledge and alignment to both standards and assessments. There are also benefits for "consulting teachers" who express greater efficacy, professional rejuvenation, and more of a "ladder" for professional growth within the institution (Fiarman, Johnson, Munger, Papay, & Qazilbash, 2009). Districts implementing PAR systems have saved money in terms of teacher turnover and dismissal costs (Papay & Johnson, 2012).

QTEL Professional Development

This section provides a general overview of QTEL, beginning with its broad theoretical underpinnings derived from sociocultural perspectives. Next, pedagogical scaffolding is characterized as generative practices that apprentice students into a discipline. The five principles of QTEL guide teachers in developing their practice. Finally, the model of accomplished teaching provides domains beyond knowledge and practice with which to consider teacher expertise.

QTEL draws on sociocultural perspectives on learning and teaching, which can be summarized in the following four tenets.

- Development follows learning.
- Participation in activity is central in the development of knowledge.
- Participation in activity progresses from apprenticeship to appropriation or from the social to the individual plane.
- Learning can be observed as changes in participation over time. (Walqui & van Lier, 2010).

These propositions challenge many of the assumptions of schooling, which have tended to focus on the individual student moving through predetermined sequences of knowledge often fragmented into discrete pieces (Au, 2007; Grossman & Stodolsky, 1995). The "social" emphasis on interactions provides discrete moments within students' participation over time within the "culture" of a discipline such as mathematics or science. Over time, participation apprentices students into the practices of the discipline, allowing students to appropriate disciplinary language, habits of mind, and ways of knowing. In mathematics, for instance, this shift is away from asking if students know their multiplication facts or standard algorithms, emphasizing instead whether students are engaged in mathematical practices that are homologous to those of working mathematicians.

Specific instances of learning occur within an individual's zone of proximal development (ZPD; Vygotsky, 1978). Traditionally, the ZPD has referred to what an individual learner can accomplish with assistance from a more capable individual. In classroom settings, it is the adult teacher who is usually placed in the role of providing this support. By contrast, van Lier (2004) presented an expanded version of the ZPD, which explicitly incorporates more interactions than the expert-novice relations characteristic of traditional apprenticeships. For example, when a more capable and a less capable peer interact, the more capable peer also learns by assuming the role of teacher. By teaching, the more capable peer may actually deepen his or her knowledge and understanding of the task at hand or deepen metacognitive understanding about ways of thinking about that particular task or concept. Alternatively, equally skilled peers working together may also learn by combining their intellectual and linguistic resources. From this perspective, joint participation in activities with others promotes appropriation of knowledge and language first through social interaction and then individual appropriation.

Pedagogical Scaffolding

This process of assisted performance is known as pedagogical scaffolding, which has frequently been misunderstood to refer to any help provided by teachers to assist learners in completing activities. Rigidly scripting what students will do in advance or breaking down complex processes into predetermined steps, however, does not promote student flexibility and adaptive expertise. Instead of just making a task easier, pedagogical scaffolding uses familiar participatory structures that enable students to engage in a process that is "spontaneous, dynamic, interactive, and dialogical" (Walqui & van Lier 2010, p. 19). Rather than providing rigid structures to complete a single, specific task, pedagogical scaffolding that is generative builds students' autonomy over time as they become more central participants in disciplinary practices.

Walqui (2006) outlined six different types of scaffolding that serve different purposes for adolescent ELLs. *Modeling* provides students with explicit examples of what they are supposed to do, either in terms of finished student work, procedures to apply, or swatches of language. *Bridging* builds connections from students' prior knowledge and experiences into more formal or specialized uses of language or concepts specific to a discipline. *Contextualizing* grounds general or abstract concepts in concrete sensory experiences or specific real-world situations. *Schema building* provides students with advance organizers or general categories with which to interpret and sort information. *Re-presenting text* engages students in creating new genres for the expression of information that they have read and understood in another format or modality. *Developing meta-cognition* occurs as students explicitly reflect on and select cognitive strategies as appropriate or effective for specific objectives and purposes.

Principles of Quality Teaching for English Learners

To provide teachers with a vision of what pedagogical scaffolding should look like and accomplish in the classroom, professional development focuses on five principles of QTEL: academic rigor, quality interactions, focus on language, high expectations, and quality curriculum (Walqui & van Lier, 2010).

More detail is provided on these principles in the later section that describes the QTEL Observation Instrument (QTELOI). An example of how the types of pedagogical scaffolding described earlier are connected to the principles can be seen through the high expectations principle, which asserts that teachers must provide their students with both high challenge and high support (Gibbons, 2009). Teachers provide high challenge when they invite students to work in their ZPD in ways that require students to move toward participating more centrally in disciplinary practices. Teachers provide high support through the different types of pedagogical scaffolding and the specific tasks on which they invite students to collaborate. High expectations include clearly communicating to students that they are capable of the work, as well as explicit models and modeling of what that work looks and sounds like, with opportunities over time for students to take on more central roles within classroom activity.

Professional Development Design and Implementation

The principles provide content focus and coherence, two of the key features of effective professional development (DeSimone, 2009). Since teachers also need active learning and collective participation, teacher engagement is embedded in their disciplines and daily work. Within each of the four disciplines of English language arts, mathematics, science, and social studies, teachers at the school engaged in four cycles of disciplinary professional development and instructional coaching in each of the two years. These cycles consisted of both professional development and instructional coaching during teachers' regular class time. A typical cycle consisted of one day-long professional development workshop in which all teachers from that discipline participated, followed by cycles of instructional coaching. During professional development sessions, teachers engaged in a variety of activities, including experiencing tasks through exemplars (lessons specifically designed to illustrate scaffolding and the principles in action) and unpacking the principles by analyzing student work and videos. The remainder of each week was spent in one-on-one coaching. Each coaching cycle consisted of three phases: co-planning a lesson, classroom observations of the implementation of these lessons, and feedback or debriefing sessions. Within each discipline, teachers learned to set lesson goals (conceptual, academic, and linguistic), select and sequence scaffolding tasks to achieve the stated lesson goals, and implement lessons that both challenged and supported students through participation and apprenticeship.

Parallel to the apprenticeship model for students, the instructional coaching also employed an apprenticeship model for teacher participants over the three-year project. During the first year, coaches modeled tasks and lessons that demonstrated the principles and supported teachers in planning lessons in "three moments" architecture: preparing the learner, interacting with the concept, and extending understanding (Walqui & van Lier, 2010). The second year focused on collaboratively planning and developing lessons, along with refining the purposes of tasks within each of the three moments of the lesson. Now in the third and final year, the coach's role will shift to developing the capacity for select teachers to serve as peer mentors. Because teachers across all disciplines engage in the same kind of scaffolding tasks, they are able to collaborate in their interdisciplinary teams that share the same group of students.

Triangulating Teacher Evaluation

In this section, we describe in greater detail the system for teacher evaluation at RASS. This teacher evaluation system consists of two major components. The first is an enhanced protocol for classroom observations referred to as the Quality Teaching for English Learners Observation Instrument (QTELOI), which is aligned to the five QTEL principles. The second component is a teacher portfolio of annotated student work sampled from different achievement levels.

Quality Teaching for English Learners Observation Instrument

This section is divided into two parts. The first part provides an overview and detailed description of the classroom-based observation instrument. The second part describes the procedures for carrying out the observations and the training for raters.

The QTELOI is based directly on the five QTEL principles: academic rigor, high expectations, language focus, quality interactions, and quality curriculum. Of these five principles, the first four can be most directly assessed through classroom observation of individual lessons or segments of lessons, while quality curriculum emerges over time and can be measured by a review of documents such as lesson and unit plans over the course of a school year or semester. This section focuses on the first four principles, which correspond on a structural level to the domains in other teacher evaluation systems. A listing of the standards within each of the domains is given in Table 2. Compared to other teacher evaluation systems, the QTELOI has relatively few individual standards, but this feature has been intentionally designed to sharpen the focus of attention on those aspects most critical to challenging and supporting ELLs.

Table 2. Overview of Four Principles as Domains and Standards.

Academic Rigor	High Expectations	Quality Interactions	Language Focus
• Disciplinary Knowledge • Higher Order Thinking	• Clearly Communicated Expectations • Support of Lesson	• Sustained and Reciprocal Talk • Co-Constructing New Understandings	• Metalinguistic Knowledge • Language Practice • Fluency, Accuracy, and Complexity • Amplified Communications

The observation instrument rubrics have also been designed with horizontally aligned bands of descriptors. As seen in Table 3, the complete rubric for the academic rigor standards, each of the standards has focus questions that are answered by detailed descriptions at each of the performance levels. It is thus possible to locate specific levels for individual subquestions within each domain, but the rating for the standard as a whole is always conducted holistically. This finer grained detail provides more specificity for reflection and feedback.

Table 3. Rubric for Academic Rigor.

Academic Rigor	1	2	3	4
Promoting deep disciplinary knowledge	Lesson does not address any central and generative ideas of a discipline.	Lesson only tangentially addresses central and generative ideas of the discipline with limited interrelatedness.	Lesson addresses central and generative ideas of the discipline with some interrelatedness.	Lesson focuses on central and generative ideas with substantial interrelatedness.
Promoting higher order thinking skills	Lesson consists of content activities that require students to only recall information.	Lesson mostly consists of content activities that require students to recall information, although there are isolated instances when students are required to combine ideas to analyze, synthesize, generalize, explain, or hypothesize.	Lesson mostly consists of content activities that require students to recall information, but there are activities that ask students to combine ideas to analyze, synthesize, generalize, explain, or hypothesize.	Lesson mostly consists of content activities that require students to combine ideas to analyze, synthesize, generalize, explain, or hypothesize.

Academic rigor. The domain of academic rigor is the most closely aligned with common classroom observation instruments. Academic rigor consists of two standards: disciplinary knowledge and higher order thinking. Instead of focusing on the recall of isolated facts, disciplinary knowledge refers to the extent to which students are invited to engage in making connections with the central and generative ideas or concepts of a discipline, such as equivalence in mathematics. Acquiring disciplinary knowledge is connected to higher order thinking skills such as generalizing, synthesizing, and hypothesizing, which cut across academic disciplines. What distinguishes QTELOI from other observation instruments are the three interconnected domains of high expectations, quality interactions, and language focus.

High expectations. In addition to the explanation of the high expectations principle given earlier, the rubric articulates two standards: clear communication of expectations and support of lesson. Teachers who clearly communicate their expectations consistently tell students that they are capable of the work and provide significant models or descriptions of what constitutes quality work and exemplary performance in a particular task. These high levels of challenge must be accompanied by contingent and responsive supports for students. The support of the lesson is thus marked by the use of appropriate types of scaffolding, multiple entry points, and apprenticeship or growing participation over time.

Quality interactions. Although other observation instruments do include standards on questioning techniques or teacher communication, the onus is typically put on the teacher. Within the QTELOI, the domain of quality interactions consists of two connected standards: sustained and reciprocal talk and co-constructing new understandings. In order for classroom talk to be sustained and reciprocal, it must go beyond questioning initiated and controlled by the teacher with only a few responses possible. Rather, talk must be sustained in maintaining a focus and development on a central concept and reciprocal in how it is a shared responsibility between the teacher and students as they jointly explore, expand, and elaborate on ideas. Interactions between students within scaffolding tasks should smoothly follow the structure of the task with the purpose of building deeper understandings together. The domain of quality interactions thus measures both the process and the content of the interactions, with an emphasis on peer interactions among students.

Language focus. Compared to the other domains, language focus has the greatest number of standards, but this specificity is particularly appropriate given the explicit supports that ELLs need. The four standards are metalinguistic knowledge; language practice; fluency, accuracy, and complexity; and amplification of communications. In each case, the target is disciplinary language that extends beyond technical vocabulary and into the structures, genres, and language practices that are characteristic of those engaged in a discipline. The metalinguistic knowledge that ELLs in particular need to develop explicitly have to do with the structure of text, choices used in different genres, and other linguistic choices that are connected to the purposes of texts. These explanations must be both clear and purposeful within the lesson. Students must also be provided with ample opportunities to interact with each using disciplinary language specific to genres, in contrast with "practice" in the sense of repetitive application or parroting. Further, teacher feedback must be judicious and targeted toward students' felicitous uses of language. While fluency, accuracy, and complexity are all important goals for language performance and development, teachers must exercise pedagogical tact in providing students with appropriate feedback that addresses the most relevant of these aspects as aligned with the broader goals of the lesson. Finally, amplification implies that instead of simplifying or narrowing the forms of language used, teachers need to employ a variety of linguistic or paralinguistic cues to provide students with alternative access points to disciplinary language. Amplification in this sense is not only raising the linguistic bar by using more complex or technical terms and structures but also broadening the different ways students can understand and use language.

Observation procedures. Raters who use the QTELOI include school administrators as well as peer mentors who are teachers apprenticing to serve as instructional coaches. The procedure is that raters first take detailed, verbatim notes about the video clip or within the classroom observation, attempting to "script" as faithfully as possible what they observe. Then, as the raters review these notes, they individually reach a rating that they need to share with the group at large and to support with evidence in written form. This process is conducted collectively so that interrater reliability is developed through collaboration, as that group will be responsible for providing ratings and peer mentoring. The procedure for rating is explained, modeled, and practiced collectively multiple times. Raters practice both with carefully selected video clips from an existing repository as well as "live" observations in the classrooms of their colleagues.

Feedback through peer mentoring. Peer mentors attend a series of professional development workshops and engage in practical experiences with coaching. Peer mentors learn to use the observation instrument to target potential areas for teacher growth to be facilitated through coaching conversations. Beyond making ratings and collecting evidence, peer mentors practice and develop their skills in selecting a domain or standard that will most effectively catalyze teacher growth. They further practice how to facilitate planning sessions to most effectively improve teacher design and implementation of tasks, lessons, and units. As part of their ongoing development, peer mentors also role-play with each other difficult conversations and engage in anticipatory reflection about how they will be able to build collaborative norms, structures, and benchmarks that will sustain the work of improving instruction aligned with the principles.

Teacher Portfolios of Student Work

To complement the classroom-based observational data collected and quantified with the QTELOI, teachers also assemble a portfolio of student work. At the beginning of the school year, they select six students to follow over the course of the year. This sample is purposefully stratified at high, average, and low levels of relative achievement within the class. At regular intervals, they give students prompts that require an extended response, for a total of four each year. These prompts have been used to serve two purposes, as students also need to complete writing samples as part of the Texas English Language Proficiency Assessment System for ELLs. Teachers then produce annotations of this student work that supply the instructional context, observations about student understanding demonstrated by their responses, and instructional decision making both about what feedback to provide students as well as how to guide future instruction. The complete set of directions for annotations is provided in Table 4. These annotations incorporate both recollective and anticipatory reflection by teachers and provide a common framework for teachers to share their work with one another and collaborate on crafting prompts.

Table 4. Directions for Teacher Annotations of Student Work.

Directions for Annotations

In your annotations, explain the context of the lesson that the sample came from, comment on what the sample tells you about the student's conceptual understanding and linguistic abilities, and discuss the direction that the sample might give you for making decisions about your own teaching. The following questions can guide you as you think about each student's work.

Part 1: Context of the Lesson
- Where does the sample come from?
- What was the unit or the lesson that it was part of?
- When was this task used and with what purpose?
- What were the objectives of the assignment?
- How did the student achieve the goals of the assignment?

Part 2: Student Understanding
- What does the sample demonstrate about the student's conceptual understanding?
- What does the sample tell you about the student's ability to write in your content area?
- Did the student's errors preclude understanding?

Part 3: Instructional Decision Making
- What direction did the student work give to your teaching?
- What guidance would you provide to the student?

Remember that you are encouraged to collaborate with colleagues as you make your annotations and that you have exemplar annotations to guide your work as well.

The process of annotation, although approached at first with some trepidation by teachers, contrasts sharply with other practices that claim to be "data driven." The district has implemented regular "curriculum-based" assessments that are multiple-choice exams correlated with the district pacing guide that are administered approximately every six weeks. Teachers are expected to conduct item analyses and construct intervention plans based on these results, even though these tests have not been validated or field tested in advance and are aligned to a shifting slate of state standards. By contrast, portfolio prompts come directly from teachers' work in the classroom with their students and more authentically reflect what students have been learning in the classroom. The nature of the responses, which are extended and open ended, is also more open to interpretation and annotation than multiple-choice items. Rather than focusing on the percentage correct or the percentage of students reaching proficiency, teachers can focus on the growth of students over time, contributing to a more generative vision of student potential than can be measured by test scores. Here, the portfolio is not a tool for accountability but rather capacity building in terms of teacher pedagogical reasoning and pedagogical language knowledge. (Bunch, 2013; Fullan, 2011)

These teacher skills for attending to, and noticing elements of, student work have also served as the explicit focus of professional development (Mason, 1998). In one mathematics workshop, teachers looked closely at student work through the lens of the four focus questions provided under the category of student understanding. Working collaboratively, they looked at samples of student work in order to answer each of the questions together. Parallel to the process for classroom observations, the annotations critically require teachers to cite textual evidence from their students' writing as they answer these questions. One participant noted a shift afterward; "…we need to pay attention mainly in how our students are developing math content language rather than their possible language mistakes in writing their portfolio samples."

Challenges and Possibilities

The teacher evaluation system collaboratively developed by QTEL and RASS faces several challenges, which are largely logistical in nature. Previously, the district had provided for "lead content teachers" who had administrative duties at the school as department heads but were also expected to attend and coordinate district workshops. After the first year of the QTEL-RASS collaboration, however, the district removed the one period release that these lead content teachers had each day. Consequently, time for the work of peer mentoring has been difficult to find, requiring a great deal of flexibility in terms of scheduling to complete one coaching cycle each week. This change did, however, more broadly distribute the work of peer mentoring, with one teacher from the middle school level and another from the high school level in each of the four disciplines, potentially increasing the overall capacity at the school. A further logistical challenge is that because the middle school population is smaller, there is only one teacher per grade in Grades 6 through 8. As a result, collaboration that explicitly focuses on content area topics is more difficult. Despite these challenges, the teacher evaluation system being developed and implemented at RASS still shows strong promise, as examined through the six domains of teacher expertise.

By de-privatizing classroom practice and having peer mentors work closely in their classrooms, teachers are altering their vision of their students as capable individuals. Because these peer mentors have reciprocally also invited their colleagues into their classrooms, teachers collectively have begun to imagine what their students are capable of, with appropriate supports. Further, through the sustained focus across the school year on the growth of individual students in the portfolio process, teachers are developing a broader and more tangible vision of the possibilities for student growth. Another emerging strategy, the capturing and analysis of video that reflects classroom interactions, is also beginning to have a transformative influence. The evaluation system further addresses teachers' motivations in multiple ways. Although there are financial incentives attached to high performance on the QTELOI, the evaluation system also contains other, social, incentives. These include the desire of teachers to collaborate, assist each other, and to assume more influential roles within the school as peer mentors.

Multiple forms of knowledge are also valued and developed by this evaluation system, but the most salient forms are pedagogical content knowledge and the more specialized form of pedagogical language knowledge. Classroom observations coupled with instructional coaching and peer coaching provide specific moments to develop teachers' ability to employ pedagogical knowledge in its various forms in future anticipator planning. Teachers' practice is also directly addressed in multiple, interconnected ways by the QTEL/OI and through coaching. This practice is named explicitly by the principles and includes a broad repertoire of scaffolding tasks that teachers can adopt, apply, adapt, and eventually design.

Throughout this process, teachers are invited to hone their skills of reflection to improve their instructional practice. Reflection is built into each coaching cycle, as there are explicit moments before, during, and after a lesson in which the coach or peer mentor and the teacher are mutually engaged. Reflection also is the process that is documented through each of the teacher annotations of student work within the portfolio. Viewing the portfolio as a cumulative whole, teachers also engage in longer term reflection on students' growth across the entire school year.

As other states and districts move toward revising their teacher evaluation systems, the work at RASS provides four key lessons:

- Classroom observations are central to gauging teachers' practice, but they must be more focused with responsibility and leadership more broadly shared.
- Measuring student achievement is relevant but needs to be authentically aligned to actual classroom activities and learning.
- Principled, quality feedback and specific support must be provided for teachers to fully attain their potential for professional growth as identified by teacher evaluations.
- Time remains the most valuable resource in terms of building teacher capacity.

As the collaboration between RASS and QTEL moves into the third year, peer mentors and administrators are taking more responsibility for carrying this work into the future. Within the unfolding national and state contexts for teacher evaluation, the continuing work at RASS demonstrates that there are viable alternatives to the test-centered trends that serve to disempower teachers. Although a great deal of work is entailed in developing the capacity and ongoing processes of such a system, the close alignment among the measures and the feedback and a principled model for instruction collectively support a system that places teachers at the center of the evaluation process. The continued commitment and collaboration of teachers and administrators at RASS have the promise to sustain this work beyond the collaboration with QTEL. The promise of this system reiterates the need to view teacher expertise as complex and multifaceted, including vision, motivation, reflection, knowledge, and practice within a collegial context that recognizes teacher agency to drive continued and generative professional growth.

References

Abedi, J. (2004). The No Child Left Behind Act and English language learners: Assessment and accountability issues. *Educational Researcher, 33*(1), 4–14.

Apple, M. (2006). *Educating the "right" way: Markets, standards, God, and inequality* (2nd ed.) New York, NY: Routledge.

Attinello, A., Lare, D., & Waters, F. (2006). The value of teacher portfolios for evaluation and professional growth. *NASSP Bulletin, 90*(2), 132–152.

Au, W. (2007). High-stakes testing and curricular control: A qualitative metasynthesis. *Educational Researcher, 36*(6), 258–267.

Baker, B., Oluwole, J., & Green, P. (2013). The legal consequences of mandating high stakes decisions based on low quality information: Teacher evaluation in the Race-to-the-Top era. *Education Policy Analysis Archives, 21*(5), 1–67.

Bunch, G. (2013). Pedagogical language knowledge: Preparing mainstream teachers for English learners in the new standards era. *Review of Research in Education, 37*, 298–341.

Darling-Hammond, L., Amrein-Beardsley, A., Haertel, E., & Rothstein, J. (2011). *Getting teacher evaluation right: A challenge for policy makers.* Washington, DC: American Educational Research Association and National Academy of Education.

DeSimone, L. (2009). Improving impact studies of teachers' professional development: Toward better conceptualizations and measures. *Educational Researcher, 38*(3), 181–199.

Fiarman, S., Johnson, S., Munger, M., Papay, J., & Qazilbash, E. (2009, April). *Teachers leading teachers: The experiences of peer assistance and review consulting teachers.* Paper presented at the annual meeting of the American Educational Research Association, San Diego, CA.

Flores, S., Batalova, S., & Fix, M. (2012). *The educational trajectories of English language learners in Texas.* Washington, DC: Migration Policy Institute.

Fullan, M. (2011). *Choosing the wrong drivers for whole system reform.* East Melbourne, Australia: Centre for Strategic Education.

Galguera, T. (2011). Participant structures as professional learning tasks and the development of pedagogical language knowledge among preservice teachers. *Teacher Education Quarterly, 38*, 85–106.

Gallagher, H. A. (2004). Vaughn Elementary's innovative teacher evaluation system: Are teacher evaluation scores related to growth in student achievement? *Peabody Journal of Education, 79*(4), 79–107.

García, O., & Kleifgen, J. (2010). *Educating emergent bilinguals: Policy, programs, and practices for English language learners.* New York: Teachers College Press.

Gibbons, P. (2009). *English learners, academic literacy, and thinking: Learning in the challenge zone.* Portsmouth, NH: Heinemann.

Glazerman, S., & Seifullah, A. (2012). *An evaluation of the Chicago Teacher Advancement Program (Chicago TAP) after four years.* Washington, DC: Mathematica Policy Research.

Goldstein, J. (2004). Making sense of distributed leadership: The case of peer assistance and review. *Educational Evaluation and Policy Analysis, 26*(2), 173–197.

Goldstein, J. (2005). Debunking the fear of peer review: Combining supervision and evaluation and living to tell about it. *Journal of Personnel Evaluation in Education, 18*, 235–252.

Grossman, P., & Stodolsky, S. (1995). Content as context: The role of school subjects in secondary teaching. *Educational Researcher, 24*(8), 5–11, 23.

Hill, H., Rowan, B., & Ball, D. L. (2005). Effects of teachers' mathematical knowledge for teaching on student achievement. *American Educational Research Journal, 42*(2), 371–406.

Holheide, L., Goe, L., Croft, A., & Reschly, D. (2010). *Challenges in evaluating special education teachers and English language learner specialists*. Washington, DC: National Comprehensive Center for Teacher Quality.

Hopkins, M., Thompson, K., Linquanti, R., Hakuta, K., & August, D. (2013). Fully accounting for English learner performance: A key issue in ESEA reauthorization. *Educational Researcher, 42*(2), 101–108.

Mangiante, E. (2011). Teachers matter: Measures of teacher effectiveness in low-income minority schools. *Educational Assessment, Evaluation, and Accountability, 23*(1), 41–63.

Mason, J. (1998). Enabling teachers to be real teachers: Necessary levels of awareness and structure of attention. *Journal of Mathematics Teacher Education, 1*, 243–267.

McNelly, T. (2002). Evaluations that ensure growth: Teacher portfolios. *Principal Leadership, 3*(4), 55–60.

Menken, K. (2008). *English learners left behind: Standardized testing as language policy*. Clevedon, UK: Multilingual Matters.

Papay, J., & Johnson, S. (2012). Is PAR a good investment? Understanding the costs and benefits of teacher peer assistance and review programs. *Educational Policy, 26*(5), 696–729.

Shakman, K., Cook, K., Riordan, J., Fournier, R., Sánchez, M., & Brett, J. (2012). *An examination of performance-based teacher evaluation systems in five states* (Issues & Answers Report, REL 2012, No. 129). Washington, DC: U.S. Department of Education, Institute of Education Sciences, National Center for Education Evaluation and Regional Assistance, Regional Educational Laboratory Northeast and Islands.

Shulman, L. (1986). Those who understand: Knowledge growth in teaching. *Educational Researcher, 15*(2), 4–14.

Smith, M. (2013, May 3). Figuring out how to give teachers useful feedback. *The New York Times*, p. A19A.

Solano-Flores, G., & Trumbull, E. (2003). Examining language in context: The need for new research and practice paradigms in the testing of English-language learners. *Educational Researcher, 32*(2), 3–13.

Springer, M., Lewis, J. L., Ehlert, M. W., Podgursky, M. J., Crader, G. D., Taylor, L. L., …Stuit, D.A. (2010). *District Awards for Teacher Excellence (DATE) Program: Final evaluation report*. Austin: Texas Education Agency.

Springer, M., Lewis, J. L., Podgursky, M. J., Ehlert, M. W., Gronberg, T. J., Hamilton, L. S., … Peng, A. (2009). *Texas Educator Excellence Grant (TEEG) Program: Year three evaluation report*. Austin: Texas Education Agency.

Texas Education Agency. (2005). *Professional development and appraisal system: Teacher manual*. Austin, TX: Author.

Texas Education Agency. (2011). *Texas examination of educator standards: 154 English as a second language supplemental preparation manual.* Austin, TX: Author.

Torres, D. (2012). *The beady eye of the professional development appraisal system: A Foucauldian cross-case analysis of the teacher evaluation process.* Unpublished doctoral dissertation, University of Texas, Corpus Christi.

Tucker, P. D., Stronge, J. H., Gareis, C. R., & Beers, C. S. (2003). The efficacy of portfolios for teacher evaluation and professional development: Do they make a difference? *Educational Administration Quarterly, 39*(5), 572–602.

Turner, E., Drake, C., McDuffie, A., Aguirre, J., Bartell, T., & Foote, M. (2012). Promoting equity in mathematics teacher preparation: A framework for advancing teacher learning of children's multiple mathematics knowledge bases. *Journal of Mathematics Teacher Education, 15*(1), 67–82.

van Lier, L. (2004). *The ecology and semiotics of language learning: A sociocultural perspective.* Dordrecht, Netherlands: Kluwer Academic.

Vasquez Heilig, J., & Darling-Hammond, L. (2008). Accountability Texas-style: The progress and learning of urban minority students in a high-stakes context. *Educational Evaluation and Policy Analysis, 30*(2), 75–110.

Vygotsky, L. (1978). *Mind in society.* Cambridge, MA: Harvard University Press.

Walqui, A. (2006). Scaffolding instruction of English language learners: A conceptual framework. *International Journal of Bilingual Education and Bilingualism, 9*(2), 159–180.

Walqui, A. (2008). The development of teacher expertise to work with adolescent English learners: A model and a few priorities. In L. S. Verplaetse & N. Migliacci (Eds.), *Inclusive pedagogy for English language learners: A handbook of research-informed practices* (pp. 103–125). Mahwah, NJ: Lawrence Erlbaum.

Walqui, A., & van Lier, L. (2010). *Scaffolding the academic success of adolescent English language learners.* San Francisco, CA: WestEd.

Xu, J. (2003). Promoting school-centered professional development through teaching portfolios: A case study. *Journal of Teacher Education, 54*(4), 347–361.

· 10 ·

HOW DO WE RELATE TO TEACHERS AS REVOLUTIONARIES IN A SYSTEM THAT EVALUATES THEM?

Jaime E. Martinez

The world of knowledge takes a crazy turn when teachers themselves are taught to learn.
—Bertolt Brecht, German playwright and poet

…it depicts a sort of war, with a clear definition of sides being drawn; teachers AKA "revolutionaries" against an evaluation system. It could be all the negativity surrounding the new evaluation system, but that was the first image that came to mind, although I like the idea of being considered revolutionary.
—Tiffanie, New York City high school teacher

As a former elementary and middle school teacher, I have a great deal of respect and empathy for teachers. Teacher evaluation, performance merit pay, measurement of student achievement, and Common Core State Standards are topics in the popular media that are often framed in terms that depict teachers and school authorities in opposition over the merits of these initiatives in school reform. As an assistant professor in a graduate school of education at a private college in New York City, I work with teachers in professional development workshops, service learning projects in public schools, and in the graduate courses that I teach. My experiences with New York City teachers in these different settings leave me concerned about their morale and dispositions toward their work. I would summarize my thoughts on how New

York City teachers are doing as follows: Teachers are stressed about learning a new curriculum that is aligned to the Common Core State Standards, while simultaneously preparing to be evaluated under a new system, while their students are given tests that are based on a curriculum they have not been fully exposed to. In my opinion, the situation is a recipe for low morale and feelings of helplessness.

In an effort to create a productive (developmental) conversation with teachers regarding the real struggles and concerns about the things happening in schools that individuals cannot change, I invite teachers to consider the following relationships to: school, students, peers, administrators, parents, stress, and how feelings of helplessness can be reorganized and transformed. Helping teachers relate to themselves as the creators of conversations, collaborators in relationships, and leaders of learning environments transforms how they feel about their work and how they organize it. In my classroom, I work with teachers to look for opportunities to do, or create, something new via the use of a new instructional technology, a new approach to pedagogy, or a different way of seeing and responding to a situation. Whether the changes are simple or complex teacher practices are intimately tied to individual history, cultural tools and social settings. I ask teachers to look at what they do in school as a creative activity that I call "creating the learning environment."

The activity of creating learning environments challenges us to consider who is in that environment and what each individual brings to it. We look at what resources are available and we work to decide what we are willing to do together. We identify the constraints and engage them creatively. Often, I start conversations about changes and new ideas when a deficit perspective is expressed during my class. "Students can't," "We don't have enough time," "Students must work harder to achieve," "They don't know," "Those parents don't," "We can't," are just some of the ways teachers express deficit perspectives. I believe the approach that I am describing and what follows create a context for teacher learning and development that is freed of a deficit orientation, acknowledges learning community stakeholder concerns, promotes creativity and critical thinking, is rigorous, and leads to improved teacher practices and dispositions.

The practices that I reference and describe originate in performatory social therapy, or simply, social therapy (Holzman & Mendez, 2003; Newman & Holzman, 1993, 1997, 2006). My use of social therapy and the philosophical, political, and practical aspects of the social therapeutic framework is grounded in over 40 years of therapeutic practice conducted by Fred Newman and Lois Holzman in diverse communities and fields of practice (Holzman, 2009). Following Newman and Holzman, others (myself included) have contributed to an increasing body of literature that describes social therapeutic practices in fields of K-12 education, pedagogy and technology (Martinez, 2011), teacher preparation (Lobman, 2003, 2010), and the emerging field of youth participatory evaluation (Sabo-Flores, 2008). I have found social therapeutic approaches useful in many aspects of my professional, personal, and political life (changing careers, becoming a better listener, becoming politically conscious), and I recommend and advocate for a broader dissemination of this theoretical framework and its practice for teaching and learning in formal school settings.

Evaluations and Outcomes

The new teacher evaluation process in New York City, the introduction of the Common Core State Standards, and the new emphasis on accountability are all intended to result in improved quality of teaching, which should improve student achievement in the subject areas in which students are tested. One of the expected outcomes of top-down reform approaches is consistency (pedagogical and curricular) across settings and practices. High levels of consistency and structure in schools can be experienced as a constraint (I certainly experienced this), such as being required to teach to a test or according to a highly scripted curriculum. This, for example, is what I mean by a highly scripted curriculum: Teachers have said to me that their principals talk about being able to walk into any classroom and know that the same lesson is being taught in all other classrooms covering the same subject at the same time. In a highly scripted curriculum, teacher decision making is limited to the options presented in the curriculum or the standards.

Improvising with the Script

It wasn't until I started teaching teachers that I realized I had developed as a revolutionary: my practices had become "revolutionary," and I was relating to teachers as fellow revolutionaries. My first revolutionary discovery occurred during my time as an elementary school teacher. I discovered that I was a performer who could perform being a teacher in different ways. I learned about performing and improvisation through social therapy performance workshops that were designed specifically to support teacher development. I learned that I could play; I could learn new responses to things that made me angry or frustrated, and I learned to solve the problem of a highly scripted and constrained teaching performance by improvising or "playing with" the scripts, that is, curriculum, schedule, routinized responses, and student behaviors (Lobman, 2010; Lobman & Lundquist, 2007; Martinez, 2011). Changing my relationship to constraints in school required collaborating with others (who may or may not have been similarly scripted and constrained), including students and my support network outside of school (people in the workshops), to create new ways of being (new performances) and the possibility of developmental learning (Newman & Holzman, 1997) for my students and myself. I learned to view teaching as a kind of performance that includes contributing creative leadership in an ongoing ensemble performance (in which everyone has an opportunity to contribute and lead).

My social therapeutic training included challenging the conception of teacher as being primarily a facilitator of knowledge acquisition types of learning. A revolutionary activity that a teacher may lead in a classroom does not need to exclude knowledge acquisition learning or be positioned as something that is an "add-on" or extra thing to do. The revolutionary activity I am referring to is a change in our ways of being in the world, a change in ontology. It is a shift from learning based on knowing, to learning as activity (Newman & Holzman, 1997). In the vignette that follows, I provide an example of a revolutionary activity from my own teaching practice.

First night of class—a warm-up game

Typically, on the first evening of teaching a graduate course, I will introduce myself to my students (in-service teachers), tell them a little about the course, and then ask them to briefly introduce themselves. After the introductions, I invite my students to stand and join me in an improvisation game. Since I usually teach in a computer lab, we start by moving the furniture in the classroom around to accommodate making a circle and I briefly introduce the rules of the improvisation game that I plan to play with the group. Most of the improvisation games I use come from Lobman and Lundquist's book, Unscripted Learning: Using Improv Activities Across the K-8 Curriculum *(2007). I usually select a game called* Whoosh! *It is fairly simple and is useful in demonstrating what collaborative activity looks like as well as raising the energy level in the room. The first time I play improvisation games with a group there are usually several initial miscues (forgetting what movement to make or what sound to make) that produce smiles and laughter as they occur. Any embarrassment that may occur during a miscue is quickly overcome as the players verbally encourage each other to continue playing: "Try again," "Do it over," "Oops, keep going." At the end of the game I will make some claims about what happened. I tell the students that their emotions have been transformed, because they are all smiling or have different expressions on their faces. I ask them how it felt to play the game: "weird," "a little uncomfortable," and "fun" are some of the responses that students share. I note that the improvisation activity lasted for less than five minutes and that whatever had been occupying their thoughts prior to the play had been changed into a very engaged way of being present in the activity with others. For students taking my course for the first time, something unexpected has happened in a formal learning environment, and for students who are taking a second course with me, a familiar routine has been enacted. And so, everyone has a different experience of participating in the same activity. I tell my students that I have played Whoosh! and other improvisation games with elementary and middle school students and that my expectation is that they will try improv games with their own students during our course. It is always rewarding when teachers report back that they have played improvisation games that they learned from me and noticed similar transformations in their own students.*

Proposing to play games with adults that you have just met, in a context like graduate school, is not easy and can be a bit scary. The first time I tried, I was very nervous, but I soon realized, as I started to play regularly with my students, that the nervousness and the awkwardness are normal and part of the shared experience. My experience is that these feelings cease to be barriers to trying something new and taking risks in group activities. As the improv activities have become part of my routine, I have come to feel that they are a necessary aspect of my preparation for the lecture and other classroom activities that follow. The games help me get ready to perform as a professor. They have become integrated into what I do to the extent that I include these activities during formal observations of my teaching with my department chair and the dean of my school.

Evaluation, Alienation, and Stress

Any type of evaluation in which you may be under will be "aced" when the love for the content you teach is rooted within you.

—*Rosa, New York City high school teacher*

A common approach to evaluation of teacher practices views teaching practices as a set of pedagogical behaviors that are aligned to criteria of standardized behavior (best practices). Within the social therapeutic framework, evaluation (as a "scientific" methodology) is understood to be something that typically alienates the activity (process) and results of the activity (product) from the people performing the activity (labor). Alienation in this context is the feeling that your work is separate from you, that it doesn't come from you and it doesn't require whatever is unique to you. In essence, you are simply a replaceable laborer carrying out a task that anyone could do if they follow the procedures or script. The outcomes of the work are directly related to following procedures correctly. Many people experience alienation as stressful or anxiety producing. If you say that you are "teaching to the test," it is a result of an alienating process—the testing regime that has taken over your work and impacted your ability to make choices about your work.

> As I walk the halls all I hear from my students is 'my teacher says I have to pass my test or I don't go to the next grade all we do is test prep I want to learn other things.'
> —Robert, a New York City elementary school teacher

One purpose of evaluation is to identify and measure causality between standardized teaching behaviors and the production of student achievement outcomes. The intent is to establish a linkage among teacher evaluation, change in teacher behaviors, and student achievement to form the basis for decisions on the professional needs of the teacher and the professional standing of the teacher (the rubric of the evaluation system that denotes status, that is, unsatisfactory, developing, proficient, etc.). The extent to which this linkage influences promotion, tenure, and dismissal decisions is a point of controversy. According to widely cited educational research on the importance of a teacher's impact on student achievement outcomes, "we know that teachers matter" (Wright, Horn, & Sanders, 1997).

> In past years I've felt that I was able to make a difference with the students and show student growth. Now I feel that I am constantly assessing data, which I feel is only being used to assess me as a teacher. It's as if the students are only there to prove if a teacher is effective or not, not for them [students] to actually become enriched, motivated, and well versed human beings of society.
> —Vanessa, New York City special education elementary school teacher

Teacher effectiveness is being judged based on the production of outcomes that are being generated in a process that teachers do not control: high-stakes testing regimes. We also know that subjecting adults repeatedly to an evaluation process that requires achieving goals in uncontrollable situations produces threats to self-esteem and social standing that can cause physiological changes related to unhealthy levels of stress in those adults (Dickerson

& Kemeny, 2004). An example of a stressor that has already impacted thousands of teachers is the publication of teacher rankings in newspapers and on websites (Santos & Otterman, 2012). There is also recent educational research that confirms that teacher evaluation has historically been perceived as ineffective (Sartain, Stoelinga, & Krone, 2010). Being exposed to an evaluation system that is believed to be ineffective and yet critical to continued employment and produces rankings that are disseminated to the public could be considered, at a minimum, a stressor that may be disruptive to the general well-being of a teacher (Sawchuck, 2012).

My understanding of all of this is that the state-mandated processes that are supposed to improve teaching also have the potential to disrupt well-being or cause unnecessary potentially harmful stress. Based on my observations, my opinion is that the process as it has initially been implemented in New York City public schools is negatively impacting many of the teachers with whom I work. Teaching practices in schools need to be improved and should be accountable to the community. What I am proposing is a revolutionary teaching practice that can improve what happens in schools, supports teacher learning and development, and is rigorous, accountable, and sustainable (from teacher well-being and administrative perspectives). The idea of a revolutionary practice is what I have learned in practice from Newman and Holzman's (1997) writings, specifically in *The End of Knowing, A New Developmental Way of Learning* and their social therapeutic blending of Marx, Vygotsky, and Wittgenstein.

Revolutionary Teaching Practice: A Marxist Revolutionary Postmodern Methodology

We all share in modernist conceptions of reality. The sun as the center of the solar system, the scientific method, mass production, and progress are all examples of modernist concepts. Appeals to reason, the scientific method, individualism, essential truths, predictability, educational systems, moral training, and stable family life are also examples of modernist concepts. Those of us who challenge notions of ultimate objective truths, stable systems, individualism, and what it means to be "normal" are taking up postmodernist positions. I have learned to be postmodern from other postmodernists, and my understanding is that revolutionary teaching practices would be located within postmodernist schools of thought. Psychologist Kenneth Gergen, a thought leader of postmodernism, describes the postmodern condition as "a state of continuous construction and reconstruction; it is a world where anything goes that can be negotiated. Each reality of self gives way to reflexive questioning, irony, and ultimately the playful probing of yet another reality. The center fails to hold" (Gergen, 1991, p. 7). This center that "fails to hold" is what I believe we experience as extremism, fundamentalism, and legislative gridlock; our collective capacity to negotiate compromises goes undeveloped, and we are left feeling that we lack opportunity, possibility, and hope.

Stanford trained philosopher, playwright, and social therapist Fred Newman, in a conversation with noted critical psychologist Ian Parker, took on the question, "What is a revolution?" at the "Performing the World 2" conference of the East Side Institute in October 2003. Parker, in his interpretation of Newman and Holzman's revolutionary performatory social therapeutic approach, believes that revolutionary activity should be "creative and fun" (Newman & Parker, 2003, October). Newman sees revolutionary activity as the "way out" of the contradictions and alienation that stop human development (Newman & Parker, 2003, October). Newman's "way out" is what I tried as a new teacher and it is what I am presenting as the route for teachers to take in response to the evaluation systems and the other challenges that they are facing. The "way out" is developmental, inclusive, full of possibility, hopeful, and as Parker suggests, "creative and fun."

Most teachers I have talked to claim a vague awareness of Lev Vygotsky's learning theories. They often refer to the scaffolding concepts that are influenced by some of his discoveries in learning and development. Ludwig Wittgenstein is not familiar to most people I talk with, and while people have heard of Karl Marx, it may trigger a negative association with communism. That was my impression of these theorists as well. I will add that readers should not worry if they do not know or are unfamiliar with the theories, because knowing, as Newman and Holzman (1997) pointed out, is not a requirement for learning and development.

Over the past 40 years, Newman and Holzman have developed social therapy as a unique synthesis of Soviet psychologist Lev Vygotsky's learning theory, Marx's dialectical materialism, and Wittgenstein's philosophy of language (Holzman & Mendez, 2003; Newman & Holzman, 1997). Social therapeutic approaches feature Vygotsky's discovery of the zone of proximal development (ZPD), in which he shows that learning happens in "advance of development" (Vygotsky, 1978, p. 89). Readers familiar with other theories of learning will recognize that this is different than a theory of learning in which certain types of learning happen at certain stages of development. In a ZPD, the learner is related to in advance of his or her current level of cognitive, social, and emotional development. This is a key feature of Vygotsky's theory of learning. His work in the 1920s and 1930s during a postrevolutionary moment in Soviet Russian history informs contemporary theories of learning that are, in part, derived from his work. These approaches to learning are known as cultural historical activity theory or CHAT (Holzman, 2006). Social therapy is located within this family of learning theories.

Zones of Proximal Development

In the vignette that follows, learning without knowing is presented.

> *Baby Jessie looks up from her crib and stretches both hands toward her mother who is holding her milk bottle. Her mother says, "Do you want your bottle?" Jessie babbles and continues to reach for her bottle as her mother places it in her hands. Jessie has many caregivers in addition to her mother and they all talk to her as if she understands what they are saying. They are constantly talking to her as they play, change diapers, feed, bathe, and interact with her. Jessie is an active participant in these conversations. She makes eye contact, smiles, listens, cries, gestures, and makes her own noises. In Jessie's near future, she will start to make sounds that sound like actual words to her caregivers. They will enthusiastically and unconsciously escalate the amount of talking and interaction; baby Jessie is finally talking back! By the time she is two years old, Jessie and the other children in her playgroup will be using sentences and language in new and interesting ways. They will become users and creators of language in the culture that they were born into. All of this and more are accomplished without a single lesson in school and without knowing how to read in order to look up the definition of a word. Jessie and her toddler friends can use smartphones but they do not seem to need to Google to explore or interact in the world.*

Vygotskians typically use the example of young children acquiring language in joint social activity to describe a ZPD. The basic requirements that make up a ZPD are at least two people and some activity that they are engaged in together. Learning happens through social interaction, and as Vygotsky describes it, learning runs ahead of the developmental level of the learner: Learning leads development. When baby Jessie is being spoken to, she is being related to as "a head taller" than her actual level of development. Baby Jessie has not developed to the point where she can respond with words. Toddler Jessie has learned; she has developed her ability to use some words, and she can respond in language interactions with actual words. Toddler Jessie's experiences become more complex as she is now capable of doing more and is being challenged in new ways by her caregivers, peers, and her increasing self-directed mobility in the world. There is no prerequisite for Jessie's participation in having a conversation, interacting socially, or climbing out of her crib to explore. She doesn't have to know something to learn language and develop as a member of her family or community. What is necessary in a ZPD are many diverse relationships and social interactions, the more, the better. Caregivers, siblings, and the community provide those critical opportunities to interact. When I relate to teachers as revolutionaries, I am relating to them as "a head taller" than their actual development as revolutionaries. Our zone of (revolutionary) development includes all of our skills, histories, and knowledge as we try to create our learning of pedagogy, technology, and content in our time together.

Karl Marx, Let's Change our Relationship

Marx was a German philosopher who was well known for his critical analysis of Western concepts of capitalism and industrial production. He is also known for his influential writings on revolution and communism. When I was first introduced to Marxist thought, I was uncomfortable with the idea of communism and how people who used Marxist ideas in their work and scholarship self-identified as Marxist. To make a long story short, I have changed my relationship to Marx. In fact, most of us have some relationship to Marxist influence, whether we realize it or not. His critique of capitalism is so insightful that capitalists and economists study his theories (Marx, 2010). There are whole schools of thought in the social sciences that use Marxist critical theory and analytical methods. If we study Marx and use his ideas in our work and implement his methods, does that make us Marxist? Does it matter? I leave these to the reader to contemplate.

Marx helps us to understand that industrial capitalism separates the laborer from the product of the labor. Marx's methodological approach provides social therapy with a method of analysis that reunites the laborer with his or her labor or the producer with the process. Social therapy helps people with feelings of alienation, engaging them in the creation of new relationships and choices. The terms that I (and social therapists) use for this type of analysis are *dialectical unity, totalities, and tool and result methodology,* to describe ways of understanding things that cannot be pulled apart for examination.

In contrast, the scientific method pulls things apart or is reductionist in its approach to analysis. As a result, thinking about relationships between things and concepts as dialectical unities or totalities directly challenges the way most of us trained in Western educational systems analyze and understand relationships—which is by isolating components. Briefly, our use of reductionist methods, categorizing and breaking things down to understand them, focuses us on the search for causal relationships between the constituent parts. This approach has been highly effective in the natural sciences and has been central to modernist conceptions. The use of reductionist methods in education and other social sciences is beyond the scope of this chapter. Suffice it to say that the results have been mixed.

Why would I suggest that we do something other than science (evaluation and determination of outcomes) to solve the problem of improving teacher training, evaluation, and development? Here is a brief example: My experiences of teaching in the South Bronx and in Lower Manhattan were quite different. The standards in both locations were the same, yet the outcomes were radically different. Why? The teaching is connected to the setting and the people in it; the teaching is part of a dialectical unity with the setting. We cannot understand what happened in the teaching unless we understand the totality in which it occurred. Quite simply, a reductionist outlook on teaching practices has brought us to the current state of affairs and cannot provide an analysis that explains why teachers can be effective in one setting and less so in another without resorting to finding a deficit in the teachers or the students. We have a history of reforms to reflect on and it should be clear from a thoughtful reflection that we need to do something new, something revolutionary.

As a new teacher, I was eager to get my own classroom. I wanted to do things my way. I saw what others were doing and I didn't agree. I thought I had better ideas about working with students. Of course, when I did get my own classroom, things didn't work out according to my plan. My students had their own plans. My students had a different experience that they brought to the classroom, the social setting. The norms and behavior management practices of our school building had provided their training. They responded to a particular behavior management system with charts that tracked behaviors. I hated the behavior management system. Some of the students didn't respond to it and wouldn't respond to me. I discovered that relationships and history mattered in a school building. The students knew that I was a new teacher and I didn't have relationships with their families or caregivers. I didn't know which buttons to push. I learned to watch other teachers interacting with the students, families, other teachers, and administrators. I didn't like much of what I saw, but when I started imitating the performances I saw going on around me and meeting expectations for how

I was supposed to behave (disciplinary, dominant male), I got results. I also felt horrible. I couldn't be myself (permissive, passive male); I had to be this other guy, the one that everyone in the building seemed to want me to be. I needed to create a new performance that would accommodate the expectations and wouldn't burn me out. I needed to develop, and that was only going to happen if I got some outside help. That's when I started the improvisation and teacher development training with my friends at the East Side Institute and I learned about social therapy.

Investigations for Teacher Revolutionaries

Ludwig Wittgenstein was an influential Austrian mathematician and philosopher, best known for two works: *Tractatus Logico-Philosophicus* (1961) and *Philosophical Investigations* (1953)., Newman and Holzman (1997) refer to philosophizing and using Wittgenstein's "language games" (Wittgenstein, 1953) to help us untangle the difficulties or contradictions we create with language (Newman & Holzman, 1997). This process of philosophizing and playing language games contributes to the therapeutic aspects of social therapy. An example follows:

What do you mean when you use the word *diversity*? Do you always mean the same thing when you use the word? Does the word change meanings for you when you use it in different contexts? How do you know that everyone listening to your use of the word diversity understands it in the same way that you do? Have you ever gotten into a disagreement with someone because you could not agree on what the word diversity meant?

When we are philosophizing, we are asking these kinds of questions. We are not trying to figure out the right definition; we are trying to untangle the misunderstandings to create meaning together. The activity of making meaning together turns out to be very helpful for creating in collaborative groups. Groups are studied in social therapy. The group studies itself by trying to create the group's activity. Social therapy as a group therapy practice attempts to help the members of a therapy group create new emotionality or deal with emotional pain. The social therapists lead the group by providing direction and helping to focus the group on activity and not the problems of the individual. In the vignette that follows, I provide one of my own experiences of social therapy.

I have no idea what is going on!

I have been in therapy a couple of times in my life, traditional therapy and social therapy. Social therapy is one of the most confusing things I have ever done with a group of people

I didn't know. I started off with one-on-one sessions with the therapist so we could get to know each other and build our relationship. During these sessions, I talked about my life and relationships. We weren't working on my "problems"; rather I was in therapy to get help with my emotions. It was a very stressful time in my life. I was in a small start-up company which I invested money in as a managing partner. I had to engage with the emotions of partners and employees as well as my own. In retrospect, I see that I needed to work on having emotions without being paralyzed by them or suppressing them. When I started with the therapy group, there were about 25 people in the room. It was a very diverse group: Black, White, straight, gay, business suits, poor people, Jews, Catholics, male, female, young, and not so young. Pick 25 people randomly off the streets of New York City and you have that room. What I remember is being shocked at what people were talking about. They were talking about their problems and emotions; some of their situations were so painful I could barely stay in the room to listen. I wanted to solve their problems! But that's not what people were doing. They were asking questions. I didn't even understand why they were asking the questions they asked. I left the session mystified. Social therapy was a struggle. I stopped after a couple of months of weekly sessions. It was a struggle to get to the meetings and I was uncomfortable being in therapy at all. The funny thing is that over the years I have had opportunities to make some sense out of what I learned in social therapy. One thing I learned was how to listen without judging or trying to solve the problem. It is really hard to listen and stay in a conversation with someone and resist the urge to tell him or her what to do. What people were doing in social therapy was helping those that were stuck make new ways forward by changing how they were looking at situations and thinking about them. According to Newman, all there is to work with in a social therapy group is painful and ugly stuff that people bring in to therapy. I've since learned that it is helpful, even growthful, for members of the group to build (a conversation, a play, a scene) with that material. I think my time in social therapy helped me learn how to be creative with negative emotions and to be a better partner in relationships.

I have provided a brief sketch of some of the main ideas and key theorists behind social therapy and some examples from my life and practices in an effort to create with the reader a shared meaning of revolutionary teaching practices and relating to teachers as revolutionaries. I invite the reader and my students to try a new performance of being a revolutionary. I am not a certified therapist, and I am not trying to provide therapy in my courses or help teachers individually with their emotional pain. With that said, I have had students say to me that they have found class discussions to be therapeutic. In a much broader sense, this chapter is my modest offer of help to all of the teachers who are feeling the stress and emotional pain of working in New York City public schools. I see us all as revolutionaries, and I am interested in helping organize our efforts to change or improve what happens in schools. I have discovered that teachers do not need to be alone or rely solely on school administrators in trying to improve practices and student experiences. I have developed a very specific response to teacher evaluation, to help provide some guidance to support thinking on how to use performatory social therapeutic approaches in what may look like an evaluation context. Consider this a thought exercise that could lead to an actual program proposal to be implemented. My interest is in getting rid of the alienation (maybe alienation cannot be gotten rid of, but we can change what we do with it) in the evaluation process and creating much-needed development in schools. In the next section, I draw on the work of a colleague and fellow revolutionary to imagine a very creative and revolutionary approach to a teacher evaluation program.

A Performatory Social Therapeutic Approach to Teacher Evaluation

Kim Sabo-Flores is a professional evaluation consultant who has received extensive training in performatory social therapeutics in addition to her graduate training in developmental and environmental psychology. In her book *Youth Participatory Evaluation* (2008), she draws on the literature of participatory evaluation, the work of Newman and Holzman, and her own work as a youth organizer and program evaluator to develop a model of evaluation that is not alienated or alienating. She describes youth participatory evaluation as follows:

> Youth participatory evaluation involves young people in the process of evaluating the programs, organizations, agencies, and systems that have been designed to serve them. The YPE process can be completely youth-driven, or it can be conducted in partnership with adults. In either case, the youth in YPE projects are provided with the support to perform as evaluators. (Sabo-Flores, 2008, p. 4)

In her book, Sabo-Flores (2008) goes on to describe how she has organized youth and program staff to develop knowledge, evaluation questions, analysis, interpretations of data, and reports of findings. According to Sabo-Flores, youth in a youth participatory evaluation project are not merely respondents to methods created by adults or consultants to an adult-led evaluation. With youth participatory evaluation, Sabo-Flores turns program accountability on its head by including youth in meaningful and significant ways in the evaluation of programs they participate in and ultimately in improving the design of those programs going forward. By involving *all* stakeholders, Sabo-Flores engages the community in a performance. It is an ensemble performance of developing as evaluators. In the performance of evaluating, with the support of skilled evaluators, the stakeholders learn to evaluate the programs they participate in to further the development of the programs that serve them, a ZPD of evaluation development. Sabo-Flores works primarily with nonprofit organizations and other nongovernmental organizations that serve youth in various ways.

Her book is structured as a guide for program staff and evaluators for forming youth participatory evaluation teams and training them to design and conduct participatory evaluation projects. Many of the fears and anxieties that often arise about evaluation are addressed. There are many performance and improv activities that are designed to help participants form new relationships to the evaluation process and develop new meanings and language for the project.

Can we take the youth participatory evaluation model as an inspiration for a new model of teacher evaluation? What might that look like? What follows is an imaginative scenario that might be created if a school or a school district used youth participatory evaluation as the model for teacher evaluation.

First day of school

Ms. Hernandez was nervous and excited. She was going to start the school year teaching her class an improvisation game called Yes, and.... *It was one of a collection of games she had learned over the summer. The idea was to develop the listening and collaboration skills in her third-grade students; they would be doing a lot of project-based group work this year and the games would provide them with practice in creating and collaborating together. She had learned the games from the evaluation training team that the school hired to run the summer Evaluation Training Institute. Ms. Hernandez was an experienced teacher and had opted out of the standard teacher evaluation process and volunteered to be part of a new pilot program. The "performance and improvisation" aspect of the training intrigued her. She had done a little theater work when she was in college and some of the language in the brochure for the program resonated. She also liked the fact that the learning environment was being evaluated. She had been through many evaluations in her career and had always been frustrated with the process. Administrators and observers never seemed to realize that their presence in the room changed what happened in the room. She always knew when they were coming and she had learned long ago that it was best to just figure out what they wanted to see and give it to them. She had also discovered that no matter how good she had become over the years, they always had to find something negative, as if the process only existed to find the fault. Ms. Hernandez was bored with the whole process and was ready for something new. Her third graders would be producing a lot of reflections this year about the classroom learning environment and they would be learning to perform as evaluators. Ms. Hernandez liked the concept. It tied in nicely with the critical writing curriculum and the science curriculum.*

Ms. Hernandez would also be working with parents to redefine their role as key stakeholders. Parent-teacher night was going to be totally different this year. Parents were not going to come in and receive reports on how their kids were doing. The students were going to provide evaluation reports to the parents on how the classroom environment was developing. The parents were going to participate in surveys at the end of the report to provide their input. When the surveys were completed, the results for the whole class would be sent home for review. Much of the data collection was going to be done using online systems that were accessible enough for the third graders and parents to use. Ms. Hernandez would also use technology to gather her own data about the learning environment and use it to support her own reflections and those that the students were developing. She really liked the idea of formulating evaluation questions and interviewing each other as an ongoing activity in the classroom. She thought the structured conversations would be very helpful to the students.

The evaluation training team had ensured that she leave the summer institute with a plan that would carry her throughout the year. The team also planned for a few check-in and follow-up observations as well. During the evaluation training, Ms. Hernandez and the other teachers who had volunteered for the program had bonded. They had created an "ensemble performance of developing as evaluators and facilitators." Their activity during the training was to evaluate the training even as they were receiving it. It was weirdly circular but it all seemed to work out. It had been a fun process, even though it was very frustrating at times. Every time the teachers started to talk about individual evaluations, the trainers kept turning the conversation back to groups or the environment. The evaluation trainers said that every time the focus was on the individual, the process lost track of the very important fact that the individual learns and develops in a social setting in relationships with others. If we were interested in helping individuals learn AND develop, attention needed to be on the group and the environment that was being created for learning and development to take place.

During the summer institute, Ms. Hernandez realized that the evaluation trainers were not talking about what teachers needed to do to prepare for being evaluated. One of the trainers laughed and said, "That program is going on in the room down the hall." Preparing to be evaluated is not the same as learning about evaluation and participating in an evaluation process. The trainer explained that the goal for the teacher is to develop professionally by attending to the development of the learning environment. If there were needs that were not being met, it was the teacher's responsibility to evaluate what needed to change in the learning environment *in partnership with administrators, students, and parents. The check-in sessions during the year were designed to provide supervision to help address areas in need of development. The trainers explained that participatory evaluation is for the purpose of understanding where things are, asking questions about where to go next, and organizing people in the environment to create what is needed. Ms. Hernandez looked at the clock. It was time to go meet this year's group of third graders, and she had her opening line for the game: "We are going to learn a new way to work together and create stories...."*

A new story for teacher evaluation is what is needed. Youth participatory evaluation may help inform a performatory, participatory approach to telling it. I believe it is a revolutionary activity that may help us create a way out of the developmental dead ends that the traditional approaches to school reform and teacher evaluation keep generating. If we want change in education that is grassroots or from the bottom up, change that reflects our diverse communities and interests, then we, revolutionary teachers, will have to take responsibility for creating that change. My experience of New York City public schools is that they are emotionally painful places to be. The current teacher evaluation reform movement may be well intentioned, but from my vantage point, it only contributes to the distress that teachers are experiencing in "hard to staff" and "at-risk" school settings.

Teacher evaluation will continue to be part of the education landscape. Performatory social therapy is a tool that teachers can use to create new performances for themselves and others in all kinds of settings. Health professionals, educators, performance artists, and a multitude of professionals are practicing these approaches throughout the world. The activity of supporting and creating new performances has been shown to help children and adults learn and develop. A performance of an evaluation process that is developmental might just be…revolutionary.

References

Dickerson, S. S., & Kemeny, M. E. (2004). Acute stressors and cortisol responses: A theoretical integration and synthesis of laboratory research. *Psychological Bulletin, 130*(3), 355–391. doi:10.1037/0033-2909.130.3.355

Gergen, K. (1991). *The saturated self*. New York, NY: Basic Books.

Holzman, L. (2006). What kind of theory is activity theory? Introduction. *Theory & Psychology, 16*(1), 5–11.

Holzman, L. (2009). *Vygotsky at work and play*. New York, NY: Routledge.

Holzman, L., & Mendez, R. (2003). Psychological investigations: A clinician's guide to social therapy. New York City: Brunner-Routledge.

Lobman, C. (2010). Creating developmental moments: Teaching and learning as creative activities. In C. M. Connery, V. P. John-Steiner, & A. Marjanovic-Shane (Eds.), *Vygotsky and creativity: A cultural-historical approach to play, meaning making, and the arts* (pp. 199–213). New York, NY: Peter Lang.

Lobman, C. L. (2003). What should we create today? Improvisational teaching in play-based classrooms. *Early Years, 23*(2), 132–142.

Lobman, C., & Lundquist, M. (2007). *Unscripted learning; Using improv activities across the K-8 curriculum*. New York, NY: Teachers College Press.

Martinez, J. E. (2011). *A performatory approach to teaching, learning and technology*. Rotterdam, Netherlands: Sense Publishers.

Marx, K. (2010). *Capital, a critique of political economy volume I* (E. Aveling, H. Kuhls, A. Thurrott, B. Mcdorman, & B. Schultz, Eds.). Moscow, Russia: Progress Publishers. Retrieved from http://www.marxists.org/archive/marx/works/download/pdf/Capital-Volume-I.pdf

Newman, F., & Holzman, L. (1993). *Lev Vygotsky: Revolutionary scientist*. New York, NY: Routledge.

Newman, F., & Holzman, L. (1997). *The end of knowing: A new developmental way of learning*. New York, NY: Routledge.

Newman, F., & Holzman, L. (2006). *Unscientific psychology: A cultural-performatory approach to understanding human life*. New York, NY: East Side Institute.

Newman, F., & Parker, I. (2003, October). In *What is a revolution?* Symposium conducted at the Performing the World 2 conference of the East Side Institute. New York, NY: Retrieved from http://youtu.be/gb7n-er_WzI

Sabo-Flores, K. (2008). *Youth participatory evaluation, strategies for engaging young people*. San Francisco: Jossey-Bass.

Santos, F., & Otterman S. (2012). City teacher data reports are released. Retrieved from http://www.schoolbook.org/2012/02/24/teacher-data-reports-are-released/

Sartain, L., Stoelinga, S. R., & Krone, E. (2010). *Rethinking teacher evaluation: Findings from the first year of the Excellence in Teaching project in Chicago Public Schools*. Retrieved from http://www.isbe.net/peac/pdf/teacher_eval_brief.pdf

Sawchuck, S. (2012). Arne Duncan: Newspapers shouldn't publish teacher ratings. *Education Week*. Retrieved from http://blogs.edweek.org/edweek/teacherbeat/2012/03/arne_duncan_newspapers_shouldn.html

Vygotsky, L. (1978). *Mind in society*. Cambridge, MA: Harvard University Press.

Wittgenstein, L. (1953) *Philosophical Investigations*, G.E.M. Anscombe and R. Rhees (eds.), G.E.M. Anscombe (trans.), Oxford: Blackwell.

Wittgenstein, L. (1961). *Tractatus Logico-Philosophicus*, D. F. Pears and B. F. McGuinness (trans.), New York: Humanities Press.

Wright, S. P., Horn, S. P., & Sanders, W. L. (1997). Teacher and classroom context effects on student achievement: Implications for teacher evaluation. *Journal of Personnel Evaluation in Education, 11*, 56–67.

CONTRIBUTORS

Gloria Rodríguez Bañuelos is a program associate for the Quality Teaching for English Learners initiative at WestEd. One of her main responsibilities is designing professional development experiences for secondary science teachers that enhance their ability to address the educational needs of English language learners. The other is to support teachers in implementing purposefully designed lessons using a one-on-one coaching model. Her professional knowledge and expertise span multiple areas, including conducting scientific and education research, evaluating science education programs, and teaching at the secondary level and higher education. Her research interests include integrating science learning and language acquisition for English language learners.

Joy Barnes-Johnson has served as an assessment specialist, curriculum consultant, professional developer, high school science teacher, and adult educator over the span of her 20-year teaching career. Joy has a PhD in urban education from Temple University, a MEd from Montclair State University, and a BS in chemistry from Johnson C. Smith University. She has written lessons for the National Teacher Training Institute and Adult Education

Department of WNET-NY (a PBS capstone station) and served as a program training facilitator for NJPAC, FANS, The New Teacher Project, as well as various other organizations. She has enjoyed the challenge of daily teaching in both high school and college environments. Her primary research interests are in equitable science teaching, urban teacher training, and out-of-school teaching and evaluation contexts. She is an active member of the National Science Teachers Association and the National Association for Research in Science Teaching. She is currently serving as a lecturer and state science fair coordinator at the University of Wyoming.

Anne Beitlers is an instructor of English methods and student-teaching seminars at New York University and has taught both undergraduate and graduate students for seven years. Additionally, she has 10 years of secondary teaching experience and has taught English, social studies, reading, and English as a second language in the sixth through ninth grades. She was a research assistant at The Metropolitan Center for Urban Education at New York University from 2008 to 2012 and worked on projects including the Black and Latino Male School Intervention Study with a focus on instruction within the participating schools. Her research interests involve teaching in an urban setting. Currently, she is examining the relationship between what teachers perceive their Black and Latino, low-income boys as needing instructionally and teachers' instructional practice.

Elizabeth A. Bloom is a professor of the Social and Philosophical Foundations of Education at Hartwick College in Oneonta, New York. In addition to teaching and supervising student teachers in the field, Elizabeth leads a very active student organization focused on social justice, Society for the Enrichment and Education of Children, at her institution. She also partners with the Alliance for Youth Development, a grassroots organization in Ghana, West Africa, where she brings students to engage in rural community development and plans to teach in the Department of Education at the University of Cape Coast in the spring 2015 semester. Elizabeth is deeply involved with community activism related to resistance to the corporate reform agenda, writes for the blog, oa4pe.wordpress.com, and works as a literacy volunteer at the Oneonta Job Corps Center Academy with young people bravely striving to overcome the obstacles imposed on them by poverty and segregation. She lives with her firefighter husband, two children, and her dogs in upstate New York.

Joanne M. Carris is an educational consultant and literacy specialist in New York City. As an educator for over 20 years, she has worked in alternative high schools, including juvenile detention center schools. In public schools, she specialized in literacy development with adolescents who were emerging readers. Joanne has a PhD in urban education from the City University of New York (CUNY) Graduate Center, a MA in bilingual special education from the Bank Street College of Education, and a MA in philosophy of education from the CUNY Graduate Center. She is the author of *Ghosts of No Child Left Behind*, which won a Choice Outstanding Academic Title award.

Haiwen Chu is a program associate in mathematics for the Quality Teaching for English Learners initiative at WestEd. He designs professional development workshops and institutes for mathematics teachers of English learners and engages them in cycles of instructional coaching. A former high school teacher at a school for recently arrived immigrant adolescents, he developed multiple project-based units that drew on students' real-world experiences to develop mathematical ideas. His research lies at the intersection of mathematics education, English language learners, and teacher education. Specific to mathematics education, his research interests include analogical reasoning, the roles of language, and task design.

Kevin Froner is a New York City principal and was the former founding director of the Youth Cabinet of America. Kevin's work has been profiled in the media and his youth-led public service announcements stretch from New York State to South Africa. Before entering education, he was a Wall Street options trader on the floor of the American Stock Exchange. Kevin is a doctoral student at the CUNY Graduate Center and has a MA in adolescent education from Hunter College–CUNY and an EdM in education leadership from Teachers College–Columbia University.

Mark Garrison is a professor of education policy and research at D'Youville College in Buffalo, New York, and is a graduate of the University of Buffalo. He specializes in the sociology of education, focusing on the political, sociological, and historical aspects of test-based educational policies and their role in reshaping public/private boundaries and modes of governance. His methodological critiques and political and historical analyses of standardized testing are regarded as unique contributions to the sociological study of assessment. He is the author of *A Measure of Failure: The Political Origins of Standardized Testing*, winner of two national-level awards; his recent work focuses on teacher evaluation, the Common Core State Standards, and the role of "Big Data" in the privatization of public education. He is an active public speaker and public critic of current education policy.

David A. Gorlewski is the director of the Educational Leadership Program at D'Youville College in Buffalo, New York. He has served as a high school English teacher, staff developer, senior level administrator, and teacher educator. David has authored and co-authored numerous articles, chapters, and books on topics ranging from classroom assessment and standards to school reform and educational leadership. These include *Using Standards and High-Stakes Testing for Students*, which won the American Educational Studies Association Critic's Choice Award in 2012; *Making it Real: Case Stories for Secondary Teachers* (both co-authored with Julie Gorlewski); and *From Theory to Practice: Case Stories for School Leaders* (co-authored with Julie Gorlewski and Thomas Ramming). David is the co-editor of *English Journal*, a publication of the National Council of Teachers of English.

Julie A. Gorlewski is an assistant professor at the State University of New York at New Paltz, where her research focuses on the interrelations between and among schooling, social class, literacy, and identity. Her first book, *Power, Resistance, and Literacy: Writing for Social Justice*, won the 2011 Critic's Choice Award from the American Educational Studies Association, and her second book, *Using Standards and High-Stakes Testing for Students*, won that organization's 2012 Critic's Choice Award. Additional publications explore the effects of contemporary reforms on teachers, students, and communities, as well as how narrative analysis can foster the critical reflection necessary for culturally responsive classrooms. Current projects focus on the development of professional dispositions in preservice and practicing teachers, interdisciplinary literacies, and the effects of standardized assessments on teaching and learning. She is the co-editor of *English Journal*, a publication of the National Council of Teachers of English.

Pamela Althea Joyce is a reading specialist and urban education consultant who earned her PhD in urban education at the CUNY Graduate Center. In addition, she earned a MA in reading at Montclair State University, a second MA in philosophy at the CUNY Graduate Center, and a BA in elementary and early childhood education at Queens College. She has been an educator for over 30 years. Her teaching experiences have ranged from preschool to college level classes. She received the Weston Award for Excellence in Teaching from the Montclair Public Schools in 2003, the Exceptional Teacher Award from East Orange High School in 1997, and the Montclair University Reading Department's Graduate Student Award in 1997. Pamela is the author of *School Hazard Zone: Beyond the Silence/Finding a Voice* and a number of book chapters that speak directly to concerns associated with disenfranchised students. She is currently a reading specialist at Montclair High School in New Jersey.

Lynda Kennedy is the associate executive director of the Louis August Jonas Foundation, which works to develop in young people a lifelong commitment to compassionate and responsible leadership. She has worked in the education departments of several New York City cultural institutions, including the Lower East Side Tenement Museum, the Brooklyn Historical Society, and the New York Public Library, where she was the first director of Teaching & Learning, Literacy and Outreach, growing services to teachers and students. For several years she worked on Federal Teaching American History grant-funded projects with the New York City Department of Education. She has served as adjunct faculty in the MSEd programs of Hunter College, CUNY, and Metropolitan College of New York. In addition, she has presented at many organizational conferences, including the National Council of Social Studies, the American Educational Research Association, and the Organization of American Historians. Lynda received her PhD in urban education from the CUNY Graduate Center and her MSEd from Bank Street College of Education.

Jaime E. Martinez is an assistant professor of instructional technology at the New York Institute of Technology and is a volunteer faculty member at the East Side Institute in New York City. He holds a PhD in urban education, a MA in elementary education, and a BA in computer science. His book, *A Performatory Approach to Teaching, Learning and Technology*, provides an account of his experiences as a New York City Teaching Fellow using technology and a performance-based approach to pedagogy that emphasizes improvisational performance, groups, leadership, and playful interactions in the process of creating technology-rich learning environments. Jaime taught in New York City elementary and middle schools as a classroom teacher and technology teacher. Prior to teaching, he was a managing director of a technology start-up company. He has nearly 15 years experience as an educator and over 16 years of corporate technology management and system integration experience.

Jennifer McDowall is a student in the Master of Arts in Teaching Graduate Program at Colgate University, and at the time of writing she is completing her final term. After more than three decades working in both the corporate sector and in the arts, she decided to seek out a profession of caring and contribution and one that, selfishly, fed her desire for continuous learning.

Nicholas M. Michelli is a presidential professor in the PhD program in urban education at the CUNY Graduate Center. Prior to this appointment, he served as a university dean for teacher education at CUNY and a dean of the College of Education at Montclair State University, where he is a professor and dean emeritus. His focus is on public policy in education, teacher education, social justice, and democracy. He has multiple publications in these areas.

Pedro Noguera is the Peter L. Agnew Professor of Education at New York University. Pedro is an urban sociologist whose scholarship and research focus on the ways in which schools are influenced by social and economic conditions in the urban environment. He holds faculty appointments in the departments of Teaching and Learning and Humanities and Social Sciences at the Steinhardt School of Culture, Education and Development, as well as in the Department of Sociology at New York University. Pedro is also the executive director of the Metropolitan Center for Urban Education and the co-director of the Institute for the Study of Globalization and Education in Metropolitan Settings (IGEMS). In 2008, he was appointed by the governor of New York to serve on the board of trustees of the State University of New York.

Kate E. O'Hara is an assistant professor in the School of Education at New York Institute of Technology. She holds a PhD in urban education as well as a MA in English education and a MA in philosophy. She is also an independent curriculum designer and instructional technology specialist working extensively with teachers in the New York City metro area, guiding them in the development of technology-integrated curriculum and the application of teaching strategies that foster achievement for all students. Her research is focused on the effective use of technology to empower users to become agents of social change and teacher education as it relates to contexts of power, oppression, and social justice. Her research employs the use of autoethnographic studies, couched within a sociocultural framework.

Barbara Regenspan is an educational studies professor at Colgate University who teaches philosophical, political, and psychological foundations of education and also supervises student teachers in social justice-focused teacher education. Her research focuses on the parallel nature of arts-based multiple perspective social education for prospective teachers of history and English and for the children and adolescents they will teach in their own public school classrooms. Her first book is *Parallel Practices: Social Justice-Focused Teacher Education and the Elementary School Classroom* (Peter Lang, 2002), and her current manuscript in press is *Haunting and the Educational Imagination*. She and her husband, David, have two 20-something children; she is a periodic activist, and she has been writing poetry for four years.

INDEX

V

W

Z

Studies in the Postmodern Theory of Education

General Editor
Shirley R. Steinberg

Counterpoints publishes the most compelling and imaginative books being written in education today. Grounded on the theoretical advances in criticalism, feminism, and postmodernism in the last two decades of the twentieth century, Counterpoints engages the meaning of these innovations in various forms of educational expression. Committed to the proposition that theoretical literature should be accessible to a variety of audiences, the series insists that its authors avoid esoteric and jargonistic languages that transform educational scholarship into an elite discourse for the initiated. Scholarly work matters only to the degree it affects consciousness and practice at multiple sites. Counterpoints' editorial policy is based on these principles and the ability of scholars to break new ground, to open new conversations, to go where educators have never gone before.

For additional information about this series or for the submission of manuscripts, please contact:

> Shirley R. Steinberg
> c/o Peter Lang Publishing, Inc.
> 29 Broadway, 18th floor
> New York, New York 10006

To order other books in this series, please contact our Customer Service Department:

> (800) 770-LANG (within the U.S.)
> (212) 647-7706 (outside the U.S.)
> (212) 647-7707 FAX

Or browse online by series:
> www.peterlang.com